DATE DUE

An Introduction

to the Behaviour of Ants

An Introduction

to the Behaviour of Ants

4698

John H. Sudd, Ph.D.

Department of Zoology, The University, Hull

 Edward Arnold (Publishers) Ltd., London

Printed in Great Britain by
Robert Cunningham and Sons Ltd, Alva

Preface

The large number of books and scientific papers that have been written about ants makes it almost impossible to write a comprehensive book about them. At the same time this enormous literature—a few years ago it was estimated to contain 35,000 papers—increases the need for an introductory account. Unfortunately many excellent books on ants are based on their authors' own experiences and do not lead the reader into the literature.

This book is the result of my own search among some of the many papers on ants; I hope it may shorten the search for other people. The core of the book is the large amount which has been published since about 1925. A good deal of this, especially between the wars, was written in German and has not appeared in English before. I have also of course included the results of work since the last war, as well as older work, back even as far as Huber at the start of the last century. Often this older work has a different significance now from that which it had for its author.

I have not tried to explain the workings of an ant's nervous system in producing its behaviour, nor those of the evolutionary processes by which the behaviour arose. Instead I have tried to give some idea of the variety of behaviour which is found, even in the small proportion of ants that have been studied. This aim of simple description is given valuable support by the four excellent photographs taken by my friend and colleague Peter Morgan.

The nomenclature of ants has been something of a problem. In general I have been a 'lumper', and I have not used subgeneric names where they do not appear to have any significance in the ant's behaviour.

It would not have been possible to write this book without the help of the Library of the University of Hull, who obtained most of the papers I have cited from other Universities and from the National Lending Library. I am glad to acknowledge illustrations from various journals. Full details are given in the references.

Lastly I must say how grateful I am for the patience of the publisher, my colleagues, and above all of my wife and family, while I have been writing this book.

J.H.S.

Hull, 1966

Contents

1 — Introduction

Ants do not make attractive museum specimens because they lack brilliant colours and many of them are small in size. They attract interest because of their behaviour and a dead ant is in many ways a dull ant. The number of manipulative tasks they do—nest-building, food collection—and the fact that they often do them as a group and not as single insects remind us of our own lives. The similarity is made to appear greater than in the case of bees and wasps because ants, like men, walk instead of flying. The comparison between the social world of ants and that of man (to paraphrase the title of a famous book) (Forel 1928) is what makes them so interesting. Drawing this comparison is made hazardous not only by the differences in structure between ants and men, but also by the very large number of different species of ants. There are thousands of species; six thousand are known and if those which have not yet been described were added there could hardly be less than ten thousand (Wilson 1963). Each of these species has its own peculiarities of structure and often of behaviour too, which make it distinguishable from other species.

One of the most striking things about ants as a group is that all the six thousand species form a single superfamily, Formicoidea, in the order Hymenoptera. In fact many systematists include them all in a single family Formicidae. Birds on the other hand have about the same number of species but these are grouped into 155 families. This has many disadvantages from a practical point of view because it means that the systematist is liable to run out of categories. He soon uses up subfamilies and tribes and arrives at enormous genera, like *Camponotus* which has about 1,500 species. For this reason subgenera and the less formal species-group are often used in classifying ants. Very often it is convenient to group related genera into tribes, and in some cases, for instance the Attini and the Dacetini, tribes are particularly useful in descriptions of behaviour.

However inconvenient it may be to have all ants in a single family it reflects an important fact about ants. The large number of distinct forms of ants are all built on a fairly constant ground plan. This suggests that ants have undergone a good deal of very rapid evolution in their history, perhaps exploiting all the forms of social life possible to them (Wilson 1963). All ants are of a fairly uniform shape, with differences between them in proportion rather than in structure. They all possess features which separate them from the rest of the Hymenoptera. Some of these, the infrabuccal pocket near the mouth, the metanotal gland and the structure of the proventricular valve in the gut, are directly connected with their social nature, for all ants are social. Other features like their shape may perhaps be related to their habit of living in the soil. A few, characters of the wings, do not seem to have any relevance to any of their habits.

This pattern of distinctness, and of variation within circumscribed limits, appears again when we turn from structure to habits. Not only are all ants social, but quite small details of behaviour in the capture of prey or in building a nest are common to many ants, just as the way the antenna is articulated to the head is. But just as antennae and heads built on the same plan may vary in their proportions in different species, so behavioural acts can vary in scope or timing or function.

1·1 The subfamilies of ants

A detailed account of the anatomy and classification of ants would be out of place in this book. In any case the range of ant forms is given in standard texts (Wheeler 1910, Bernard 1951a). A recent view of the classification of ants divides them into two groups of slightly different descent (Brown 1954). One group originates in the Myrmeciinae and gives rise to the Pseudomyrmicinae, as well as to the more highly evolved Dolichoderinae and Formicinae. The other line begins in the Ponerinae and includes the highly specialised Dorylinae, Cerapachyinae, Leptanillinae and the large important group of Myrmicinae. There are thus nine subfamilies in all.

The Myrmeciinae are all Australasian, mostly large and all carnivorous. Like Australian mammals they include some very primitive forms which previously occurred in other parts of the world too. The genus *Prionomyrmex* found in Baltic amber is a member of this subfamily with living relations in Australia for example. The Pseudomyrmicinae are slender ants which specialise in living in hollow twigs in the tropics of Asia, Africa and America. Both these subfamilies are rather wasp-like in appearance, and have a good many primitive features in their thoraxes, and in possessing a powerful sting. The Ponerinae are also primitive in structure. Some of them live rather unobtrusive lives below the soil, but some are large and bold, and a few in the tropics, like *Euponera senaarensis* and *Odontomachus* species, are extremely successful ants. The remaining subfamilies are more highly evolved. The Ponerine stock probably gave rise to three subfamilies of specialised structure and habits. The Dorylinae or driver-ants have peculiar males and females and live in large colonies which get their food by a special method of raids. The Cerapachyinae share some of these habits and may link Ponerinae and Dorylinae. Leptanillinae are probably raiders in the same way but their colonies seem to be small though very little is known about them. The largest and most successful group to arise from the Ponerinae is the subfamily Myrmicinae. This varied group has a waist with two nodes. In all the Hymenoptera the first segment of the abdomen is joined broadly onto the thorax, and in the stinging forms there is a narrow waist between the first and second abdominal segments. In ants there is always a second waist between the second and third segments, and the second abdominal segment is small and forms a petiole or scale. In many of the lower subfamilies the third segment is marked off from the fourth by a groove, but in the Myrmicinae (and in the Pseudomyrmicinae and some Dorylinae) the third segment is as small as the second, and forms a second node or post-petiole. It will be clear from this that what appears to be the abdomen of an ant is actually at most the third to last segments only, and in some subfamilies only the fourth to the last. This part of the abdomen is often called the gaster to avoid anatomical inexactness. The Myrmicinae are very varied but for our purpose they can be divided into three groups (Bernard 1951a). The least specialised Myrmicinae have thin, twelve-jointed antennae which are not very distinctly thickened into a club at the tip. These lower tribes include large and common genera like *Myrmica* and the various harvesting ants such as *Messor, Pogonomyrmex* and *Pheidole*. They nearly all nest in soil. Slightly more evolved are a group of tribes which includes *Crematogaster, Leptothorax* and *Solenopsis*, and many of these ants nest away from soil. The remaining tribes of Myrmicinae are highly specialised and usually have spiny bodies and heads. Cryptocerini with flattened bodies live in twigs, Dacetini are predators of a special kind and Attini are the leaf-cutting ants of the New World.

Two subfamilies remain, and they are sometimes referred to as 'higher ants' (some authors include the Myrmicinae in higher ants too). Both subfamilies have only a single petiole and both have lost the sting possessed by other ants. In the Dolichoderinae the defensive function of the sting is taken over by anal glands, which open near the anus by a slit. The Dolichoderinae are connected to the Myrmeciinae by *Aneuretus* and its relations, which still have well developed stings and are sometimes placed in a tenth subfamily of their own. The Formicinae have turned the vestiges of their sting into a device for spraying venom on enemies. This large, successful group falls into three sections according to the complexity and efficiency of the proventricular valve. The least specialised include *Melophorus* and *Plagiolepis. Myrmoteras* is a curious genus resembling *Odontomachus* or *Strumigenys* superficially. The higher tribes include some large ants, predominantly tropical (*Camponotus,*

Oecophylla and *Polyrachis*), and the medium to small *Formica* and *Lasius* which are more common in northern lands.

1·2 Ant societies

Typically an ant colony consists of a mother queen and her progeny. Most of the progeny are daughter workers, female ants that are infertile or less fertile than the queen. They devote themselves to collecting food and to feeding it to the queen. The brood of the colony, consisting of eggs, larvae and pupae, are usually produced by the queen and they too are fed as larvae by the workers. At certain times of the year the colony also contains young fertile females and males. In most species both sexes have wings when they first emerge from the pupa and they are called alate ants. The workers on the other hand never have wings. The females lose their wings after they have mated, which they usually do outside the nest, often during or just after a mating flight in which the males take part too. After this the males die but some of the females succeed in founding families of their own.

In a typical colony workers, brood and alates are the progeny of a single queen. Many ants however adopt extra queens into the colony after a mating flight. In this sort of colony the blood relationship between the queen and the rest of the colony is not so simple and there may be several queens, not necessarily related to one another.

Contacts between parent and progeny are not in themselves a criterion of social life. In many wasps and some bees a female builds a nest and collecting food feeds it to her own young in the nest. A solitary wasp like *Ammophila pubescens*, may have behaviour which is at least as complex as that of ants. The socialness of ant life lies in the way that workers carry out portions of this sort of parental behaviour for larvae which are not their own. Rearing the young is the task not of a single natural mother but of a group of foster-mothers (Richards 1953). Most of the parental behaviour which a mother *Ammophila* lavishes on her own young—nest construction, hunting and feeding the larvae—is done by the workers in an ant colony. Only the laying of eggs is left to the mother, except in the first days of a colony before there are any daughter workers.

Naturally most of this book is about the behaviour of worker ants. Chapter 2 contains information about the equipment of sensory and effector organs which ants use in their behaviour. Chapter 3 describes some more sophisticated ways in which ants use their sense organs to find their way about. Chapters 4, 5 and 6 are concerned with the main tasks that a worker ant undertakes in its life—building, hunting and nursing. In chapter 7 we turn from workers to the life of alate ants in mating and in the foundation of colonies. Chapter 8 is about the way a colony is organised and how workers alter their behaviour to suit the circumstances of the colony.

2 — Effectors and senses

It is very obvious that any animal's behaviour is made up of movements of its limbs—in the last resort muscular contractions—and of the activities of its glands. How the animal performs any piece of behaviour, like digging or eating, depends on what sort of limbs and other effector organs it has got. The movements of its effectors have to be fitted in to the animal's world. This is the task of the nervous system and of the sense organs. The way the animal's behaviour is locked into its life and environment must depend on what sort of sense organs and what sort of nervous system it has. Effectors and sense organs then are also parts of the 'machinery' which is thrown in motion when the animal behaves. This chapter introduces some points of the anatomy and physiology of ants, which concern their behaviour. It is also convenient to describe a few simple pieces of behaviour at the same time.

2·1 Effector mechanisms

In ants, as in all insects, the most important effector organs contain cuticular mechanisms—joints, levers, cutting edges, etc., which convert the contraction of the muscles into movements which are useful to the ants. The cuticle of an ant covers the whole of its outer surface and is produced by an underlying layer of epidermal cells. On the head and thorax the cuticle is relatively thick, hard, and rigid. The separate sections of the limbs and the separate plates which cover the dorsal and ventral surfaces of the gaster have the same properties. Each of these hard parts or sclerites is joined to those surrounding it by a joint membrane. This is simply part of the cuticle which instead of being hard and rigid is softer and more pliable, so that one sclerite can move on the next. The muscles are as a rule attached to the inner surface of the sclerites, and the sclerites can form flat plates, or as in the legs and mouthparts, more or less tubular jointed projections. The three most important effector systems in ant behaviour are the mouthparts, the legs and the sting.

2·1·1 *The mouthparts*

The mouth of an ant is surrounded by a set of cuticular limbs and flaps which form the mouthparts and enclose a chamber, which is really outside the mouth and in which food is manipulated. The roof of this preoral chamber is formed by a small flap, the labrum, and its floor by

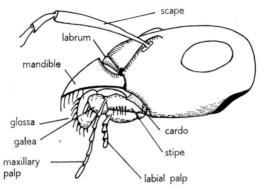

FIG. 2·1 Head of a *Formica lugubris* worker from the left side. (Original)

the labium and maxillae, and the latter close the sides too. The mandibles, unlike those of the cockroach or locust, meet each other in front of the labrum and therefore outside the preoral chamber. As a result the food cannot be chewed in the preoral cavity. As in all Hymenoptera the labium and maxillae are closely connected and both

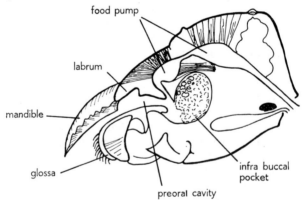

FIG. 2·2 Sagittal section through the head of an *Oecophylla longinoda* queen. (Original)

are attached to the head by the basal lever joint or cardo of the maxillae. The whole floor of the preoral chamber can be shuttled in and out as this lever swings backwards and forwards (Bugnion 1929). This movement rams small particles of food (also dust etc. removed from the ant's body as it grooms itself) into a recess at the neck end of the preoral chamber—the infrabuccal pocket. The pocket is lined with thin cuticle and can be compressed by muscles so that liquids are forced out of the food. The same muscles suck the juices into the gut by means of two pump chambers on the pharynx. The duct of the labial gland opens into the upper side of the labium and the pharynx itself opens directly above in the roof of the preoral chamber. Food regurgitated from the crop and the secretion of the labial gland flow on to the labium and can be licked up by other ants and by larvae. The inner blade or lacinia of the maxilla partly covers this area of the labium, and may be important

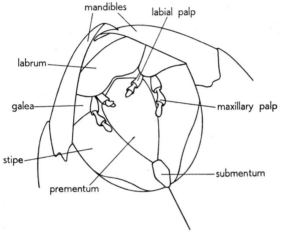

Fig. 2·3 Ventral view of the closed mouthparts of an *Oecophylla longinoda* queen. (Original)

in separating regurgitated and secreted offerings when one ant feeds another.

The mandibles of ants are used for many purposes as well as feeding: holding prey, carrying nestmates—larvae and eggs, excavating nests (Plate 1b). At these times the preoral chamber can be kept tightly closed. The basal parts of the labium and maxillae fit together behind and the maxillary galeae and the labrum in front, so that only their basal parts can be seen from outside. The sensory palps of the mouthparts still protrude.

Some ants, especially *Pogonomyrmex* but also many other desert species have their mandibles and the undersides of their heads decorated by long downward-pointing bristles. These have been called ammochaetae or psammophores. The function of these has been said to be to clear sand from the tibial strigil, which in turn cleans the antennae, or in holding dry sand when the ant is excavating the nest. Both these suggestions have been discounted and the hairs have been said to protect the mouthparts from blown sand (Creighton 1950). This in turn seems unnecessary as the mouthparts can be closed so tightly.

2·1·2 *The thoracic legs*

The thorax of an ant carries three pairs of legs, each pair representing one of the three body segments which make up the thorax of an insect. In a worker ant the divisions between these segments cannot be seen on the surface, and almost all of the thorax (and the first abdominal segment) makes a rather rigid box. The first pair of legs however are attached to a propectus which is slung underneath the upper part of the

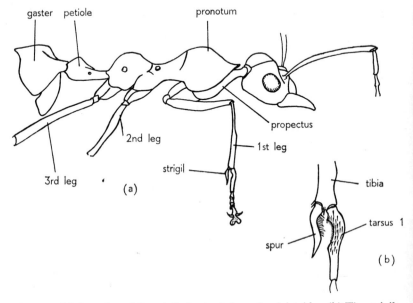

FIG. 2·4 (a) A worker of *Oecophylla longinoda* from the right side. (b) The strigil, or cleaning apparatus on the tibia of the first leg of an *Oecophylla longinoda* worker. (Original)

first thoracic segment. The propectus is joined to the rest of the thorax only by a folded sheet of soft membrane and by muscles, and the front legs therefore can be moved more freely than the two hinder pairs. The head is connected to the propectus by a neck joint, and ants produce most of the rotation of their heads by movements of the propectus. Each leg has nine joints, a large basal coxa, a small trochanter, a long femur, a long tibia, and five tarsal joints the first or basal one longer than the rest. The distal end of the tibia carries a curved structure, the strigil, which together with a notch on the basal tarsal segment forms an apparatus for cleaning the antennae. Each leg also bears two claws and a central adhesive pad or arolium.

The legs are used of course not only for walking but in digging and in other ways. They are the source of the forces ants apply to objects around them, just as the mandibles are the main link through which these forces are transmitted.

Plate 1a. A *Formica lugubris* worker cleans its left antenna on the strigil or spur of the foreleg on the same side.

Plate 1b. A *Myrmica ruginodis* worker carries a well-grown larva. The ant uses its abdomen to prevent the larva slipping away as it grips it.

(a)

Plate 2. A contrast in the relations of ants and aphids.
(a) A *Formica lugubris* attending aphids on a birch shoot. Several aphids are in a tail-up position offering the ant drops of honeydew.
(b) *Formica lugubris* with the large aphis *Tuberolachnus salignus* on willow. The aphis is rejecting the ant's attentions by kicking it and the ant's head is plastered with secretion from the aphid's siphuncles.

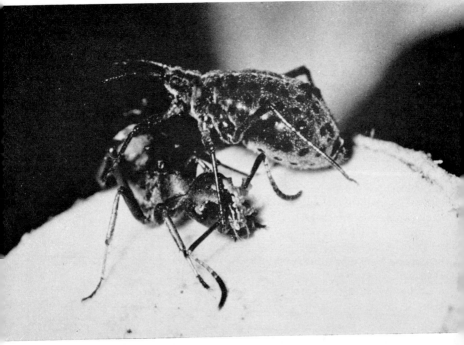

(b)

2·1·3 Some simple pieces of behaviour of worker ants

Ants become dirty in all sorts of ways. Many of them nest in soil and in rotten wood. They may be soiled by pollen in visiting flowers (Jung 1937) or smeared with food (honeydew or insect blood) in collecting food. They can also be covered with defensive secretions of their prey or with hairs and scales from them. In all these cases ants are at pains to clean their bodies. Cleaning behaviour can be produced experimentally by dusting ants with gypsum, painting them with gum or

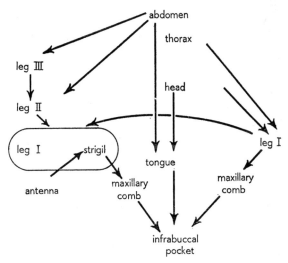

FIG. 2·5 A scheme of the cleaning movements of ants. The arrow shows the transfer of material from the part cleaned to the part which cleans it. (Original)

with irritants like acetic acid. They will not clean themselves in response to a single touch with a horse-hair, though repeated touching does release washing behaviour. Sudden changes in temperature, and light, may also start washing (Jung 1937), which is also likely to occur regularly when an ant is about to begin a foraging trip (Sudd 1957, Wallis 1964).

The general effect of self-grooming behaviour in ants is to transfer dirt from the body surface to the strigil or tibial comb of the forelegs, and thence to the maxillary comb, or directly to the mouthparts. From the maxilla food is moved over the labium to the infrabuccal pocket. Some of the movements which result in this are common to all ants. The antenna is always cleaned by being drawn through the strigil on the foreleg of its own side (Plate 1a, fig. 2·6). Each foreleg is then cleaned on the maxilla of its own side (Jung 1937). In *Formica fusca* the left antenna is cleaned on the left leg while the right leg is being cleaned on the mouthparts (Wallis 1962a). *Daceton armigerum* on the other hand cleans both antennae simultaneously and then both legs (Wilson 1962b). Sometimes the leg is stroked over the antenna rather than the antenna through the strigil. Cleaning the antennae is the most frequent of cleaning movements and is evidently of great importance to the ant. The second and third legs are cleaned less often. Usually the foreleg wipes the other legs of its own side while the ant stands on the second and third legs of the other side and on the tip of its gaster. The two forelegs are

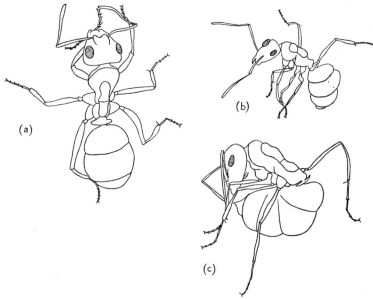

FIG. 2·6 The postures of a *Formica fusca* worker cleaning itself: (a) cleaning right antenna and left foreleg, (b) cleaning other legs, (c) cleaning the gaster. (Wallis 1962a)

then rubbed together before they are cleaned by the mouth. *Formica fusca* may wipe its third legs with the second leg and then clean the second leg (Wallis 1962a). *Daceton armigerum* shows two variations of the normal leg cleaning movements: sometimes only the middle leg or even only the two forelegs are cleaned. *Erebomyrma urichi* queens rub their front legs together and some primitive ants rub the hind legs together too (Wilson 1962b). The last operation seems to be the remains of much simpler methods used by other insects.

Ants clean their bodies less often than their limbs. The sides and underneath of the thorax may be cleaned with the first legs and the abdomen wiped with the middle and hind legs, or in *Daceton* the foreleg. The commonest abdominal cleaning movement is cleaning its tip, with it bent forwards through the legs.

As well as cleaning themselves workers clean each other, their queens, eggs and larvae too. This behaviour is brought out by a chemical on the ants' surfaces, which forms part of the chemical language of ants (section 2·5·1). It is not certain that the statement that ants cannot clean their own head and thorax (Forel 1928) is true. Unlike self-grooming this social grooming is done directly with the mouthparts which lick and sometimes nibble over the partner's cuticle. Dirt which is removed in this way ends up in the infrabuccal pocket just the same, as the number of larval spines found there show (Wheeler & Bailey 1925).

Ant nests are normally kept reasonably clean by the workers. Many ants cover up sticky fluids with earth. They normally eat any larvae that are sickly (Brian 1957a) and many Ponerine and Myrmecine ants (but no Formicine) eat the faeces of larvae (Le Masne 1953). (As the midgut of ant larvae does not open to the rectum until the prepupa is formed, all the faeces are extruded in one dark mass or meconium, contained in many layers of peritrophic membrane.) Dead workers and the chitinous remains of insects are carried by the workers to a midden or cemetery outside the nest. The stimulus releasing this, in *Pogonomyrmex* and *Solenopsis*, at least, is the rancidity of the flesh. Filter paper squares soaked in oleic acid are carried to the midden too. Even living workers smeared with oleic acid are carried out, and when they return to the nest they are carried out again (Wilson, Durlach and Roth 1958).

While all ants transport larvae and pupae inside the nest many carry adults too. In *Formica* sp. nestmates are carried under the body of another worker. The transporter first grabs the outside of the other's head at its strongest point near the mandibular articulation. The transported ant folds up its legs and is carried upsidedown but head first under the thorax of its nestmate. There is reason to think that in spite of this curious position the transported ant can learn a light-compass course on the way (Forel 1928, Dobrzanska 1958). This method of transport may be typical of all Formicines, it is found in *Formica, Campanotus, Cataglyphus* and *Rossomyrmex* (Forel 1928, Arnoldi 1932). In some Myrmecines (*Tetramorium, Leptothorax*, Forel 1928; *Myrmica, Cardiocondyla*, Arnoldi 1932) the companion is carried by the mandibles but inverted over the back of the transporter. *Crematogaster* (Arnoldi 1932), *Pogonomyrmex* (Wheeler 1917b) and *Tapinoma* (Forel 1928) however carry nestmates by the petiole. Whether this reflects a taxonomic difference is doubtful. Very light prey is often carried in a higher position than slightly heavier prey.

2·1·4 *The sting*

The sting of an ant consists of a pair of stylets which run inside a sheath. Each stylet originates inside the ant's gaster where it is attached to a series of plates, the gonangulum, the modified tergite of the ninth segment of the abdomen, and the second gonocoxa (Scudder 1961). From here the stylets curve inwards and ventrally, and lie together in the midline to form the shaft of the sting. Each stylet is guided in its curved course by another curved branch which runs from the gonocoxa and eventually joins its fellow from the other side of the ant's body to form a sheath (Janet 1898a). The movements of the sting do not seem to have been studied in ants, but the stylets are probably levered out of the sheath by muscles which move the gonangulum and the ninth tergite relative to the gonocoxa. As the gonocoxa is connected to the sheath the stylets move inside the sheath rather like a Bowden cable.

The venom of the sting is produced by a venom gland which opens by a protuberance which is firmly corked into the inner end of the

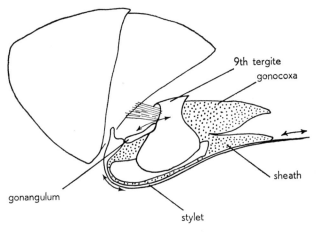

FIG. 2·7 The sting of a *Pheidole crassinoda* worker. (Original)

sheath (Janet 1898a). There is a long, often branched, venom gland opening into a large reservoir. Near the distal end of the reservoir opens Dufour's gland, the source of various signal substances.

Ants appear at first sight to be well protected against enemies. They defend themselves by biting alone (*Anomma*), by stinging, or both biting and stinging (Ponerines and Myrmecines), or by spraying a venom with or without biting (Formicinae). Dolichoderine ants produce repellent oils from abdominal glands (Stumper 1953). The mere bite of some ants such as *Oecophylla longinoda* is painful, and large workers of *Anomma nigricans* can draw blood from the foot. Many worker ants cannot easily be removed once they have bitten. Their jaws remain shut even if the head is cut off, and after a battle between ants of different colonies some survivors can be seen with severed heads fast on their legs. This and the very large forces which can be transmitted by the closed mandibles, suggests that some undescribed 'catch' mechanism exists.

In ants the sting is very often not used in hunting, except in attacks on large insects, and is used more for defence. Some ants such as *Odontomachus, Brachyponera senaarensis, Solenopsis saevissima* and most

Pseudomyrmecines sting more readily than others, and these usually have effective stings. In *Solenopsis saevissima* the venom is a water soluble aliphatic ketone and contains no protein (Blum et al. 1958). The venom of *Pseudomyrma pallida* on the other hand contains a protein; proteinaceous venoms may be characteristic of lower families (Blum and Callahan 1963) or perhaps of flesh-eaters; honeydew ants e.g. *Formica* produce fatty acids (Stumper 1953) such as formic acid.

In stinging most ants seize the enemy, whether it is another ant or a larger animal, in their mandibles and apply their sting close to the bite. *Myrmecia gulosa* is unable to sting if its mandibles are cut off, and it is clear that the mandibles provide the purchase for thrusting in the sting (Beard 1963). Often some venom enters by the bite even in ants which have a piercing sting. The venom of *Solenopsis saevissima* is not only poisonous to insects when it is injected by the sting: it kills insects when it is painted on the outside of their bodies and even has a residual effect about as strong as DDT and an antibiotic action (Blum et al. 1958).

Dolichoderine ants have no sting and only small sting glands. The defensive function of the sting has been taken over by anal glands which produce a complex of scented compounds. These not only have repellent and insecticidal properties but in *Tapinoma nigerrimum* two components polymerise to a viscous oil which immobilises small enemies (Stumper 1953).

In most Formicine ants the vesicle of the sting gland is enlarged and opens through a wider tube. The vesicle contains a mixture of formic acid and various other substances. In wood ants the contents of the vesicle may account for 20% of the ant's weight (Stumper 1953). When the muscles of the vesicle contract a spray of acid at about 50% concentration (Stumper 1953, Otto 1960) is forced out of the wide orifice near the anus between the small plates which represent what is left of the sting. *Formica* sp. and *Oecophylla longinoda* bend the gaster forwards between the legs and can spray up to 20-50 cm. The spray is rather fine with droplets of about 1 mg. (Otto 1960). The acid kills soft bodied insects rapidly on contact, and also kills insects as a fumigant in confined spaces (Osman & Kloft 1961). On hard bodied insects it penetrates the cuticle and kills the underlying epidermis and fat, and is also harmful when it enters the trachaeae. On human skin it raises a blister which persists for 10 days. All these effects can be ascribed to formic acid alone; dried venom, from which formic acid has all evaporated, is not very toxic (Otto 1960). The secretions of *Formica rufa*, *Camponotus maculatus*, and *Cataglyphis bicolor* are physically identical with formic acid (Stumper 1953).

When ants are so well equipped with defensive weapons it is rather surprising to find that many of them are eaten freely by birds, reptiles and amphibia. The large African *Paltothyreus*, which has a powerful sting, was the most common ant found in toads' stomachs in a collection from the Congo (Wheeler 1922), and it is eaten by birds and lizards too

(Sudd 1962a). When toads in Oklahoma were dissected their stomachs actually bristled with the stings of ants which were sticking through from inside. The stomachs of older specimens of toad were heavily scarred, apparently by old stings (Smith and Bragg 1949). Many other examples of vertebrates preying on ants have been listed (Bequaert 1922, 1930).

2·2 Sense organs

Sense organs play several parts in the machinery of ant behaviour. First of all they ensure that the ant's behaviour is relevant to the circumstances in which it finds itself. For example the behaviour of capturing prey only appears normally in the presence of prey, and the behaviour of feeding larvae only in the presence of larvae. This is called the releasing function of sense organs. Certain features, movement, smell, and possibly shape, of prey are detected by sense organs and the sense organ in some way sets in train the rest of the machinery to produce prey capture. But present circumstances are not the only things which decide what behaviour should appear at any moment. Not all ants will attack prey or feed larvae when they meet them. Whether they do so or not depends on many factors which can be loosely put under the heading of 'mood'. This includes obvious things such as whether the ant is hungry, or has food to give. 'Mood' is affected too by the age and size of the ant as well as by other poorly understood factors. Some of these may work through sense organs, others do not.

If a particular piece of behaviour does appear, it needs to be guided so that the ant's jaws close on the prey and not in mid-air. The sense organs are responsible for this orientating function too, and they may use either the same sensory impressions that released the behaviour, or different ones to do so. Very often the ant needs not only reports of where the prey is but also reports of where its own jaws are, to be sure that it strikes the prey. The sense organs also lead ants to search for prey in places where they are likely to find it. For instance the ant's movements may be directed towards the light or up vertical surfaces as it searches for prey. Messages from the sense organs ensure that some species of ant hunt by day, others by night. Altogether the functions of the sense organs in ant behaviour can be summed up by saying that they make sure that the 'right' behaviour occurs at the 'right' place and the 'right' time.

Ants are not particularly suited to physiological research but fortunately most of their sense organs are similar in their anatomy to types that are found in other insects. In larger and more accommodating insects the organs can be studied by recording their electrical responses to changes in the outside world (Dethier 1963). Each sense organ is more or less specialised to report the presence of only one sort of change. Eyes respond when light acts on them, organs of chemical sense in the presence of particular substances, and mechanical sense organs when they are deformed by forces such as air pressure and gravity or by contact. Sense organs which report on the outside world are naturally mostly set in the ant's cuticle, but a good many other sense organs in the cuticle report instead the position of limbs and joints and the strains in the cuticle. Organs which report on the outside world are called exteroceptors, those which report the state of the animal's own body are called proprioceptors.

2·2·1 *Hair sense organs*

The central part of each sense organ is a sense cell which is connected to the central nervous system by a nerve. Each sensory cell is associated with a special part formed from the cuticle, and it is very often the cuticular part which makes the organ sensitive to one particular class of stimulus. The microscopic appearance of the sense organs was well described by early ant anatomists (Janet 1904, Forel 1928) whose surmises as to function were not always accurate. The simplest organs are sensitive hairs each set in a cuticular socket. Single hairs act as organs of touch and respond when the hair is bent. They may be specialised in function like the long hairs borne by *Strumigenys* and other long-jawed Dacetines. These are of just the right length so that anything touching their tips will be transfixed by the jaws when they close (Brown and Wilson 1959). This is an example of a sense organ bringing behaviour into the correct spatial relationship with an object.

The same sort of hair organ can be bent by air-currents and also by airborne sound vibrations. No other sort of organ of hearing has been described in an ant. Provided they were insulated from vibration through the ground, *Myrmica rubra, Lasius niger, L. fuliginosus* and *Formica rufa* were in no way disturbed by sounds at frequencies of 50-11,000 cycles per second, when they were placed at the point where pressure changes due to the sound were at a maximum. If they were placed where displacement was maximum they did respond to sounds of frequencies of 790-840 c.p.s. (Autrum 1936).

Hair-organs also occur in hair-plates. These are patches of rather short stout hairs and are found at the antennal joints, the neck, the coxal and trochanteral joints and between thorax and petiole and petiole and gaster. The bristles are bent to different extents as the joints move, and so they can report on the position of the joint. They also can measure the alinement of the ant's body with the vertical. Many aquatic animals, and also man, have organs called statocysts to do this. The organ contains a heavy stone-like statolith, and the direction in which gravity acts is measured, in relation to the animal, by the way the weight of the statolith bears on sensory cells in the wall of the statocyst. No insect has a statolith; instead insects measure the direction of gravity by the way one part of their body bears against the next. Ants are able to aline their bodies directly up or down a vertical surface, or at any angle to the vertical. They can do so only if at least one antenna, or the neck, or the petiole and gaster, or any four coxae are free to move and have intact hair-plates. On a vertical surface *Formica polyctena* can aline itself within 14° on average, though some individual ants

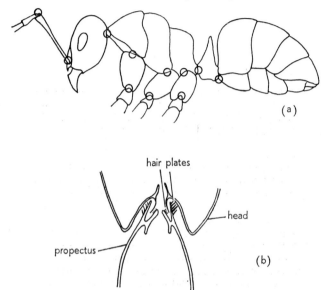

(a)

hair plates

head

propectus

(b)

FIG. 2·8 (a) Location of hair-plates on the body of *Formica polyctena*, (b) two pairs of hair-plates in the neck joint. (Redrawn after Markl 1962)

were accurate to 1°. They can maintain a less accurate orientation even on a surface inclined at only 3·5° to the horizontal (Markl 1962, 1963).

2·2·2 *Chemical senses*

Other hairs act as organs of chemical sense, corresponding to taste and smell in man. In other insects chemosensory hairs are short and thin-walled, but in ants no particular type of hair has been shown to be sensitive to chemicals. The sensitivity of ants to sugars has been tested by offering them solutions of different sugars in water; some are licked up, others are not. In this way it is possible to see which sugars are acceptable to ants and which are not, either because ants do not taste them or because they do not set feeding behaviour in motion. At the same time the relative attractiveness of different sugars can be found by comparing the weakest solution of each that will just induce an ant to feed. This sort of experiment shows great differences between ants. *Manica rubida* accepts only seven sugars whilst *Myrmica rubra*, which is not so much limited to insect flesh in nature, accepts twelve. In other cases there is no particular connection between the sugars an ant accepts. Ants which have been starved in the laboratory will accept very weak solutions; in the field only stronger solutions are usually taken. The sugar solutions are tested by sense organs on the mouthparts and ants, unlike butterflies, have no taste organs on the feet at least in *Manica rubida*. There are sense organs which can respond to sugars on the antennae. *Manica rubida* will not reject a solution of an unacceptable sugar merely after testing it with its antennae, all fluids are licked and then accepted or rejected on the testimony of organs on the mouthparts (Schmidt 1938). Acceptance or rejection is not affected by removal of the antennae or the maxillary or labial palps (Forel 1928), so that the sense organs must be in the preoral cavity itself. After training however *Manica rubida* workers can discriminate sugars with their antennae alone, and reject them before they have licked them (Schmidt 1938). Wood-ants will accept saccharine but *Messor barbarus* does not (Stäger 1935a).

In the blowfly *Phormia* sensory hairs on the labium each contain three to five sense cells some of which are stimulated by 'acceptable' substances such as sugars and water, and one only by unacceptable substances like alcohol (Dethier 1963). The sense of 'taste' in ants probably works on the same lines but no-one has investigated it in this way.

Our knowledge of the other chemical senses of ants is even less precise. Ants, like most insects, use their antennae to investigate food, other ants, the ground over which they walk and all the other objects they meet. If their antennae are cut off their behaviour is distorted, usually so much so that it gives little hint as to the functions of antennal organs. Now that we can isolate some of the chemicals ants use to signal to one another it may be possible to study their antennal sense more closely.

Because the antennae are moveable and have sense organs all over their surface it has been suggested that ants can perceive spatial arrangements of chemical stimuli, rather as we can perceive patterns of colour or texture. This is the so-called topochemical sense (Forel 1908). The sense could only work with substances that diffused very little or the pattern would be very much blurred. In fact there is very little evidence that ants can detect patterns of this kind. The observations which supported the original idea can be interpreted in other ways yet the phrase 'topochemical sense' is still occasionally used.

The antennae are relatively longer in small species of ant than in large ones and in small individuals compared with larger ones of the same species. The ratio of antenna length to body length varies from 0·12 to 0·95 in different species. Since large ants usually have better sight than small ones, the size of the antennae may compensate small ants for relatively poor distant vision. The antennae of blind ant species are no longer than those of sighted ants of the same general shape and size. Blind Doryline species however have two to four times as many hairs on their antennae as eyed species (Stumper 1955).

2·2·3 *Temperature and humidity senses*

Other hair organs are probably responsible for detecting temperature changes and the humidity of the air. Once again the type of organ which does this has not been identified in ants, although they have very decided responses to both temperature and humidity. Early experiments with *Aphaenogaster fulva*, *Camponotus pennsylvanicus* and *Acanthomyops latipes* showed that these ants moved sluggishly below 15°C and that heat stupor began to set in at about 35°. They were rapidly killed by exposure to 50°. Inside this range they would elect to rest in a temperature of 24-27° (Fielde 1904).

The temperature at which wood-ants preferred to settle depended on the temperature at which they had been kept before the experiment. Ants cultured at 15°C chose 27°C, but ants cultured at 19° preferred 31-32°. Their preference was not affected by the humidity of the air in the apparatus. Wood-ants are said to respond, by moving away, to a rise of only 0·25° (Herter 1924, 1925). Their preferred temperature varies a good deal with the time of year. In spring both *Formica polyctena* and *F. lugubris* choose temperatures of only 22°, but their choice is for 32° by the end of April. This change checks with the ant's movement into the warm upper part of the nest at this time of year. However there is quite a lot of variation from ant to ant. In spring some prefer cool, others warm places: in summer all of them settle down at 27-30°. The queen's choices are the reverse of this. In summer she selects 21-22° but in spring and autumn she prefers a warmer temperature, about 29° (Gösswald & Bier 1954). In winter all the ants collect into a winter cluster at about 21° and an even lower temperature may be chosen in deep winter. These experiments have all been made in apparatus which offered the ants a range of temperatures along its length. The preferred temperature is the temperature of the region where they settle. In some cases both the control of temperature and its measurement were rather crude and it would be a mistake to take the figures strictly.

Ants also have a humidity sense, though as is usually the case temperature and humidity are hard to disentangle. Low humidities cause the death of ants from excessive loss of water, especially when they are combined with a high temperature. Most ants like *Formica* and *Lasius* species survive for 30-40 days if they are kept without food at 20° in air saturated with water vapour. In air at 50-60% relative humidity and the same temperature they survive for only 2-3 days, a reduction to about one sixteenth. A more resistant species like *Leptothorax unifasciatus* can survive for about 9 days at this low humidity, although it will not live so long as other ants at high humidities. Most *Leptothorax* species live in twigs and crevices and cannot avoid dry conditions by retreating deeper into the soil as an earth-nesting ant does (Gösswald 1938a). *Proformica nasuta*, an ant nesting in the dry soil of steppes and of some Mediterranean lands, is also able to survive low humidities moderately well (Stumper 1961). The larvae of ants lose water to the air even faster than adults, and queens lose more water than workers. The pupae of ants on the other hand are far more resistant to desiccation than the other stages (Peakin 1960).

The behaviour of ants in apparatus which allows them to choose a humidity, is what one might expect from what has just been said about their susceptibility to desiccation. Most species, if tested at temperatures reasonably near to what obtains in their nest (15-20°), show a very marked preference for saturated air. After they have been in the apparatus for a day or so many species become more active especially at higher temperatures (above 16° in the small *Plagiolepis pygmaea* but not until 25° in the tougher *Formica* and *Myrmica* species). As a result they leave their preferred temperature and spread more evenly through the apparatus. This is perhaps due to the activating effect of temperature on a hungry or desiccated ant. *Leptothorax unifasciatus* is again an exception, for it always preferred low temperatures early in the experiment and only went to moist air after several days of desiccation (Gösswald 1941b). *Lasius flavus*, an ant which hardly ever appears above ground, always preferred moist air (Peakin 1960). Responses to humidity, like those to temperature, are evidently affected by mood. Workers of *Camponotus herculeanus* captured while foraging, but not those from the nest, had a clear preference for dry air for 9 hours after their capture. By 23 hours after their capture they preferred moist air, even if they had meanwhile been kept in moist air. Feeding them with sugar actually accelerated the change in preference. This may be connected in some way with the return of successful foragers to the nest (Pertunen 1955).

2·2·4 Some proprioceptors

Some sense organs in the cuticle have a similar arrangement of cells to that of a hair organ although there is no hair. An example is the campaniform sensillum. As its modern name suggests this has a bell-like dome set in the cuticle instead of a hair. Older workers on ants referred to it as a champagne cork organ (Forel 1904) or an umbilicus. The dome is thinner than the cuticle which surrounds it and any deformation in the cuticle is magnified in the dome. The movement of the dome excites the sense cell inside so that strains or distortions of the cuticle are reported to the central nervous system. Very often the dome is strengthened by a rib more sensitive to distortion in one direction. Campaniform organs can be found all over the bodies of ants. They are especially common on the mouthparts, the anterior part of the neck, the thorax, the base of the femur and on the tibia. They are also said to occur on the biting edge of the mandible (Janet 1904). All these places are concerned in transmitting forces from part to part of the ant, or from the ant to its food or building materials. They must aid it in controlling the amount of force it uses.

An even more modified form of hair organ is called a chordotonal organ. This consists of a set of cells slung across one or more of the joints of the ant. It too reports the position or loading of the joint. In *Myrmica rubra* chordotonal organs occur in the antennae (Johnston's organ), between the top and sides of the prothorax, mesothorax and metathorax, in the tibiae (the subgenual organ) and in the petiole and post petiole. There are none in the abdomen (Janet 1904). Johnston's organ reports the forces acting on the antenna, and it has been thought to detect the direction of gravity. Ants walking on a vertical surface can be made to change direction if an electromagnetic force is applied to an iron filing stuck to their antenna (Vowles 1954b). Ants without antennae however can still show responses to gravity which are in fact due to the hair plates. The antennae possess three hair plates, but hair plates on other parts of the body are equally able to detect gravity (Markl 1962, 1963). Johnston's organ probably registers the effect of air currents on the antenna as it does in blowflies (Burckhardt 1960), dung-beetles (Birukow 1958) and the honeybee (Heran 1957). Johnston's organ does not seem to respond to steady forces like that of gravity, but only to changes in force (Markl 1963). Another chordotonal organ lies in the blood-space of the tibia of each leg and contains, in *Camponotus ligniperdus*, 18-20 sense cells. It gives an electrical response to ground vibrations in the range from 100 to 3,000 cycles per second. Its sensitivity in ants is high, though not so high as in cockroaches. In ants this subgenual organ responds to accelerations of from $0·2-0·07$ g; in cockroaches the corresponding organ can detect accelerations as small as $0·00006$ g. Insects like beetles and flies have poorly developed subgenual organs and respond to larger accelerations—$0·2-1·5$ g over a frequency range of 50-300 c.p.s. (Autrum and Schneider 1948). Ants in artificial nests and in the field are notoriously sensitive to jolts transmitted through the ground and there can be little doubt that the subgenual organ is responsible for this.

2·3 Eyes

Ants, like other insects, have two types of eye when they are adult. Larval ants never have eyes of any kind, and no-one has suggested that they are sensitive to light. Most ants have a pair of compound eyes placed towards the side of their heads. Most queen ants, males and the workers of larger species also have three simple eyes or ocelli on the upper surface of their heads.

The compound eye can be seen from outside as a part of the cuticle which is transparent and divided into a number of facets, each more or less hexagonal in shape. Beneath each facet lies a complete lightsensitive organ called an ommatidium. The optical parts of the ommatidium are the cuticular lens and the specialised cells which secrete it, and a transparent cone which lies beneath the lens cell. The sensitive part of an ommatidium consists of seven retinal cells arranged to form a seven-sided prism with one end almost in contact with the cone.

Where the seven retinal cells all touch one another along the axis of the ommatidium, is a rod, the rhabdome. Each ommatidium forms an image of a small portion of the ant's field of view. These individual images are only used by the ant as dots in a mosaic picture, built up over the whole eye. Whatever detail of light and shade or of colour exists within each little image is lost. The sharpness or acuity of the overall picture depends on the number of facets in the eye and on the angle of view each ommatidium covers.

The number of ommatidia corresponds to the number of tiles in the mosaic picture. It is usually more in male and in queen ants than in workers. It also varies with the size of the ant. Larger species have more ommatidia than small ones, and larger individuals more than small ones of the same species. Ants which spend a good deal of time underground commonly have few or no facets. In wood-ants the workers have about 600 facets while the equally large worker of *Anomma nigricans* has none, and the small worker of *Pheidole megacephala* has about 30-50. A good many medium sized ants, like species of *Myrmica* and *Lasius*, get along with 100-200 facets. Among driver-ants the eye is reduced to a single lens on each side of the head in *Eciton burchelli*, and this is connected to the brain in much the same way as the eye of a *Formica*. In other species of *Eciton* and in *Dorylus* there is no eye and the optic centres of the brain form and then degenerate in the pupa. Male Doryline ants however have eyes with a very large number of facets (Werringloer 1932). Some other ants which rarely come to the surface like *Carebara*, *Paedalgus* and some species of *Proceratium* are also eyeless. The workers of some *Strumigenys* species have eyes with only sixteen facets and degenerate optic lobes like those of Dorylinae (Stärcke 1941).

Sharper and sharper vision can be obtained by crowding the ommatidia closer and closer together on the curved surface of the eye. Unfortunately the diameter of an ommatidium cannot be made less than a critical size, related to the wavelength of light. As a result a small eye cannot have an acuity equal to that of the best large eyes simply by having as many ommatidia (Barlow 1952). Smaller ants usually have therefore fewer facets than large ants, and are more likely to depend on antennal senses than on their eyes. Even those with large eyes and many facets probably cannot see much detail. After all 600 is quite a small number of ommatidia compared with the 4,000 or more in each eye of the honeybee, let alone the 115,000 cone cells in the central fovea of the human eye. The coarse-grained vision of ants is better suited to detecting movements. Many ants, like wood-ants and *Oecophylla*, can detect movements of a disc 22 mm. in diameter at a distance of 15-20 cm. (Homan 1924). The eyes of ants can also detect changes in the ant's own position relative to a fixed object like the sun. This property is used in the light-compass reaction (chapter 3).

Ants' eyes can detect the plane of polarisation of the light which falls on them. *Myrmica ruginodis* (Vowles 1950), *Lasius niger* (Carthy 1951a),

Tetramorium caespitum, *Tapinoma erraticum*, *Formica fusca* and wood-ants (Jander 1957) can orientate to the plane of polarisation, in place of an ordinary light-compass reaction. The lens and the cone do not act as analysers to detect the polarisation (Autrum & Stumpf 1950). The accuracy of the orientation to polarised light in *Myrmica ruginodis* is 27°. As this is the angle between the first and the fourth sides of a regular heptagon the seven retina cells may be responsible for detecting the plane of polarisation (Vowles 1954b).

2·3·1 *The ocelli*

The function of the ocelli, in ants that have them, is not known. Their focal length is too long for an image to be formed on the retina (Homan 1924). The fact that they are absent in many worker ants but found on their queens, which rarely leave the nest, suggests that they may affect the avoidance of light. Winged females of *Camponotus ligniperdus* normally move away from the light. If their ocelli are blackened they react positively to light by moving towards it. When these winged queens are kept in the dark for a day, those with ocelli blacked-out only become active after thirty seconds exposure to light. Ones with unpainted ocelli become active at once when light is let in (Müller 1931).

2·3·2 *Colour vision*

It is not very likely that ants can distinguish different colours of light as bees do. The few ants that are brightly coloured themselves, however, do have large eyes (*Myrmecia* and *Pseudomyrma*) and may be able to recognise the pattern of their own species (Wheeler 1915). The sensitivity of ants to different wavelengths has been tested by older workers (Lubbock 1882, Forel 1904) who found that ants would hide their brood under red glass as if it was opaque but that they behaved in ultra-violet light exactly as they do in light visible to man. If *Solenopsis saevissima* is trained to run on a scent trail with a light on one side, when the light is changed to the other side of the trail some ants reverse the direction in which they run. The proportion of the ants that respond depends on its brightness and also on its colour. There are most reversals when the light has a wavelength of 360 (ultra-violet), 505 (green) and 620 (orange) mμ (Marak and Wolken 1965). This simply means that light of these colours affects ants more strongly than light of the same intensity at other wavelengths. The ants may or may not be able to distinguish between colours.

2·4 Rhythms of activity

Most ants are more active at some times of day than at others. The best known of these activity rhythms are those of foraging. Of course it is harder to study rhythms inside the nest in conditions which are anything like the natural ones, but there is little reason to think that nursing behaviour has similar rhythms. Foraging rhythms confine the outside activity of ants to times when temperature and humidity outside the nest are least harmful to them, and also when their food is most easily obtained. When a piece of behaviour recurs at the same time each day it is said to show a circadian rhythm. Not all rhythms are of this kind: ants show a seasonal or annual rhythm in the date of the mating flight each year, and in the time of hibernation in sub-arctic ants. Another rhythm again is the alternation of statory and nomadic phases in the life of *Eciton* (chapter 5).

2·4·1 Circadian rhythms

Except in the hottest climates, many species of ants forage in the daytime. They may continue to collect food very late on mild summer nights however. Some of them are very inclined to break off in the middle of the day. *Formica subnitens* has a fairly regular midday break (Ayre 1958a) and so does *F. polyctena*, at least on clear days (Bruns 1954). On dull days they may keep on foraging all day (Otto 1958). Rain stops wood-ants foraging altogether. They are usually more active in the afternoon than in the morning, and this may simply reflect the greater number of insects to be caught then (Lange 1962). *Anoplolepis custodiens* in South Africa is also more active in the second half of the day (Steyn 1954). Midday rests, as one might expect, are even more frequent among ants of hotter lands. Mediterranean species of *Messor* do not collect seeds in a laboratory nest between 0600 and 1600 hours and they are most active from 2100 till 0300 (Ehrhardt 1931). In Palestine, *M. barbarus* does almost all its foraging between midnight and 0900 except when humidity is unusually high (Buxton 1924) or temperatures unusually low (Bodenheimer and Klein 1930) in the day. In Eritrea it is exclusively nocturnal (Escherisch 1907). Two other ants of African savannahs, *Pheidole crassinoda* and *P. sulphurata* do not hunt at midday especially when dry-season fires have bared the soil (Kemp 1951). American desert ants like *Veromessor pergandei* (Tevis 1958b) and *V. andrei* (McCluskey 1962) have similar habits, and 54 out of the 58 species of ant which live in the Sahara are nocturnal (Bernard 1951b). Some ants from moister climates in the tropics, *Camponotus maculatus* and *C. langei* are nocturnal too (Wheeler 1922). *C. maculatus* does not forage any less at full moon (Kaschef and Sheata 1963). Deserts seem also to have a certain number of diurnal species however. *Cataglyphus bombycina* (Pickles 1944) and its near relation *Myrmecocystus* in America (Cole 1957) are examples from actual deserts. *Camponotus rufo-glaucus* and *Ocymyrmex weitzeckeri* (Kemp 1951) from savannahs. These ants often have a silvery coat of short hairs which may protect them from the sun. No-one has measured the body temperatures of dead ants to see if this is so.

2·4·2 The basis of rhythmic activity

In some insects a circadian rhythm is not merely the direct result of changes in temperature and other conditions through the day, for the insect will continue to show peaks of activity at the same time of day if it is imprisoned in the dark at a constant temperature. This shows that the rhythm is at least partly under the control of an internal 'biological clock'. If the insect is kept, not in constant conditions but in a simulated day and night regime, the rhythm will be gradually reset. This shows itself as a drift of the peak of activity until it occurs at the same time of 'simulated day' as it originally did by true time (Harker 1961, Cloudesley-Thompson 1961).

Few experiments have been done with ants kept at constant conditions so it is hard to say how far ants rely on biological clocks. The typical diurnal rhythm of *Veromessor andrei* does more or less persist in the dark at constant temperature (McCluskey 1963) but that of *Formica polyctena* does not (Otto 1958). Apart from this contradiction it is clear that ants' activities are very much altered by the immediate effects of light and temperature. *Atta cephalotes* for example normally forages all day long. The time at which it commences leaf collection in the morning can be delayed by shading its nest entrance at 0530-0600 hours, the time when the first workers usually appear. As no amount of light before 0530 will make foraging start however there must be some sort of clock in this species which brings workers to the nest entrance to inspect the light (Hodgson 1955).

Further evidence that ants possess 'clocks' comes from experiments on their time sense. If ants are fed regularly at the same time each day for three to five days they learn to search for food then on succeeding days. *Lasius fuliginosus* and wood-ants can be trained in this way (Autrum 1936) and it is claimed *Myrmica rubra*, *Lasius niger*, *Formica fusca* and *Camponotus ligniperda* can be trained to search for food at intervals of 3, 5, 21, 22, 26, and 27 hours as well as 24 hours (Grabensberger 1933). Extremely careful control and rather elaborate analysis of the results would be needed to substantiate the last claim. Once ants have been trained in this way they can be made to come early or late by feeding them with stimulant or depressant drugs (Grabensberger 1933, 1934a). This itself suggests that ants have a metabolic clock.

Another implication of these experiments in ant learning is that we might expect ants in the wild to learn to forage when food was most plentiful. This simply adds to the complexity of studying ant rhythms. The daily activity of an ant colony may depend on minute to minute conditions, on an internal rhythm itself partly dependent on past conditions, and on the individual past experience of the ants in the colony.

2·5 The languages of ants

Although ants are very well equipped with eyes and other organs they get quite a lot of their information about the outside world indirectly. Some of the organs of ants, though they are technically effector organs, are used to make signals to other ants, usually nestmates. The signals

are physical—sounds or movements—or chemical—gland secretions—
in nature and they make up three sorts of 'language': one of scent, one
of sound and one of touch. Investigating these languages is extremely
difficult. When we see one ant affected in some way by the behaviour
of another ant it is easy to conclude that the two ants are communicat-
ing with each other. Finding out what sort of signals they are using is
a different matter. The ant which is sending the signals will almost
certainly be doing several things at once, and any one or more of these
may be the signal which is carrying a message to the other ant. The
way to find out which of the ant's actions carry a message is to reproduce
the effects of them each in isolation. If one of these effects is followed by
the response in the second ant's behaviour then probably we have discovered a word in that particular language. Even so we have to allow
in some way for the possibility that the second ant was going to behave
in that way in any case, with or without a signal. A chemical signal can
be produced in isolation by holding cotton wool soaked in the signal
substance near ants, and a sound can be recorded on tape and played
back to them. The language of touch however is almost impossible to
reproduce.

2·5·1   *The chemical language*

The 'alphabet' of the chemical language is made up of the secretions
of different glands. Some of these secretions have a more or less immediate effect on behaviour and affect other ants through their sense
organs. Another sort, which we are not concerned with here, has slower
effects on development and in a more general way on behaviour;
probably this sort has a drug-like action and the ants actually have to
eat the chemicals. Both classes of substance resemble in some ways the
hormones which circulate in the blood of insects, as well as in other
animals. The old name of ectohormone, for a chemical-messenger-
substance which circulates outside an animal's body instead of inside it
has now been replaced by the name pheromone (Karlson and Butenandt 1959).

Some ant pheromones are merely attractant substances which allow
ants to collect in clusters. Air in which *Solenopsis saevissima* workers have
been kept will attract clusters of ants, and most of this effect can be
shown to be due to the carbon dioxide it contains (Wilson 1962a).
Workers of *Lasius alienus* and of *Pheidole pallidula* cluster about their
queens in response to substances on the queens' cuticle. The substances
can be extracted from queens in ether, petrol or alcohol and painted
on to pieces of sponge or pith. The ants cluster round the treated
sponge and lick it (Stumper 1956). *Solenopsis saevissima* collects round
pieces of cork treated with chloroform or petrol extracts of its own
workers and licks them or carries them to its nest (Wilson 1962a).
These attractant and grooming substances are probably produced, or
at least liberated, over the entire surface of the ants' bodies.

IBA C

Some other substances however are produced by larger, localised glands; ants have many of these opening to the surface of their bodies (Janet 1898b, Pavan and Ronchetti 1955). The substances they produce are of at least two types. One sort is used to mark trails of scent. By following these an ant can retrace its own steps or guide those of its nestmates. The glands which produce these substances are all at the posterior tip of the ant's body. Trail-making is discussed in more detail in chapter 3. The other sort of secretion is used to spread alarm through a colony, for example if the nest is disturbed. In large colonies the smell is sometimes strong enough for us to smell it. This has led some people to think that what they smell when they are digging up a nest is the 'nest odour', by which ants recognise their nestmates (chapter 6). This is not so; these strong odours are in fact common to all members of the species and not peculiar to the nest. Alarm substances are rapidly diffusing substances usually with a molecular weight between 100 and 200 (Wilson and Bossert 1963). They are most often produced by glands near the main defensive weapons of ants—the mandibles and the sting (Maschwitz 1964). The mandibular gland has a large reservoir opening near the base of the mandible on each side. If the head of a *Pogonomyrmex badius* worker is crushed the secretion of the mandibular gland is released. In about 13 seconds it diffuses outwards to a distance of 6 cm., and ants within a circle of this radius run about in alarm with open mandibles. The scent falls below its effective threshold concentration in about 35 seconds. When the substance is released naturally by an alarmed worker the amount, and therefore the speed and extent of its spread, will be less. Some alarm substances have been identified chemically. Citral is produced by *Atta rubropilosa* and in smaller quantities by *Acanthomyops claviger*, which also produces citronellal. *Lasius fuliginosus* has the much more complex dendrolasin as its alarm substance (Wilson and Bossert 1963). Mandibular gland alarm substances exist, but have not been isolated in *Myrmica rubra*, *sulcinodis* and *ruginodis*. Any of these species will respond to the alarm signals of the other two. The crushed heads of *Messor barbarus*, *Pheidole pallidula*, *Crematogaster scutellaris*, *C. auberti* and *Tetramorium caespitum* alarm their own species but have no effect on others. *Formica polyctena*, *F. fusca* and *F. cinerea* also have mandibular gland alarm substances, but *Ponera coarctata* has none (Maschwitz 1964).

A very interesting pair of glands opens at the rear of the thorax. These, the metapleural glands, are found in all ants except the parasite *Teleutomyrmex*. Unlike the mandibular and sting glands they are not found in any other Hymenoptera. Each has a number of small budlike glands which open into a large incompressible chamber in the cuticle, through a sieve-like plate. Probably this ensures that their secretion only reaches the outside as a vapour, for the gland chamber never contains any liquid (Janet 1898b). The powerful stench of *Paltothyreus tarsatus* originates in these glands. It is only produced by maltreated

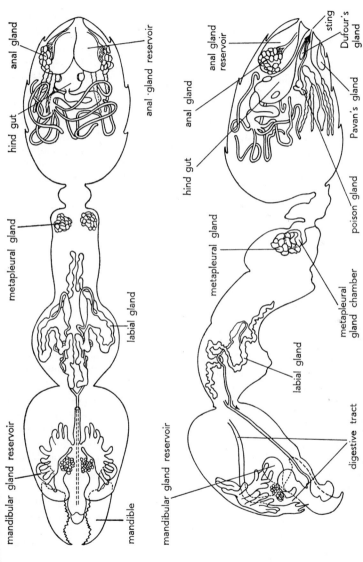

FIG. 2·9 Glands which produce chemical signals. (From 'Pheromones', E. O. Wilson. Copyright © May 1963 by Scientific American Inc. All rights reserved. (After Pavan and Ronchetti)

ants and causes flight or attack in other *P. tarsatus* workers (Sudd 1962a). The metapleural glands are enlarged in some tree-ants which attack in swarms, for example in *Pseudomyrma*, *Pachysima* (Wheeler 1922), *Crematogaster diformis* and *physothorax* (Bingham 1903).

Alarm signals are also produced from glands at the hind ends of many ants, even those which also produce trailing substances. Scents from the sting region can often be applied to the ground and in this way a point of danger, instead of the general presence of danger, can be marked. If the abdomen of a *Pheidole pallidula* worker is wiped along the ground a scent trail which other workers will follow is produced. At various points along this artificial trail workers suddenly show alarmed behaviour (Goetsch 1934). Whether this is only due to excessive amounts of trail substance or to a distinct trail substance is not clear. In *Tapinoma* and other Dolichoderine ants the enlarged anal gland produces a specific alarm substance methylheptenone, as well as repellent secretions aimed at attackers, not nestmates (Wilson & Bossert 1963). In the Formicinae Dufour's gland produces an alarm substance. That found in *Lasius niger* and *fuliginosus* and in *Plagiolepis pygmaea* acts intergenerically, and the alarm of one species affects the others (Maschwitz 1964).

2·5·2 *The sound language*

Many insects especially grasshoppers and crickets, produce sounds by stridulation. A shrill chirp is made when one cuticular part, bearing a peg or pegs, is rubbed over another ridged part of the cuticle. The cuticle of many ants, and even ant larvae, is ridged especially in Myrmicinae and Ponerinae. Where another part of the body could be rubbed over the ridges, for example between petiole and post-petiole in *Myrmica rubra* (Janet 1897a), or petiole and gaster in Ponerine ants (Sharp 1893), it has been described as a stridulating organ. It is rather exceptional for an ant to make a noise we can hear. *Messor* species and *Aphaenogaster testaceus* do stridulate when they are picked up. The sound they produce is in bursts, that is, it is probably modulated like the songs of grasshoppers (Krausse 1910). The large African *Megaponera foetans* produces a shrill whistling noise as it hunts in bands over the forest floor. This does not serve, as has been claimed, to hold the band together, for the ant only stridulates when it is disturbed (Bequaert 1912). A worker which was buried in sand stridulated and immediately other workers ran to it and began to dig (Collart 1925). As this behaviour is very similar to that of *Pogonomyrmex badius* in response to the mandibular gland secretion of an injured worker, it may be that chemical language is involved too. The alarm signal of *M. foetans* is effective over distances of several metres however (Santschi 1923), and this is a long way even for a strong odour such as it possesses. The only evidence that it responds to sounds is that little boys in Eastern Nigeria point it out as an ant which 'goes mad' if they whistle at it. I have never seen this done.

Although other ants make no sound, some people have supposed them able to stridulate and thought that stridulation was responsible for recruiting nestmates to a find of food. This of course we now know in many cases is due to the chemical language. *Myrmica rubra* and *ruginodis* make movements of their petiole and gaster which might produce a noise. No airborne sounds can be detected however. Ground vibrations on the other hand are produced by *Myrmica* (though not by *Formica* and *Lasius* species). No sounds were produced when the ants were feeding but only when they were trapped caught, held, attacked, poisoned or heated. None of the sounds produced the least response from other ants even when they were played back through a speaker which made the nest floor vibrate (Autrum 1936). So though our common European ants do stridulate either the sound is meaningless 'elimination of nervous energy' (Autrum 1936) or, like the sounds some beetles and moth caterpillars make, it is intended not for fellow ants but for predators. A vibration might be as potent a warning to an arthropod predator as black and yellow stripes are to a bird.

2·5·3 The antennal language

The story that ants talk by touching antennae is probably the most deeply rooted idea most people have about ants. It is also a story of considerable age. Yet the evidence that ants do have an antennal language is extremely thin. The story first appears in Huber's great little book (Huber 1810). He rightly says that ants must be able to communicate with their nestmates and he believes he has found their language in the contact of heads and mandibles, and above all, of the antennae, sensitive to touch and perhaps to unknown senses too. He bases this mainly on the noticeable part played by the antennae when one ant feeds another by regurgitation. He also thinks that the antennae can be used in spreading an alarm, in announcing the arrival of sunlight into which the pupae should be moved, for indicating a route during migration and in other ways as well. Later the idea of an antennal language was considerably expanded and different messages were supposed to be encoded by variations in the violence, frequency, duration and target of antennal strokes (Forel 1928). Sometimes detailed vocabularies were published; two blows on the antennal flagellum were supposed to be an incitement to leave the nest and forage, two on the top of the head a request for regurgitated food (Grabensberger 1933). Wasmann, on whom many of these ideas have been fathered, was in fact a good deal more cautious. Although he thought that messages might be encoded by the violence of the blows, the main function of antennal strokes was to excite the attention of another ant so that it was attracted to certain objects or activities. Above all, antennal blows served as a 'follow me' signal, by which the 'imitative drive' was excited. He added that antennal examination allowed ants to detect scents adhering to their fellows, and that scents might be produced by ants according to their state of excitement. In this way it was possible that the excitement might be communicated from ant to ant (Wasmann 1899). The existence of these scents was pure speculation on Wasmann's part, as he admitted, but the fact is that more and more of the 'transfers of excitement' that he listed turn out to be due to pheromones, in the form of scents. The recruitment of foragers which had seemed the best example of antennal language can be produced by the same pheromone that guides trail-following ants (section 3·3). In the sharing of food the role of the antennae seems to be secondary (section 6·1).

2·6 The central nervous system

One essential part of the machinery of behaviour remains—the central nervous system. All the information the sense organs can draw from the outside world, whether it comes to them directly or through signals from other ants, is passed by them to the central nervous system. The effector organs begin work when they receive orders to do so from the central nervous system. The central nervous system of an ant is concentrated to form a brain in the ant's head and there is also a chain of further concentrations, or ganglia, along the mid-ventral line of its body. These ganglia contain the cell-bodies and nuclei of nerve cells. They are linked with each other, and with the brain, by cords or commissures. These do not contain any cell-bodies, only axons or nerve fibres connecting different cells. Each ganglion outside the head contains cells which send out motor nerve fibres to the various muscles in its own part of the body. The segmental arrangement of ganglia in an ant is modified so that there are three ganglia in the thorax which supply motor nerves not only to the three segments of the thorax but also to the first two segments of the abdomen. (One of these segments is itself an integral part of the 'thorax' in an ant, the second forms the petiole.) There is a ganglion in the petiole which supplies nerves to the succeeding (third) segment of the abdomen. The rest of the abdomen has five ganglia. Each of these body ganglia has sensory nerves running into it, and probably the ganglia themselves contain many of the connections which are needed to co-ordinate the movements of, for instance the legs in walking.

The brain is a solid lump of nervous tissue and the oesophagus runs through the middle of it on its way to the neck. The part of the brain below the oesophagus contains three concentrations of nerve cells which represent the ganglia controlling the mandibles, the maxillae and the labium. The part above the oesophagus is drawn out on each side into optic lobes which merge with the inner end of the nervous parts of the compound eye. More anteriorly are two masses of tissue containing nerve cells which control the movements of the antennae, and sensory fibres from the antennae run into the same part of the brain. There are also smaller regions which connect with the ocelli in ants which have ocelli.

These arrangements mean that the brain receives sensory nerves directly from the two major sense organs, the eyes and the antennae,

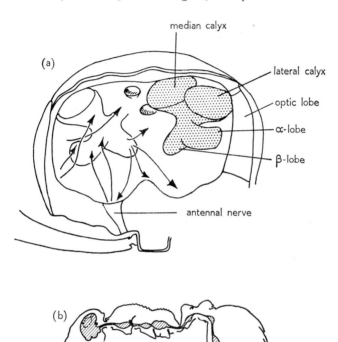

Fig. 2·10 (a) The brain of a *Formica lugubris* worker showing the mushroom bodies. The tracts to and from them are drawn in after Vowles (1955). (b) The central nervous system of *Myrmica rubra* (After Janet)

and sends nerves directly to control two major effectors, the mouthparts and the antennae. The connection between these special senses and the effector organs is probably made in the mushroom bodies or corpora pendunculata. These masses of nervous tissue lie above and slightly behind the optic lobes in the brain. On each side there are two cup-shaped bodies, the lateral and median calyces, which are joined by short stalks to two horn-shaped lobes, the alpha and beta lobes. The mushroom bodies are largely made up of nerve fibres. Some of these originate from nerve cells in the calyces, and run to other parts of the mushroom bodies. Fibres from nerve cells outside the mushroom bodies run to the calyces and to the alpha lobe. These are sensory fibres connecting the mushroom body with the optic and antennal lobes of the brain and with more posterior parts of the nervous system via the suboesophageal parts of the brain. No fibre which originates in the mushroom body leaves it. Instead the beta lobe is connected to the central body of the brain, to the motor centre of the antennae and to both sides of the suboesophageal ganglia, by fibres from cells in these various places (Vowles 1955b).

The anatomy of the brain cannot tell us how it works. Obviously the nervous centres of the special senses of the compound eyes and the antennae are connected with motor centres through the tracts of the calyces. The cells from which the fibres in these tracts start are placed near to the outside surface of the brain where they are most exposed to the blood. (Like all insects ants have no blood vessels, the brain is merely bathed in blood, not permeated by it.) Hormones in the blood, and the amount of food substances in the blood, would affect these cells rather quickly. They would therefore be well-placed to effect the way that the ant responds to sights and smells from the outside world.

3 — Ant navigation

Ants can use their sense organs and effectors in simple orientations like those described in chapter 2, to lead them to a particular sort of place. For example they might use them to find damp and dark places. Sometimes this is not enough, for the ant needs to find not just any damp dark place but the particular damp dark place where it has a nest. This is not such a simple matter, for the ant can never find its way by responding to stimuli which are produced by all damp dark places. It must use stimuli which are somehow peculiar to its own nest. Now the marks which lead it to its own nest often have no more direct biological significance to the ant than the number of a house has to the comfort of its owner. They 'stand for' the nest in a coincidental way, and are only connected with it by some activity of the ant. This is quite a different matter from an ant choosing to rest in a certain favourable degree of temperature. For that reason it is convenient to use the word 'navigation' for this route-finding by coincidental marks.

Because the stimuli which guide an ant back to its nest have no in-built biological significance they were often a stumbling block to early natural historians. The simple ideas that ants found their nest after a journey by the sight, smell or sound of it were soon disproved by 'displacement experiments'. These showed that many ants were unable to find their way home if they were moved to an 'unknown' place, although they usually could return from greater distances on their own journeys. Perhaps an unknown sense of direction existed. 'Has it a special organ and if so where? That is none of my business. It concerns those physiologists who specialise in the internal anatomy of ants' (Cornetz 1911). The problem was largely solved in a paper in the same volume of the journal from which this quotation came. Santschi (1911) showed that ants could use two senses, antennal chemical sense and vision, to find their way to and from their nests. It turned out that 'the' way ants navigate does not exist, for even ants which resemble each other closely in size and form sometimes use different methods even in the same laboratory conditions. If a worker of *Lasius niger* is set the task of carrying back to its nest pupae which are placed in the middle of a large turntable it can find its way home, even if the table is turned between its outward and homeward trips. However it loses its way completely in the dark, or in red light. Clearly it uses its eyes to find its way. *Lasius fuliginosus* on the other hand is not in the least hampered by darkness but becomes lost if the table is turned, or if the surface of the table is cleaned. Although its eyes are if anything larger than those of *L. niger*, it depends on a chemical sense to find its way, at least in these particular circumstances (Carthy 1951 a and b). These two ants are typical of the two main types of ant navigation. In one the ants orientate to distant marks, often the sun, which they sense with their eyes. In the other type of navigation ants use nearby objects, often on the ground they are running over. Most often they detect the objects by a chemical sense, though they sometimes appear to use touch. (Santschi 1923.)

3·1 Visual navigation

The discovery that ants use their eyes in navigation put an end to a long controversy. Some workers were reluctant to admit that ants could return to their nests using visual clues they had learnt on the outward journey. Memory was a 'psychic capability' which ants could not possess (Bethe 1898). On the other hand some were ready enough to allow ants such faculties, but did not believe that their eyes were good enough to recognise distant landmarks (Forel 1908). In fact an eye with 100 or more facets is well able to discriminate angles for navigation by a light-compass method. In this orientation the ant sets its body so that a certain group of ommatidia always point to the sun or landmark. As a result it moves in a fairly straight path—a bee-line in fact.

Experiments of three kinds demonstrate visual route-finding in a particular ant. In turntable experiments (Lubbock 1882, Bethe 1898) the ant is made to run on a piece of card which is turned while the ant is on it. The ant turns against the movement of the turntable and so maintains a true orientation. The experiment shows that the ant is not depending on nearby objects, for nearby objects turn with the turntable. The second sort of experiment is the displacement experiment. In these an ant is caught at one place and carried to another where it is released. An ant which depends mostly on a visual orientation strikes out from the new place on a course parallel to its old course (Cornetz 1911, Santschi 1911). This experiment also shows that the ant is using distant landmarks, and that the nest itself is not one of them. Experiments which go further and show that the ant detects these distant objects by vision, involve moving the objects so that the ant's orientation changes. The most striking of these experiments is Santschi's mirror experiment (Santschi 1911). In this an ant running in the sun is shaded by a small screen while the sun's light is reflected on to it by a mirror. The ant turns so that its body lies at the same angle to the reflected light as it formerly did to the direct light of the sun. These experiments can generally be carried out in the field to show how ants are actually orientating. More critical experiments in the laboratory show how ants can orientate. For instance, an ant can be trained to orientate to an electric light; when the light is replaced by another in a

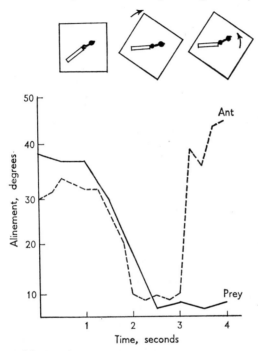

FIG. 3·1 A turntable experiment with a *Myrmica rubra* worker. As the card over which the ant runs is turned, the ant turns itself and its prey to maintain the alinement of its body. (Sudd 1965)

different position the ant changes its orientation. A negative result does not show that the ant cannot orientate visually; it only shows that some other method was more important at that time. A positive result does not mean that it has no other ways of orientating. Research on ant navigation has to be along two lines. Laboratory experiments show how ants can orientate, field experiments how they orientate in particular contexts. The two are complementary.

3·1·1 *The mechanism of visual orientation*

Visual orientation is best known and very highly developed in wood-ants (Jander 1957). In laboratory experiments wood-ant workers can orientate to a single light or to a black disc. In the field they orientate not only to the sun but to other landmarks as well so that the mirror experiment does not usually work. Their ability to use two landmarks simultaneously has been shown in the laboratory. They were trained to run with a lamp 20° above the horizontal on their left. Then some were trained to run with a lamp 40° above the horizontal on their right as well. Tested with a lamp 40° above the horizontal the doubly trained ants orientated with it on their right, the singly trained ants with it on their left. They could also be trained to orientate to the north in one part of a

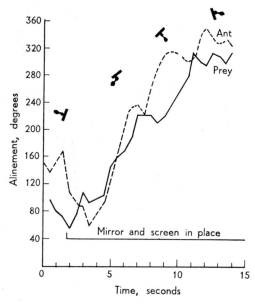

FIG. 3·2 Santschi's mirror experiment with *Myrmica rubra*. When the ant is screened from the sun and the sun's light is shone on to it from the opposite side, it turns and drags its prey in the other direction. (Sudd 1965)

garden and to east, south and west in three other parts. This sort of learning persisted for up to five days (Jander 1957).

These menotaxes or light-compass orientations (in which the ant's body lies at an angle to the light) are related to simpler phototaxes (in which the ant's head points directly at or away from the light). Inexperienced ants which are just beginning to forage show simple phototaxis. When they leave the nest they travel directly into the light. When they return they move directly away from it. In a positive phototaxis the insect's head points at the light. As soon as the image of the light falls on any part of the eye except a few forward-looking ommatidia—the fixation spot—the ant turns so that the image returns to the fixation spot. When the light enters ommatidia to the right of the fixation spot the ant turns to the right; ommatidia to the left of the fixation spot produce turning to the left. In a phototaxis the ant will only go forward without turning when it is pointing its fixation spot straight at the light. In light-compass orientation the fixation spot need not point directly at the light. As a result there is a turning tendency due to the illumination of ommatidia to one side or the other of the fixation spot. This is counteracted by a 'course order' which produces an exactly equal turning tendency in the opposite direction. Instead of turning towards the light the ant points at an angle to the light and

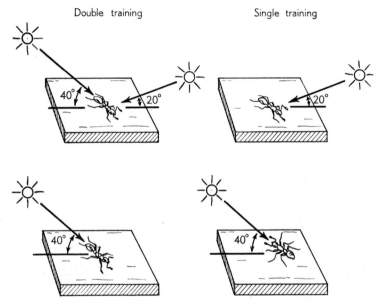

FIG. 3·3 Wood-ants can be trained to orientate in one direction to a light 20° above the horizon and in the other direction to one 40° above the horizon. (After Jander 1957)

this angle is decided by the course order (Jander 1957). With a certain amount of modification (Mittelstaedt 1962) this 'compensation theory' of menotaxis allows the ant to orientate at any angle to the light. It also allows the ant to reverse its course for the homeward trip. If the underlying phototaxis or basotaxis is changed from positive to negative the compensated course also turns through 180°. This ability is in fact possessed even by untrained ants, which have been reared in the dark. On their first trip in the light they are able to follow an opposite course on their return.

The correction to the course can be learnt on either the outward or inward journey. Ants can follow a crooked course outwards and return by something near the shortest straight line course. In the past this was explained by a kinaesthetic sense. Sense organs in the muscles and joints of the ant recorded the distance it travelled, and all the turns it made. These were added together to give a resultant course. In the laboratory wood-ants can only do this calculation if they are provided with an orientating light all the time. The turns are therefore recorded by the eyes and not by a muscle sense. Something of the way the ant

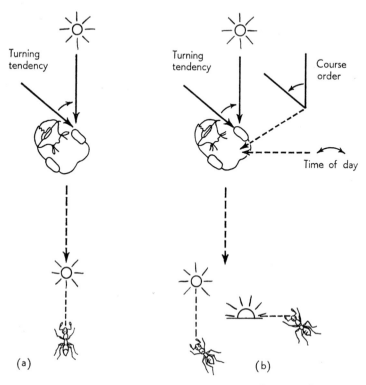

FIG. 3·4 The interaction of a basotaxis and a course-order to produce a meno-taxis. (a) In phototaxis the ant turns towards (or away from) the sun, and moves in a straight line to or from it. (b) In menotaxis the turning tendency due to the basotaxis is cancelled by a course-order so that the ant moves at an angle to the sun. The course-order is corrected for the sun's movement so the ant keeps a steady course whatever the time of day. (Based on Jander 1957)

performs the calculation can be seen from experiments with two lights. Ants were trained with a light that shone for 30 seconds at an angle of 135° to their course. This light was then replaced by another that shone for only 10 seconds from an angle of 225°, the two lights were shone in alternation like this for the whole training period. When these ants were later tested with a single light that burned all the time they orientated to it on a course of 159°. This is near the third side of a triangle which has one side at 225° and another three times as long at 135°. In other words it is the resultant straight line course (Jander 1957).

Ants may remain out of the nest tending aphids for several hours. All this time the sun is moving about 15° through the sky each hour and if the ant set the same course by the sun it would be a corresponding number of degrees wide of its nest on its return. Older experiments suggested that ants did make this error. Recently the experiment has been repeated however. The mean error of workers of *Lasius niger* which

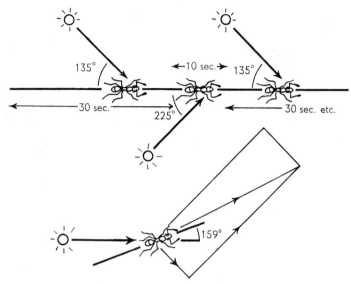

FIG. 3·5 After training with alternately a light at 135° for 30 seconds and a light at 225° for 10 seconds, a wood-ant orientates to a single lamp at 159°, near the resultant of the two earlier courses. (Based on Jander 1957)

had been imprisoned in a light-tight box for two hours was only 0·7°, not 30°, and for wood-ants the error was 1°. Both these species then can correct their course for the passage of time and no doubt other ants do so too (Jander 1957).

Wood-ants can orientate not only to the sun but to landmarks like trees and buildings and to the moon. Wood-ants (Jander 1957), *Myrmica rubra* (Vowles 1950) and *Lasius niger* (Carthy 1951a) can also set a course by the pattern of polarised light in the cloudless parts of the sky. This is related to the position of the sun in the sky. Like bees then, these ants can continue to run on a menotactic course when the sun is hidden by clouds.

3·2 Navigation by gravity

The ability of ants to set their bodies at an angle to the vertical was mentioned in discussing the action of hair plates (section 2·2·1). This also is a sort of menotaxis, in which the body is kept at a constant angle to gravity instead of to a light. *Myrmica rubra*, *M. ruginodis* (Vowles 1954a), *Formica polyctena* (Markl 1964) and *Crematogaster scutellaris* (Goetsch 1934) can orientate in this way. Probably many other ants can do so too.

Formica polyctena can be trained to run to food from the centre of a vertical turntable and back again in red light. After $\frac{1}{2}$ to 3 hours training they can run at any angle to the vertical. However their course always deviates slightly from the target. When the food is anywhere above the centre of the turntable the courses of ants to the food are likely to be slightly too near the vertical. Below the centre their courses to the food are biassed downwards. Ants returning from the food to the centre of the turntable on the other hand are biassed downwards if the goal is 60° or more from vertically above the centre of the turntable (Markl, 1964). This seems to be the result of imperfect compensation of a basotaxis to gravity. Inexperienced wood-ant workers are positively geotactic, that is they tend to walk downwards (Jander 1957).

When *Myrmica rubra* or *M. ruginodis* workers are startled they make a short straight escape run. During the run they will orientate to gravity on a vertical surface or to light on a horizontal one. If they are running on a board which can be swung from horizontal to vertical while they are running they change immediately from light to gravity as their orientating stimulus. In doing this they confuse angles of $x°$ with $360 - x°$, for example 30° and 330° (Vowles 1954a). This is not due to a defect in the mechanism of orientation to gravity, for ants trained to fetch food on a vertical surface do not confuse these angles (Markl 1964). Orientations to the direction of gravity, the direction of light and the plane of polarisation of light are 'coupled' (Jander 1957); the ant does not have to learn the relation between them. The defect may lie in the coupling.

3·3 Navigation by scent trails

When an ant is navigating menotactically it usually walks in a fairly straight line, and its path is parallel to that of other ants rather than superimposed on them. Some ants, including common European ones, can be seen moving in files, one behind the other but not necessarily close behind, on paths which may be curved. Early naturalists were already acquainted with the follow-my-leader habits of processionary caterpillars, and thought that ants too might be following some kind of trace left on the ground by other ants. This idea was supported by interruption experiments. In these the ground in front of an ant is rubbed, in the classic experiment with a finger. When the ant reaches the rubbed place it stops short and recoils. Other ants on the same path stop at the same place and there is usually a delay before any ants cross over the interruption. The disturbance is not due to the smell of fingers, for the same result can be got by wiping with cotton wool, or even by sticking adhesive tape on the ground in front of the ants.

An interruption experiment really only shows that ants will not cross clean ground. It does not show what was on the ground or how the ants use it. The origin of the marks can be seen by watching the development of a trail from the start. The workers of many small ants look for food singly. When one of them finds something which it cannot move to its nest unaided it leaves it and goes back to the nest. Shortly after a number of its nestmates come out of the nest and run to the food (chapter 5). The tracks of these 'recruits' are very nearly the same as the track of the 'scout' back to the nest. If the scout is persuaded to run

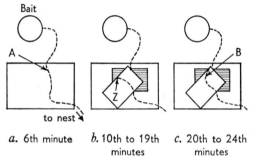

a. 6th minute   *b.* 10th to 19th   *c.* 20th to 24th
minutes   minutes

FIG. 3·6 An interruption experiment, showing that *Monomorium pharaonis* lays scent trails. (Sudd 1960a)

home over a sheet of paper and the sheet of paper is turned the track of the recruits is displaced with the paper. The scout does not lead the recruits to the food, in fact the scout may be captured as soon as recruits begin to leave the nest and their path will be the same (Eidmann 1927a, Hingston 1928). Scouts of *Tapinoma nigerrimum* press the tips of their abdomens to the ground as they return to the nest, and probably smear the secretions of glands on the ground as they go. Smears which are made in the same way by *Lasius fuliginosus* can be made visible by dusting them with lycopodium powder (Carthy 1951b). Artificial trails can be made by drawing a line from an established trail with the tip of the abdomen of a freshly killed ant (Goetsch 1934).

The last experiment can be done with the contents of different glands dissected out of ants. Some interesting differences between ants emerge from this. In Myrmicinae, where the sting is well developed, trails can be made with the venom gland itself in the Attini and in *Tetramorium guineense* (Blum and Ross 1965), or with the contents of Dufour's gland in other members of the subfamily. In the Dolichoderinae, which have no sting, Pavan's gland can be implicated (Wilson 1963). The Formicinae, equally stingless, produce a trail substance from their hindgut (Carthy 1951b, Blum and Wilson 1964). *Eciton hamatum*, which has a sting, also produces its scent from its hind-gut (Blum and Pontecarrero 1964). The Myrmicinae extrude the sting and use it like a pen to lay trails. The posterior border of the sixth sternite in the Dolicho-derinae and the circle of hairs around the anus in the Formicinae serve the same purpose (Wilson 1963).

Apart from these gross differences between subfamilies, each species of ant which lays a trail seems to produce its own peculiar trail sub-stance. Each of three species of *Solenopsis* which has been tested follows artificial trails of its own secretion far more strongly than the secretion of the other two (Wilson 1962a). The substances are species-specific in a number of Dolichoderine ants too (Wilson and Pavan 1959). Oddly the secretion of Dufour's gland from the vestigial sting-glands of the Dolichoderine *Monacis bispinosa* is followed very readily by *Solenopsis saevissima*; *M. bispinosa* itself follows trails made from its Pavan's gland. In many cases the scent the ant follows is not the major constituent of the secretion. Presumably each species can elect to follow a different trace (Blum and Ross 1965).

These experiments show that ant trails are due to a scent deposited on the ground from specialised glands, and not to any other kind of mark. Probably scent trail behaviour began with one ant following another closely, even in contact with it like the tandem of mating ter-mites. This sort of behaviour still exists in some species of *Camponotus* (Wilson 1959a, Hingston 1928) especially those which forage under the sun of a tropical noon. When *Monomorium pharaonis* workers are running on a trail which branches each worker is independent of the rest in selecting a branch to follow. Workers which are running very closely behind another worker however are likely to follow it into the branch it chooses (Sudd 1960d). This seems to be a remnant of tandem behaviour. In most species however there has been evolution in be-haviour and biochemistry so that the distance between ants can be tens of centimetres. No trail substance has so far been identified chemi-cally so that we do not know whether the substances different ants produce are similar chemically or not.

The ants which have been shown to lay scent trails are listed below. Those in which artificial trails have been produced are marked *: in the remainder scent trails have been demonstrated by interruption or turntable experiments.

> *Eciton hamatum** (Blum and Pontecarrero 1964)
> *Solenopsis geminata** (Goetsch 1934)
> *S. saevissima** (Wilson 1962)
> *Monomorium pharaonis* (Sudd 1960a)
> *Pogonomyrmex* sp. (Goetsch 1934)
> *Crematogaster scutellaris** (Goetsch 1934)
> *C. sordidula** (Goetsch 1934)
> *Pheidole crassinoda* (Sudd 1960c)
> *Ph. pallidula** (Goetsch 1934)

Myrmica rubra (Eidmann 1927a)
Manica rubida (Goetsch 1934)
*Atta rubropilosa** (Wilson 1963)
Tetramorium caespitum (Goetsch 1934)
T. guineense (Blum and Ross 1965)
*Liometopum occidentale** (Wilson and Pavan 1959)
Dorymyrmex goetschi (Goetsch 1934)
Tapinoma erraticum (Goetsch 1934)
T. melanocephalum (Goetsch 1934)
T. antarcticum (Goetsch 1934)
T. sessile (Wilson and Pavan 1959)
*Monacis bispinosa** (Wilson and Pavan 1959)
*Iridomyrmex humilis** (Wilson and Pavan 1959)
*I. pruinosus** (Wilson and Pavan 1959)
Acantholepis frauenfeldi (Goetsch 1934)
Plagiolepis pygmaea (Goetsch 1934)
Lasius niger (Bethe 1898)
L. emarginatus (Goetsch 1934)
L. fuliginosus (Carthy 1951a)
*Paratrechina longicornis** (Blum and Wilson 1964)
*Myrmelachista ramulorum** (Blum and Wilson 1964)

Most of the ants in this table are small, under 6 mm. long. Larger ants, for instance wood-ants, are sometimes found only on constant paths, but these are not formed in the same way as the scent trails of smaller ants. There is no evidence that the roads of wood-ants are marked by scent. It is better therefore to call these 'routes', and not to assume that they have a similar basis to the trails of smaller ants (Santschi 1911).

3·3·1 Following scent trails

We know few of the details of how ants respond to the trail of scent. Since they sometimes touch the ground with their antennae, or reach out as if searching for the scent, it is likely that they use their antennal organs of chemical sense to follow the trail, and not organs on their feet. (The only experiment in which ants' antennae have been cut off was with *Formica nigricans*, which does not use scent trails—Forel 1908.) At first it was thought that the ants followed the trail by using a contact chemical sense but ants can in fact follow a trail without touching the ground and they can also follow it as much as 10 mm. to the side of where it was laid.

Some recent experiments with *Solenopsis saevissima* are most easily explained in terms of a trail that exists in the air rather than on the ground. A successful scout leaves a trail of scent on the ground behind it. The scent evaporates and diffuses outwards in the air. If we assume that an ant following this scent can only detect it when its concentration is greater than a threshold value, the trail will end, in effect, where this concentration occurs in the air. This will be a surface which encloses a sort of tunnel of scented air. A section of the tunnel at right-angles to the ant's path will be a semi-circle. Where the scent is newly laid the semicircle will be small, as the scent diffuses outwards the semicircle first grows, and then, when there is no longer any unevaporated

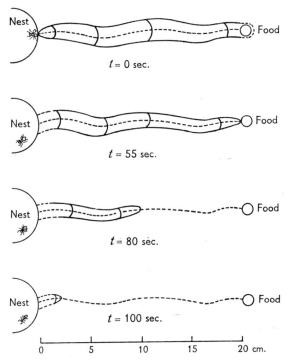

FIG. 3·7 The scent trail of *Solenopsis saevissima* laid from food to nest. The scented air fills a sausage-shaped space up to 40 cm. long and 2 cm. wide. Outside this space the scent is too dilute for the ant to respond to it. (Wilson and Bossert 1963)

scent, it begins to shrink. So at any time the tunnel is a sausage-shaped portion of space, about 42 cm. long. Its greatest width occurs about 15 cm. behind the ant which is laying it. It is about 2 cm. wide there. Outside this space the air contains less than the threshold concentration of scent. The trail fades out at the end where it was first laid after about 100 seconds, so that the tail of the sausage disappears as its head is extended. The width of the sausage depends on the amount of scent released by the ant, on its rate of diffusion and on the threshold. The length of the sausage depends on all these and also on the speed at which the ant laying the trail was walking (Bossert and Wilson 1963).

We do not know how exactly the ant behaves inside the tunnel of scent. Probably, once it has got into the scented space, it remains there by turning back whenever it finds itself passing through the threshold concentration at the skin of the sausage. It keeps moving because the scent, or extracts from the Dufour's gland, not only guide ants, but activate them as well (Wilson 1962a). Detailed descriptions of the ants' movements are lacking.

3·3·2   *The accuracy of scent trails*

We know rather more about the accuracy of the guidance which a trail gives to recruits (Wilson 1962a). There are two sources of in-accuracy; errors of the scout in laying the trail and errors of the recruits who follow it. As a result the place where the scout stops searching for food on the trail and turns back may be beyond, or short of, the food (a range deviation) or to left or right of it (a direction deviation) or, of course, both. Looking first at direction, if recruits got no guidance about direction and were equally likely to travel out from the nest in any direction, we should have almost no certainty that the path of a recruit would lie in a particular sector of, say, 1°. On average we should expect one recruit in 360 to do so. If on the other hand the trail gave such accurate guidance that all the recruits travelled on the same path within 1°, we should be absolutely certain that any recruit's path would end in this 1° sector. The chance that it would do so would have increased from 1 in 360 to 1 in 1, a 360 times increase. The trail does not really guide recruits as accurately as this and instead of all recruits reaching the 1° sector, the points where their paths end are spread out on both sides of the sector. Because of this dispersion we cannot be absolutely sure that a recruit's path will end in our 1° sector. There is still a residual uncertainty, which has the amount $\sqrt{2\pi.e.\sigma}$, where σ is the standard deviation of the positions where paths end, a measure of their dispersion. Instead of the trail's guidance increasing our certainty by 360 times it has only increased it by $360/\sqrt{2\pi.e.\sigma}$. The change in certainty the trail produces is called technically its information. Infor-mation is usually expressed as the binary logarithm of the increase in certainty. In our example every binary unit (or 'bit') of information halves the uncertainty so that 1 unit is needed to guide a recruit into the right semicircle, two for the right quadrant and so on.

The amount of guidance as to range can be found from the greatest distance, d, over which ants will follow trails. (If there was no guidance about direction ants would stop at points evenly scattered between the nest and this distance.) If the points are actually scattered around the target distance with a standard deviation σ_r then the change of cer-tainty is $d/\sqrt{2\pi.e.\sigma_r}$, and the information is the binary logarithm of this.

Actual measurements of the dispersion of recruits of *Solenopsis saevis-sima* in range and direction show that the trail contains about 2 units of information about distance, enough to decide which of four equally likely stretches of the range the target lies in. The trail contains different amounts of information about direction according to the distance of the target from the nest. The actual error, as a distance to right or left, is about the same at all ranges. When the error is measured as an angle it must appear greatest when the range is least. When the target is 50 mm. from the nest the trail carries about 4 units of information, when it is 100 mm. away about 5 units. These are enough to fix the position of the target in arcs of 22·5° and 11° respectively. If the trail gave no guidance at all to recruits we should expect 1 recruit in 4 to reach the right quarter of the range and 1 in 16 of these the right arc of 22·5°. Altogether only 1 in 4 times 16 would be in both the right part of the range and the right arc. The information required to make it certain that any recruit will be right in both these respects is $\log_2 64$, or 6 units. Now we can see why units of information are expressed as logarithms, for the total information in the trail is found by adding 4 units for direction to 2 units for range. Information measured in this way is useful for comparing the amounts of information which can be transmitted by different methods. For example the dances of the honey-bee can be shown to carry 2·5-4 units of information as to direction and 1·1-1·25 units as to distance (Haldane and Spurway 1954). The total of up to 5·25 units is very close to the capacity of an *S. saevissima* trail (Wilson 1962a).

3·3·3 *The choice of direction*

Modern work has shown that the trail tells recruits nothing but the position of the food. Any information they possess about the amount of the food, they do not get from the trail (chapter 5), and they do not seem to be informed of the nature or flavour of the food (Sudd 1960a). Even the amount of information they get about the position of the food has been disputed. An ant which encounters the trail at either end will, if it only persists in following, reach the other end, but which end will an ant that stumbles on the middle of the trail go to? Will it distinguish between the nestward and outward directions on the trail? Older accounts stated that it would, and ascribed this to a polarisation of the trail, on the analogy of the compass needle which not only alines itself north-south, but points one end consistently to the north. This idea seems to have begun with the misinterpretation of an experiment made by Forel in 1886. He took home-going wood-ants from one of their routes and replaced them on the same route about a metre away. 'After having made several very short loops, they started off without mistake, en route in the proper direction to their nest, never in the opposite direction.' (Forel 1908.) Since wood-ants do not have scent-trails of the ordinary type this experiment has no bearing on the polar-isation of scent-trails. Wood-ants usually take a correct direction like this by visual navigation, whether thay are placed on a route or not. Forel appropriated the observation to support his supposed topo-

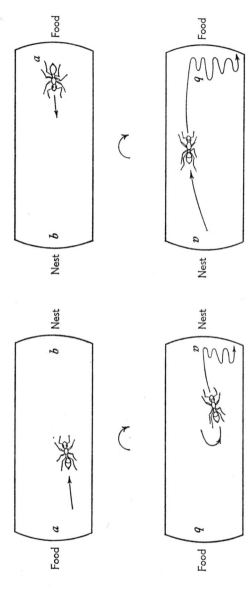

FIG. 3·8 Bethe's experiment. An ant which is near the pivot of the turntable when it is turned corrects its alinement. If it is near the end of the turntable however it does not correct but runs to the end of the turntable where it becomes confused. (Original)

chemical sense but it has no bearing on this either. A firm statement that the trail possessed a polarity was based on experiments with *Lasius niger* (Bethe 1898). Interruption and turntable experiments showed that this ant followed scent-trails to and from its food. One of these trails ran over a zinc turntable on a wooden plank (apparently the turntable was on a vertical surface). If the turntable was turned while an ant was running on it from *a* to *b* and was near the pivot, the ant turned against the movement of the turntable. As a result it went towards *a* though still running in the same direction (figure 3·8). This showed clearly that the ants were taking note of light or gravity as well as following the trail. It also showed that the ants did not detect any polarity in the middle of a stretch of trail. If on the other hand the ant was near one end when the turntable was turned, it did not correct its course but went on running from *a* to *b*, although this now took it towards the nest. In either case when the ant reached the end of the turntable it shied, running backwards and forwards at the edge. It is very clear from this that whatever caused the ants to shy was to be found at the joints on the track. The experiment was nevertheless used for 50 years to show that the trail was polarised throughout its length. Shying is actually typical of interruption experiments, and the experiment has been repeated, with precautions to avoid bad joins at the end of the turntable, and ants ran smoothly over the joins however the turntable was placed (Chauvin 1948). Many suggestions were made to explain the supposed polarity of the trail. Some involved a gradient in the intensity of scent along the trail (Brun 1914), though on a long trail either the gradient would be so slight as to be undetectable or it would reach zero before the end was reached (Chauvin 1948). Most other suggestions were that the shape of the scent patches betrayed the direction in which the trail had been laid. Oddly the smears left by *Lasius fuliginosus* are drawn out to a tear-drop shape by the movement of the ant which lays them, but the ants seem to be unable to appreciate this (Carthy 1951b). Although *Myrmica rubra* seems to be able to find the direction of its nest in the dark after running over a very small section of trail (McGregor 1948), there is no evidence that it can do so from a single scent spot. More probably it learns the direction of the nest with respect to gravity for other ants can orientate even on a slope as low as 3·5° (Markl 1962).

3·4 *Integrated navigation*

There is a good deal of evidence that ants use several systems of navigation at once. Experiments which seem to show that ants can detect a polarity in scent trails only work when the ants are able to use other sorts of navigation too. 'Ants which are set down in the middle of a route which is unknown to them are incapable of distinguishing between the two directions from that point' (Brun 1914). The ants only make a correct choice when they are replaced on a trail near to the place where they were captured (Santschi 1911, Sudd 1960b). After *Solenopsis saevissima* has been trained to run on a scent trail lighted from one side it will turn round and retrace its steps if the trail is illuminated from the other side (Marak and Wolken 1965). All these observations imply that ants use visual navigation at the same time as they are running on trails. *Crematogaster scutellaris* workers evidently use gravity instead when they are returning home up a vertical wall. They will follow portions of their trail which have been displaced by turning a piece of paper over which they ran, only when the paper has been turned less than 40°. When it has been turned between 40 and 75° they are disturbed, and when it is turned more than 75° they leave the trail and run vertically up the wall (Goetsch 1934). Recruits running from the nest on an established trail behave in the same way but they follow a newly-laid trail slavishly.

Evidently the general direction of the trail is learnt and ants will not follow departures from it. The trail itself is equivocal about direction; instead of leading an ant to one small arc it may lead to either of two arcs. This equivocation is a deficiency of one unit of information, and one unit should accordingly be deducted from estimates of the amount of information in the trail. The deficiency is made up by information coming from visual and gravity senses. Even in the worst equipped ants these are capable of showing which of two semicircles to go to.

In all probability a 'pure' orientation to odour is as rare among ants as it is in other animals (Jander 1963).

4 — The nests of ants

Almost all social insects build nests of some sort, and so of course do the solitary wasps and bees to which many of them are related. Unless the adults carry their young with them they need some base to which they can return with food for the young. They get other advantages from a nest too, such as protection from attack and from weather and a place to store food for bad seasons. The honeybee achieves these ends by building elaborate wax combs for storing honey and rearing its brood, and these structures also play a part in controlling development, for queens are reared in a special sort of wax cell. Honeybee workers can control the temperature of their nest even when the outside temperature is very high or very low.

In contrast the nests of ants often seem to be simply holes in the ground and the young are reared in a set of rather poky chambers. Most ants' nests in reality however have an architecture of their own, which represents so to speak the 'frozen behaviour' of the ants that built them. The arboreal nests of ants like *Crematogaster* and *Azteca*, in their less geometrical way, are as striking as those of the honeybee. A large nest of the leaf-cutting ant, *Atta*, will bear comparison with any piece of insect architecture.

A peculiarity of many ants is that a single colony may possess several nests, or may build branch nests during favourable seasons. A colony which is spread over several nests in this way is said to be polydomous. The wood-ants are notorious for this habit.

4·0·1 Nestless ants

Some American army-ants do not dig a nest when they stop raiding at nightfall. These ants are nomadic for part of their time, raiding by day and resting at night (section 5·1·4). At these times they merely form a bivouac, a cluster of worker ants surrounding the queen and her brood. The cluster always hangs down from a tree or branch, or inside a hollow tree or log. In shape it may be a cylinder, a curtain or a conical stopper inside a cavity (figure 4·1). The ants generally choose places for their bivouacs which offer some sort of protection from extremes of temperature and humidity, but this probably comes about because they avoid sunflecks and draughts on the rain-forest floor (Jackson 1957). A cluster begins to form when returning foragers meet, and often collide with, an evening exodus of workers from the previous night's bivouac. A 'confusion centre', a sort of traffic-jam, forms and ants eventually break out of this in a new direction in a column, whose front moves rather hesitantly, as if led from behind. The front spreads

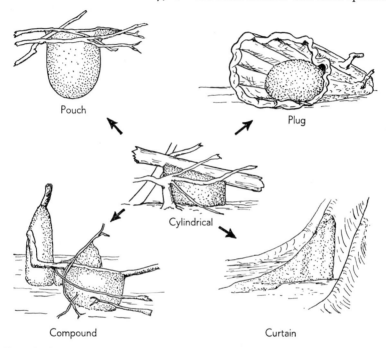

Pouch

Plug

Cylindrical

Compound

Curtain

FIG. 4·1 Some of the shapes taken by bivouac swarms of *Eciton*. (Schneirla, Brown and Brown 1954)

out and may be forced over tree-roots and buttresses. When an ant runs over a log it is likely to stop on the overhanging surface with its forelegs and body dangling from the middle and hind legs. If it is left alone it will shortly recoil and turn back. Before this happens as a rule another ant runs over it and in turn stops hanging by its hind legs from the first ant. If another ant runs over the second and yet another in turn over this a string of ants begins to form. In *Eciton hamatum* the strings can grow up to 28 cm. long, in *E. burchelli* rather longer. Neighbouring strings become cross-linked when ants settle between them, and ropes, curtains and cylinders eventually form. How the queen and brood get inside the cluster is not known but they are always near the top with the smallest larvae near the centre and the larger ones outside them (Schneirla, Brown & Brown 1954).

In the relatively constant weather inside a tropical forest these nest-less ants succeed in keeping their brood at a temperature between 24° and 28°, that is one to two degrees above the temperature of the forest floor, with only a few degrees variation between day and night (Jackson 1957). Rain forest is perhaps the most favourable place one could choose for this and it is rather doubtful whether a bivouac could provide conditions as good as this in a slightly more severe climate. Many other Dorylinae, for instance *Anomma* in Africa, dig holes in which they bivouac (Raignier and van Boven 1955).

4·1 Types of nest

Among ants that do build nests the appearance of the nest depends on the material from which it is made and the style in which it is built. While some ants only build their nest in certain materials, living leaves or twigs for instance, most ants are less particular. Nests may be begun in soil and later extended into rotten wood, or begun in wood and extended into soil as in *Camponotus herculeanus* (Eidmann 1928b). They may begin in soil or in tree stumps and later spread to other materials as in wood-ants (Chauvin 1958). But even ants which nest in soil may have their preferences for particular types of soil. Although only 35% of the land in the Middle Main district of Germany has dry soil, 87% of all the region's nests of *Lasius niger* are found on the dry soils (Gösswald 1938a). Many similar examples could be chosen to show that ants select particular sites because of the properties of their soils or vegetation (Hayashida 1960, Brian 1964). Exposure to sunlight is also important. *Formica exsectoides* (Cory and Haviland 1938), *F. polyctena* (Otto 1958) and all Attini (Weber 1941) prefer shade, and other species prefer sun (Brian and Brian 1951).

The way in which the nest is built can be used to classify nests as well. Some ants nest in ready-made cavities, usually above ground, in hollow twigs and in crevices in trees or rocks. Others construct their own cavities in all sorts of materials. Crevice nesters are able to place themselves near to supplies of food, especially if they nest in trees, but they have limited contact with the soil and the store of moisture it holds. Ants which dig nests in earth on the other hand can usually get moister conditions by digging deeper (Gösswald 1938a). Nests dug in soil are the commonest and probably the most primitive kind of nest in ants. Certain types of soil nest are therefore common to a good many species of ants. Nests away from soil are less common and more hazardous and some types of nests are peculiar to particular species or genera of ant.

It is difficult to generalise about the methods ants use to work their materials. There may perhaps be two contrasted ways of working, either of which can be used with most sorts of material. Some ants' nests are made of holes which they dig either in natural materials or in heaps of materials they have collected. Other ants build their nests of walls which enclose spaces. This second method has greater possibilities for building nests away from soil.

4·1·1 Excavated nests

Ants which dig nests in soil use their mandibles as trowels to scrape away earth, form it into pellets and carry it away. They use the convex outer face of their mandibles to consolidate their building by forward and downward thrusting movements (Forel 1920). *Formica fusca* is described using its forelegs, terrier style, to dig and its mandibles to

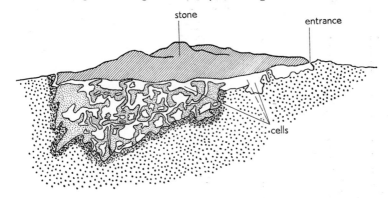

FIG. 4·2 A nest of *Crematogaster sordidula* under a stone, an example of a horizontally laid out nest. (Soulié 1961)

remove the spoil (Forel 1920, Wallis 1962a, Sakagami and Hayashida 1962). The same manner of digging is supposed to be an adaptation for digging in dry soil in the desert-dwelling *Cataglyphis* (Forel 1920). Perhaps *Formica fusca*, which sometimes favours rather dry sites, can vary its way of digging to suit the state of the soil. Ammochaetae are also said to be an adaptation for handling dry soil (section 2·1·1). Many ants however dig chiefly when the soil is moist (Goetsch 1928, Chen 1937b, Tevis 1958, Hodgson 1955).

Casts of underground nests can be made by pouring plaster, solder (Markin 1964) or latex (Brian and Downing 1958) into the nest entrance. The casts suggest that digging is differently orientated in different species. Some species produce a rather shallow maze of more or less horizontal tunnels, others dig vertical shafts. The underground nests of *Lasius alienus* and *Tetramorium caespitum* belong to the first type. They are made up of tunnels at a depth of only 2-5 cm. which lead to sites where root-feeding aphids are tended. The nest of *Lasius niger* has so many tunnels that it looks spongy. A *Tetramorium caespitum* nest also has a few vertical shafts. (Brian and Downing 1958.) In other ants such as *Acropyga* (Bünzli 1935) and *Crematogaster auberti* (Soulié 1961) the tunnels follow tree roots where scale insects feed. In the second type

of nest horizontal tunnels are rare. The nest of *Formica fusca* has no
horizontal feeding galleries for this ant feeds above ground. Instead
the nest has many vertical shafts with short lateral brood cells. The nest
may go down as deep as 70 cm. in sandy heathland (Brian and Downing 1958). Deep vertical nests are common in dry regions and in deep
soil a regular lay-out can sometimes be seen. The nest of *Prenolepis*

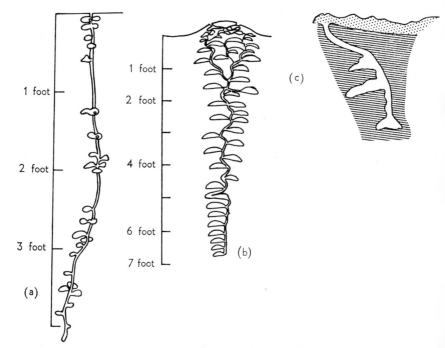

FIG. 4·3 Some types of vertically arranged nests: (a) *Prenolepis imparis* (after
Talbot 1943), (b) *Pogonomyrmex badius* (after Wray 1938), (c) excavations in captivity made by *Messor* (after Meyer).

imparis opens by a single hole only 0·5 cm. wide, but may descend over
a metre. Chambers a few cm. long and 1 cm. high radiate from the
shaft. Each chamber has a floor which slopes down towards the shaft so
that water (and the fluid poured down to trace the nest) does not drain
into the cells (Talbot 1943). Similar nests are made by many seed-
eating ants. The nest of *Pogonomyrmex badius* can be two metres deep
(Wray 1938) and *Veromessor pergandei* sometimes digs down to three
metres. The nest of the latter ant can stretch some way horizontally
too. About ten times a year a new entrance tunnel is opened to exploit
a different patch of seeds. Maps of the different holes they use cover an
area up to 16 metres in diameter. Even allowing for the slant of the
entrance tunnels the underground nest must therefore be about 10
metres in diameter (Tevis 1958). The nests of species of *Messor* in the

Old World are similar in form. Even in captivity *Messor* will build nests of a shaft and side chambers (Meyer 1927). There must be striking differences of orientation underlying these varying types of nests, but no-one has investigated them.

4·1·2 Mound nests

Ants also differ from species to species in the way they treat the soil they excavate in making their nests. Some ants carry the soil to a distance to deposit it whilst others leave it in a circle or crescent round the entrance hole to form a 'crater'. The craters are of course largest where nests are large or deep so that a good deal of soil has to be disposed of. They are most common therefore in desert and semi-desert areas. Other ants organise the spoil from their excavations into a mound, which often contains galleries and chambers. Earth mounds are most common in temperate lands; in the tropics 'ant-hills' are almost always the work of termites, and even as far north as Tenessee mounds built by true ants are uncommon (Dennis 1938).

No modern naturalist has studied the behaviour of ants when they are building or extending their earth mounds. Some interesting lines of investigation were suggested by Huber 150 years ago (Huber 1810). The mounds of *Lasius niger* consist of chambers and tunnels, story upon story. Each layer is about 8 or 10 mm. thick, and the floors and ceilings between are only 1 mm. thick, and follow the curve of the mound. Each room in the nest has a little vaulted roof supported on columns and little walls. When *L. niger* adds to the mound it brings pellets of earth from below ground. Each worker places its pellet to form the foundations of the walls and pillars, which are of fine soil. When the walls and pillars have reached a height of 8-10 mm. the ants join them together with a ceiling. Very often grass stems and leaves are built into the mound and strengthen it. *Formica fusca* builds up its coarser mound by a very different method. The workers begin by spreading a thick layer of earth over the top of the mound. In this they trace the plan of a new story in relief. First they dig grooves, all of an equal depth, and leave large masses of soil between them. These form the foundations of walls which are raised in height and later covered with a ceiling (Huber 1810). The mound of *F. fusca* is made of holes, that of *L. niger* of walls. How this is related to the difference between horizontal and vertical building, in which the same two species also contrast, we know too little to say.

There is no doubt that the mound raises the temperature of the nest, by increasing the amount of sunlight it intercepts, especially when the sun is low in the sky. At the latitude of Bern a hemispherical mound may intercept twice as much of the sun's radiation as a flat disc of the same diameter. Early in the morning it may collect three times as much (Steiner 1929). As a result the daytime temperature in the soil near the top of a mound of *Lasius flavus, L. niger* or *Formica fusca* may be 3-7° higher than in the soil around the nest (Steiner 1929, Cloudesley-

Thompson 1958, Peakin 1960). The raised mound however, like any other sun-bather, is exposed to winds, and in bad weather its temperature may be below that of the soil nearby (Steiner 1929). *Myrmica rubra, Tetramorium caespitum, Tapinoma erraticum* and even *Lasius niger* often only build temporary summer mounds in Britain, and desert them in winter (Donisthorpe 1927), to be destroyed by the winter's rain. Mounds like those of *Lasius flavus,* and some mounds of *Lasius niger* which are permanent, are usually no less deserted by their owners in winter when the ants normally burrow many inches down in the soil (Peakin 1960).

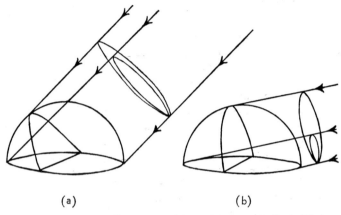

(a)   (b)

FIG. 4·4 Insolation of a mound nest at the equinox in the latitude of Berne: (a) at noon a mound receives 1·2 times the radiation on a flat disc of the same diameter, (b) at 0700 hrs it receives 3 times as much. (After Steiner 1929)

Although the mound collects heat in the day, it loses it at night. Most ants must be thought of as like a housewife who does not rely on exact thermostatic control of her oven but uses a higher or lower shelf according to the temperature she wants. Rather in the same way a nest with an earthen mound offers a selection of temperatures and humidities, varying from hour to hour and from place to place in the nest. The ants move themselves and their brood to take advantage of these differences (Steiner 1929, Peakin 1960, Scherba 1959).

4·1·3 *Thatched mounds*

Temperatures under stones are not usually high. While the upper surface of a stone in sun can be 21° above the soil surface little of this heat gets through the stone to the lower side (Steiner 1929). The nests of ants on high alps are not, as one might expect, under stones. Instead they are built in the cushions and rosettes of alpine plants. Often these are sheltered from the east wind by a stone (Stäger 1935b).

At lower levels where plant material is easier to get some ants cover their nests with it. *Myrmecia gigas* often thatches its mound in this way in open country (Clark 1951), and the nests of *Messor* are often covered by chaff from the seeds they eat (Goetsch 1929). Many ants in fact carry back rubbish to their nests. *Pheidole crassinoda* workers seize all sorts of inanimate things during the excitement of a mass attack on an insect, and *Formica lugubris* carries stones and twigs in the same circumstances. In *Formica rufa* about 50% of all loads brought to the nest in June are plant material, and in *F. nigricans* 20% (Schwenke 1957). This seems more than one would expect if collection was merely casual. In a wood-ant nest in its natural surroundings the mound is built of whatever elongated vegetable matter is most easily obtained: pine or spruce needles, heather sprigs, petioles and leaf veins of broad-leaved trees (Chauvin 1959a and b). The colony may take exception to alterations in the sort of material provided. Nests of *Formica lugubris* have been transplanted from spruce forests in the Lombard Prealps to forests of pine and larch in the Appenines. (This was done to replace *F. nigricans* and other species by those which are more beneficial in forests because they destroy caterpillars and other pests.) The transplanted ants were reluctant to use pine and other materials for their nest. At first they travelled considerable distances to fetch spruce needles although pine was to be had much nearer to their nests. Only after some time did they begin to collect pine needles, and at first these were simply left at the base of the mound and only later incorporated in it (Pavan 1961). It looks rather as if collectors of material are habituated to take certain sorts by preference. Either they learn rather slowly to take other kinds, or they are replaced by younger less prejudiced ants.

Wood-ants carry material for their nests by the same methods that they use for carrying prey, and two or more ants may carry the same piece of twig. At the nest building material is not carried in at the base as prey is; instead it is carried up the outside of the mound, often nearly to the summit. Pine needles are laid down pointing in any direction. At the base soil from underground digging is mixed with the material, and the nest is often surrounded by a ring of small stones (Chauvin 1958).

Ants of the *Formica exsecta* group, in Europe and America build superficially similar mounds, but their mounds are earth inside with a thin layer of thatch on top (Steiner 1929, Scherba 1959). The earth in the mound is not just what has been dug out from below; some of it has been carried from as far away as 30 metres (Wheeler 1906b). The differences in structure between these mounds and those of true wood-ants are reflected in living conditions inside them. In a shallowly thatched *F. exsecta* mound the surface temperature may be high in sun, but inside it is much less away from the surface. The temperature inside however is always more than it would be in soil at the same depth, and a temperature of 22° or more can be found somewhere in the mound any time from May to October (Steiner 1929, Scherba 1962). The tempera-

ture fluctuates a good deal and this is the price that *F. exsecta* pays for
the raised temperature of its nests.

The larger, better insulated mounds of wood-ants offer much more
even temperatures. The temperature at the surface shows an enormous
change of temperature according to the time of day; on a sunny day it
may rise to 32° at noon and fall to 15° by early morning (Steiner 1924).
The surface temperature reflects very closely the amount of the sun's
radiation falling on the mound ('black bulb temperature') and has
little relation to air or soil temperatures (Katô 1939). Inside the mound
the temperature varies much less than this. At a depth of 15-30 cm.
below the summit of the mound temperatures are in the range 23-29°
day and night (Steiner 1924, Katô 1939, Raignier 1948) and at a depth
of more than 30 cm. the temperature is within a degree or so of 25°,
especially in nests which have some shade from the afternoon sun
(Steiner 1924, Raignier 1948). Wood-ants manage to get the best of
both worlds: at the top of the nest very high daytime temperatures are
available for 'forcing' pupae, and in the depths of the nest constant
favourable temperatures can be found. (The complicated responses of
wood-ants to temperature were described in section 2·2·3.)

These conditions of temperature depend on the shape of the nest and
on insulating properties of the thatch. Both of these depend in turn on
the behaviour of the ants. However the behaviour of wood-ants has a
deeper effect than this on the temperature of their nest. Deserted nests
are not so warm as inhabited ones, so that the fermentation of the
vegetable matter probably does not add much heat to the nest. An inhabited mound was poisoned by pouring $3\frac{1}{2}$ litres of carbon disulphide
over it; its temperature fell until it was consistently 4-5° below nearby
inhabited mounds (Raignier 1948). Bee-hives are warmed by the
bodily heat produced by the metabolism of the bees in the colony, this
is probably not important in ants' nests, compared with the large input
of solar energy they receive (Steiner 1929). Real ant mounds vary their
temperature much less than the imitation mounds made by a Japanese
worker (Katô 1939) who tipped pine needles into a heap of the same
size and shape. This is probably due to two differences between real
and imitation mounds: the texture which the ants build into the body
of the mound and the way they manipulate its surface to control heat
losses. The texture of the mound is produced and maintained by behaviour which can be seen if a few wood-ants are placed in a jar of
pine-needles. The ant thrusts its head and thorax under some of the
material and then lifts it up so that an open zone is formed. The movement is a little bit like that of a golden hamster fluffing up its nest.
Openings are made in the nest surface by the same method, and by
dragging out fragments of the thatch. In a general sort of way the
building behaviour of wood-ants therefore resembles that of *Formica
fusca*: the mound is built of holes not of walls. Openings near the top
of the nest are not used by foragers, who enter and leave the nest near

its base. The holes may be ventilators, or they may be used mainly by builder ants. They are reduced in size towards the end of the day and not opened at all on cold and misty days (Huber 1810). They are not very obvious on nests in Britain.

In spring the first act of the newly awakened workers is to carry out fine material that has washed into the mound during winter. This leaves spaces between the coarser material they let remain. The work

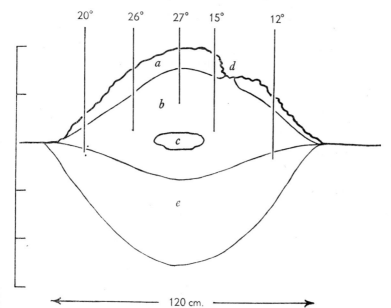

FIG. 4·5 Section of a mound nest of a wood-ant, a—fine material, b—coarse material, c—original stump, d—a ventilation door, e—old rotting material. The temperatures are those which might be recorded in summer 25 cm. below the surface with the doors shut (on left) or open (on right). (After Raignier 1948 and Zahn 1958)

begins at the summit of the mound so that a hollow appears there; later the work is extended downwards so that the mound has a cylindrical or conical core of spongy material. After this the ants begin to collect coarse material and bring it to the mound and build it into the sponge. Finer material is left on the outside of the mound, and openings in this lead into the open-work core (Zahn 1958).

Later in the year the surface of the mound is turned over continually by the large number of ants which are always to be seen on it. This circulation of material preserves the smoothness of the mound surface, which no doubt reduces the risk of the mound being damaged by rain. Small 'foreign objects' are removed (surprisingly match-sticks are foreign objects) and larger ones are buried. The symmetry of the mound can be destroyed by inserting small planks radially in its surface: certain sectors of the nest seem to receive more material than others and the surplus is not redistributed. If the planks do not meet at the apex of the mound the materials are spread out evenly. Apparently the inequalities only reflect the direction from which material is brought to the nest. When the mound is left alone the excess on the side where most is brought in is moved round to give the nest a smooth outline. Raised portions are rapidly demolished and hollows filled in more slowly (Chauvin 1958, 1959a, 1959b, 1960).

The turning over of material is influenced by the weather. In captivity the height of the mound is altered by radiant heat. With an infrared lamp 48 cm. away the ants form a rather flat mound, when the lamp is 100 cm. away they pile the material into a heap. Heated from only 36 cm. the mound became flat again (Lange 1959). This checks with the shape of mounds in nature—in woods they are tall, in the open flatter. The mounds of *F. ulkei* are steep on the shaded side, and flat on the sunny side (Scherba 1958). Building is accelerated by watering the mounds (Zahn 1958, Scherba 1961), just as digging is in burrowing ants.

All these pieces of behaviour act to conserve equable conditions in the mound by maintaining the insulating properties of the thatch, and by altering the amount of radiant heat the nest intercepts, and the amount it loses by convection. Opening passages to the interior also increases the amount of heat lost or gained by the core of the nest to or from the outside. It has also been suggested that worker ants bask on the mound until they are really hot and then dash into the nest carrying their heat with them (Zahn 1958). Although the number of ants involved in this could be large enough to contain a fair amount of heat, it is doubtful how long such a small creature could hold heat.

4·1·4 Nests of leaf-cutter ants

The ants in the tribe Attini live by growing fungus inside their nests (section 5·6). The fungus evidently requires rather special conditions and Attine ants are found only in the warmer parts of the New World. Even then the nests of the larger species are more complex than any other sort of soil nest. One might guess that this too is because of the exacting requirements of fungus culture.

Smaller members of the tribe build simple nests. In *Trachymyrmex* these can be of the vertical type with side chambers, which is more typical of places drier than a tropical forest (Wheeler 1907). No doubt this sort of nest is able to keep a higher internal humidity. Some species of *Cyphomyrmex* and *Myrmicocrypta* build superficial nests in wet humus, and *C. rimosus* has been found nesting in humus on an epiphytic plant 92 feet above ground (Weber 1941). *Apterostigma mayri* may nest in nutshells, like some crevice-nesting *Leptothorax* species (Weber 1946).

The large species of *Atta* have populous colonies however and build deep and complex nests. The first nest built by a newly fertilised queen is a simple cavity with a raised crater, which is however sealed (Eid-mann 1932). As daughter workers appear the nest is extended outwards until it is marked at the surface by a disc of turned-up soil from 5 to 47 square metres in area. A number of craters, like the nest-openings of other ants, surround the disc. Attempts to kill the ants, which do a lot of harm to crops from which they strip the leaves, by pumping insecti-cidal smoke down the craters are disappointing. Although smoke comes

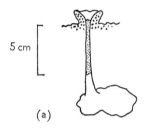

(a)

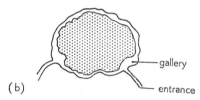

(b)

Fig. 4·6 (a) Burrow dug by a solitary queen of *Atta*, (after Eidmann 1932 and Jacoby 1953), (b) a fungus chamber from a nest of *A. sexdens* (after Jacoby 1955).

out of other craters the ants are not usually harmed. This is a result of the complex structure of the nest.

There seems to be a good deal of variation in the form of the nests according to the soil and slope. Investigations have not all been equally thorough, and some describe details which others do not mention. Very large nests of *Atta sexdens* seem to have a constant lay-out. The structure of a very large nest was studied by pouring liquid cement into the craters. When the cement had set the whole nest was exposed by re-moving soil from around the cement. The volume of the nest is shown by the amount of cement used—1·5 cubic metres. This was made up of about 120 metres of tunnels averaging 3 cm. in diameter (900 litres), and 100 fungus chambers each holding 6·5 litres (Jacoby 1953). The nest is in two parts, a tangle of tunnels above extending into the disc, and a vital zone with fungus chambers below. The tunnels of the upper zone are only used for carrying earth from excavations up into the disc. The craters are not used as entrances; leaves are brought to the fungus chambers through almost horizontal entrance tunnels which run underground from distant entrances in several directions. The entrance tunnels join a ring tunnel which circles the nest 60-80 cm. below ground, just about at the top of the vital zone. The tunnels of the upper zone also run out of the ring tunnel. Leaves which have just been brought into the nest are first stored in large side-chambers on the ring, and later carried by oblique tunnels to the fungus chambers. Each

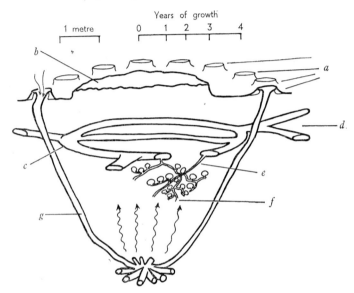

FIG. 4·7 Diagrammatic section of a large nest of *Atta sexdens*: a—craters, b—disc of excavated soil, c—ring tunnel and diameter tunnel, d—entrance tunnels, e—oblique tunnels with f—fungus chambers in vital zone, g—marginal tunnels. The arrows show the supposed air circulation. (Based on Jacoby 1953, 1955)

fungus chamber is shaped like a rather deep toadstool, with a floor below and a domed top. A space not filled with fungus is left right round the chamber where floor and dome meet, and the oblique entrance tunnel opens into this space like a rather oblique stem. Small tunnels connect different chambers. The whole nest forms an inverted cone 1-4 metres in diameter and 2-3 metres deep, imbedded in the soil. This underground cone is surrounded by a cage of tunnels leading down from the craters round the disc and meeting just below the deepest part of the nest. These marginal tunnels do not join directly to the fungus chambers (Jacoby 1955).

No-one has measured temperatures in a nest of just his type, but in a nest of *Atta cephalotes*, which seems to have been shallower, the temperature below the disc was 25-28° and in the fungus chambers 26-29°.

This was 15° or more above soil temperature. The relative humidity in the nest was always above 90% and the concentration of carbon dioxide was about four times as great as in fresh air (Stahel and Geijskes 1940). In the large nests of fungus-growing termites high temperatures and concentrations of carbon dioxide and low concentrations of oxygen are found. These are dealt with by a circulation of the air inside the nest driven by a temperature difference of 5° between the top and the bottom of the nest. In at least some termite nests the air is regenerated without loss, losing heat and carbon dioxide and gaining oxygen through the thin walls of external galleries in the raised mound (Lüscher 1956). This system is impossible in the subterranean nest of *Atta sexdens* and the marginal tunnels probably provide a change of air, as in fact a basal tunnel does in some termite nests. Without a cooling flow of air the heat produced by the fungi would accumulate and the nest might eventually catch fire, like a damp haystack. As the colony grows new marginal tunnels are dug and the ring tunnel and its connections move out inside them. The old craters are hidden by the expansion of the disc.

4·2 Nests above ground

Although ants began their career as crawling earth-nesting insects they would hardly have become so successful if they had not exploited the rich possibilities of collecting food, especially honeydew, on woody plants. Wood-ants manage to collect food on trees but they have to walk long distances to do it. It is not therefore very surprising that many species have moved their nests into the trees. This is especially true in the tropics, which, above all, are the world of the tree. No ant in the genus *Azteca* nests in soil, *A. instabilis* and *velox* live in rotting wood, some others in chinks in bark or in hollow twigs, while *A. aurita* and *A. trigona* build hanging nests of 'carton' high up in the trees. This series from wood to crevices to manufactured nests is repeated in a good many other genera too (Forel 1905). An ant which builds its nest above ground can no longer draw on the moisture in the soil. Because of this some of these ants are specially resistant to desiccation, others nest only in moist situations above ground. Others again go out of the nest and collect water.

4·2·1 Crevice nests

The simplest sort of nest above ground is in a ready-made crevice in a tree, in rocks or in buildings. Nests of *Leptothorax acervorum* are common on moorland under bark and in fallen twigs and branches. They have been found in a number of other cavities too including hollow flints (Donisthorpe 1927). Other species of *Leptothorax* live in fallen galls or acorns (Wheeler 1910). *Leptothorax* is able to live in moderately dry conditions and seems to specialise in nesting in places where other ants will not nest (Gösswald 1938a). Sometimes the nesting site of this sort of ant must be only a temporary one because the twig or acorn will rot away in a few months. Ants with this sort of habit are often spread over the world by man. Their nests can be accidentally included in cargoes, and they are able to spread from them to all sorts of crevices about houses and ships. Three or four ants are common in houses in Nigeria but *Monomorium pharaonis* alone is able to nest in furniture and in cracks in woodwork (Sudd 1962b). This ant is cosmopolitan, living in all houses in the tropics and centrally heated buildings in colder lands. Colonies have been said to nest in soil in Asia (Stitz 1939) but this is not well authenticated. *M. pharaonis* does nest away from buildings under tree bark and in similar places in Texas (Mitchell and Pierce 1912) and in the Florida keys (Wilson 1964), but it is certainly not a native of either place. *Prenolepis longicornis* seems to live in houses in a similar way in India (Assmuth 1907). A more recent traveller is *Plagiolepis allaudi* which has been entering the U.S. on plants from West Indian ports. It came originally from Africa and evidently brought its crevice-nesting habits with it as it has been found under bark and in the deserted tunnels of wood-boring beetles (Smith 1957). All these species tolerate low humidity. In the laboratory *Monomorium pharaonis* will nest in wooden cells where the humidity is only 58-66% (Peacock, Waterhouse and Baxter 1955). After the ants have taken up residence however they probably raise the humidity, for in nature workers carry large quantities of water into the nest (Sudd 1960a, 1962b).

Crevices higher up in trees are used for nesting by many species of ant. Conditions in a crevice vary a lot, especially in moistness. Many species of *Pseudomyrma* live in hollow twigs in the warmer parts of the U.S. *Ps. apache* however lives in parts of Arizona which are very dry and also have a low winter temperature. It seems to be able to do this because it chooses sizable limbs of evergreen oaks and other trees rather than twigs. The limbs often point upwards and collect moisture, and large limbs give more protection than twigs against the low night temperatures (Creighton 1954). Most of the other tree-nesting ants of Arizona including *Leptothorax silvestri* also nest in limbs rather than twigs (Creighton 1953a).

Ants which nest in crevices often go to some trouble to close or restrict the opening into the crevice. One way of doing this is common to ants which are not closely related. In *Colobopsis* (a subgenus of *Camponotus*) the large workers in some species have the front of their large heads flat and roughened. In *C. truncatus* of Europe and *C. etiolata* of America these large workers do not often leave the nest but they remain in the openings of the nest and close them with the 'phragmotic disc' of their heads. They move aside to let smaller workers out or in. Small colonies of *C. truncatus* in Europe however often have no large workers, and in those that have, they do other work besides door-keeping

(Goetsch 1934). In a different subfamily *Cryptocerus texanus* also has large workers with similar flattened heads. Their heads cannot block the nest entrances though, because if the head was placed with its phragmotic disc vertical the jaws would be below floor level. The thorax is heavily armoured on its shoulders which stand above the level of the top of its head, so that the large worker cannot pass through holes which are small enough to be closed by its phragmotic disc. In actual fact it uses both its head and its thorax to close the doors (Creighton and Gregg 1954). It is unlikely that there is a secret knock which returning workers deliver on the top of the head of the door-keeper. In *Cryptocerus texanus* and in *Camponotus* (*Myrmaphaenus*) *ulcerosus* which has similar habits, the door-keeper's antennae are visible from outside, and it could recognise returning workers by smell. Although the large workers of *Pheidole militicida* have no special phragmotic area on their heads, they still close passages in the nest with them. This is probably the main contribution which the 'soldiers' make to the defence of the nest (Creighton and Gregg 1959).

4·2·2 *Nests in specialised parts of plants*

Most crevice-dwelling ants live in hollows produced in plants by rot or by insect damage. There are however plants which have hollow stems, leaves and thorns as a matter of course and in many of these ants nest. The two most important sorts of plants are under-story trees in tropical forests and *Acacia* of thorn-scrub in arid lands, but a few are large trees. Some of the ants which live in these spaces are simply those which would move into any suitable cavity however it had been formed; species of *Crematogaster*, *Tetraponera*, *Monomorium*, *Leptothorax* and *Cataulacus*. Others like *Viticola tessmanni*, *Pachysima aethiops*, some species of *Pseudomyrma* and *Azteca muelleri* are only found in particular plants and can be called obligate plant-ants. In the same way some of the plants form their cavities merely as an adaptation to rapid growth in the competitive conditions of forests. A thick stem with much pith concentrates the mechanical strength of the trunk at the edge where the weight of the tree is felt: later the pith dries and disappears. The plants themselves appear quite able to live without the ants so that they cannot be called obligate ant-plants. It is hard to see what the plants get from the association with ants and the ants are sometimes said to be parasitic on the plants or to cause damage to them, for example by attracting woodpeckers (Escherisch 1911). Ant-plants are generally healthy, unlike those inhabited by ants which like rotting wood. The ants may preserve their trees from attack by leaf-eating animals including of course leaf-cutting ants (Schimper 1898). The *Acacia* (wattle) of Australia is rarely inhabited by ants and is often thornless. Those of similar regions in Africa and America usually have both ants and thorns. This may possibly be connected with the rareness of browsing mammals in Australia and of course with the poorness of the Australian ant-fauna too (Brown 1960). West African plants like *Barteria* and *Newbouldia* which are inhabited by ants are certainly protected from attack by man, and they are almost always left alone when an African farmer clears the bush.

Although the stems, branches and so on of ant-plants seem in most cases to become hollow without the help of ants, the ants often put in some work in turning the cavity to a nest. The small African forest tree *Barteria fistulosa* has its trunk and most of its branches full of pith. Some

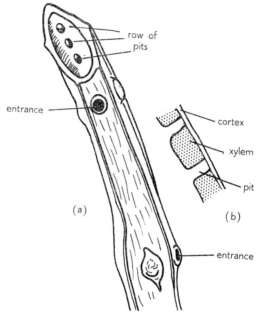

FIG. 4·8 (a) Stem of *Vitex staudti* inhabited by *Viticola tessmanni*, (b) section of stem wall. (Redrawn from Bequaert 1922)

of the branches develop swellings at their bases and, losing their pith, they become hollow. The walls of these hollow branches remain relatively soft. Young queens of *Pachysima aethiops* bite their way into the hollow after their mating flight, and the entrance hole then partly closes up as the tree forms a callus. The first workers produced in this incipient nest reopen the entrance hole and clean out the joints and pith from the cavity to form a continuous gallery. Although several queens may settle in the tree there is eventually only one mature colony to each tree. This has many aggressive workers but only one queen (Bequaert 1922). A related ant, *Viticola tessmanni*, lives in the hollow stems of a climber *Vitex*. Again the pith disappears of its own accord. Later the young queen and the workers bite entrance holes. A pair of these is made in each joint of the stem just below the node. The entrances are always in the two opposite sides of the quadrangular stem in which there are fewer vessels and fibres. As this is related to the position of the paired opposite leaves, the entrance holes occur, like the leaves, turned through 90° in successive joints. Inside the stem are two rows of pits, alined with the entrance hole in each joint. The ants seem to have bitten out these pits through the xylem as far as the cambium.

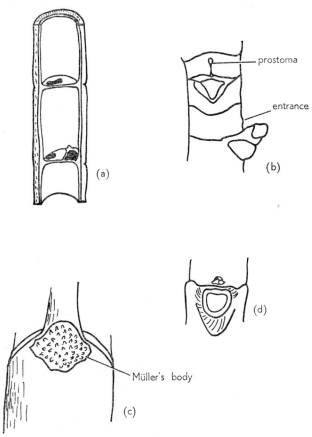

FIG. 4·9 (a) Stem of *Cecropia adenopus* split to show the joints bored by *Azteca mülleri*, (b) outside of stem showing prostoma, (c) leaf-base showing Müller's body, (d) stem of a species not inhabited by ants. (Redrawn from Schimper 1898)

A callus grows into each pit from the cambium and is alleged to provide the ants with food (Bailey 1924).

The South American trumpet-tree, *Cecropia adenopus*, has a hollow trunk and branches in which *Azteca muelleri* nests. The queen ant invades the tree when it is only a few feet high. She bites an entrance hole through a thin spot or prostoma in the rind, which occurs above each node where an axillary bud has pressed against the stem. Later the

workers bite out the nodes and occupy the whole tree except the growing branch tips. Only part of this space is used for the nest, which is
built inside the trunk but enclosed in an envelope of 'carton'. Larger
nests are sometimes enclosed in a swollen part of the trunk. The swelling
is produced by the ants, who bite away the inner wood so that the walls
of the trunk bulge outwards under the weight of the crown. The ants
remove small growths, Müller's bodies, from cushions at the base of
the leaves and may use them as food (Schimper 1898).

Several species of *Pseudomyrma* live in hollow thorns of *Acacia* in Central and South America, and in East Africa species of *Sima, Crematogaster* and *Meranoplus* have the same habits (Keller 1892, Forel 1892,
Emery 1892). The thorns swell out into gall-like growths but again this
does not seem to be the result of anything the ants do to the tree. Just
as only some of the branches of *Barteria* become hollow, only some of
the thorns of *Acacia* swell (Keller 1892) and some unidentified disease
may cause this. The American *Acacia sphaerocephala* produces Belt's
bodies on its leaves and the ants collect them.

The epiphytic plant *Myrmecodia* in Java has a swollen bulb in which
many small tunnels develop: these are in fact usually inhabited by
Iridomyrmex myrmecodiae but they may originally have served in the
absorption of water by the plant. As the ants deposit their faeces in
these tunnels the plant may conceivably get some benefit from the
nitrogen they contain. This would be especially valuable to an epiphyte,
provided that the nitrogen did not eventually come, through plant-lice,
from the epiphyte itself (Miehe 1911).

True plant-ants then seem to have behaviour which allows them to
exploit particular plants. Their entrance holes in particular are placed
in spots which are to some extent preformed by the plant. The ants do
not necessarily find these spots first shot, for tentative borings might well
be removed when the cavity is subsequently cleaned out. The lines of
internal pits which *Viticola* makes inside its vine are interesting from this
point of view. On the face of it they seem to show that the ants distinguish two of the sides of the stem from the other two. In other ways
their use of the nest is simply what one finds in any other crevice-nester.

4·3 Nests in trees

Rotting wood is as good as, or better than, soil to a lot of the soil-nesting
ants. Some species are so fond of rotting wood as a nest material that
they can be thought of as tree ants. Several of them have in fact got
relations which have moved on to a true arboreal life. The large carpenter-ants (*Camponotus ligniperda, herculeanus* and *vagus* from north to
south in Europe and *C. pennsylvanicus* and its relations in America) build
their nests in wood. The nests are founded by single queens in crevices

of bark, in deserted beetle tunnels or in the soil (Eidmann 1928b), and perhaps sometimes in rotting wood (Riordan 1960). If the nest is in a tree, the daughter workers excavate a nest down into its roots and into the soil, but also very often they dig upwards inside the tree. Each year they dig a little higher until eventually the nest may reach as high as 10 metres. When the wood is soft the nest is an irregular cavity but in sound wood it consists of passages which follow the growth rings, leaving the hard autumn wood intact. Knots are bitten out to connect one ring to another. Carpenter-ants do not build floors inside their nests; instead the larvae hang from the walls on their special hook-like hairs (Eidmann 1928b). In winter the colony retreats down the tree to not more than 20 cm. above the soil, often below it. In both the northern species (*C. ligniperdus* and *herculeanus*) the nest is sealed over-winter and to some extent lagged round, with sawdust, and the workers form a cluster round the queen. If colonies are kept in the laboratory in wooden nests at a steady temperature of 24° the cluster is still formed. *C. herculeanus* will also seal its nest at this temperature but *C. ligniperda* will not (Hölldobler 1961). These are very necessary adaptations in a tree-dwelling ant which is found far north in Scandinavia, though not, unfortunately, in Britain.

Lasius brunneus may sometimes nest in soil, but more usually does so in rotting wood. Like *Camponotus pennsylvanicus* it sometimes nests in house timbers, though it is doubtful how far either will attack wood which is entirely sound. A floor-beam has been found honeycombed by *L. brunneus* for 1½ metres, where moist walls had allowed rot to start (Green and Kane 1958). *Lasius umbratus* generally nests in soil, at the foot of a tree in some cases. Some nests however contain cells built from a mixture of soil and fibres apparently scraped from the roots of plants which pass through the nest (Donisthorpe 1927).

Lasius fuliginosus builds a much more refined nest, occasionally in soil or in houses but typically in hollow trees, especially oaks. The nest is built of 'carton', a sort of reconstituted wood, much darker and denser than the paper which wasps make. The carton of *L. fuliginosus* consists of little pieces of wood fibre set in a yellowish homogeneous cement. A black or yellow coloration spreads a little way into the sound wood of the tree to which the nest is stuck (Forel 1920). It looks as if the carton is made by chewing up wood fibres, possibly from rotten or well soaked wood, and adding to the fibre a secretion from a gland in the head. Unfortunately there are no direct observations of how *L. fuliginosus* makes carton.

The construction of a carpenter-ants' nest is essentially that of an ant which digs holes to form a nest. *Lasius fuliginosus* on the other hand builds walls, in this case of carton, to divide up an existing cavity into cells about 1 to 2 cm. cube in size. This method is extended by many other ants which build cellular nests in open air on the leaves and branches of trees.

4·4 Aerial nests

Soil may be carried up trees and used to build small nests by *Pheidole megacephala* and by *Macromischoides aculeatus*. Sometimes *M. aculeatus* builds its nest among leaves and even sometimes between two leaves which are stuck together. In this case first of all the ants coat the whole leaf with fibres as if to mark out the foundations of new cells. (This

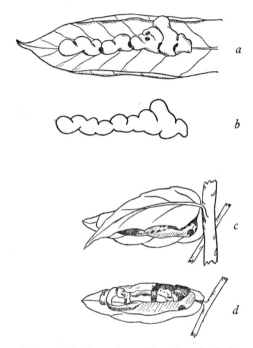

FIG. 4·10 Nest of *Macromischoides aculeatus* (a) under a leaf, (b) outline of walls, (c) between two leaves, (d) upper leaf removed. (Ledoux 1958)

description is very like Huber's account of the extension of a *Lasius niger* mound.) Later more workers come and stick elongated pieces of leaf and moss around the foundations to make a wall. When the cell is on the underside of a single leaf a roof is put on in the same way, but when the nest is between two leaves the walls simply join on to the second leaf. The nest then has a leaf for a floor and another for a ceiling and is very elastic and weather-proof (Ledoux 1958).

Ants in the very large genus *Crematogaster* build an interesting series of nests, ranging from nests in soil to carton nests high in trees. *C. sordidula* in southern Europe builds rather sponge-like nests in soil under stones (figure 4·2). It is possible that it uses its saliva to strengthen the earth (in fact this is a possibility that needs testing in all earthen nests), but the basis of its nest is earth. *C. auberti*, from the same parts, also builds a soil nest but of a more complex kind. *Crematogaster scutellaris* shows the beginnings of arboreal habits: almost all nests are in wood. Small nests, and possibly the first nests of newly fertilised queens, are made under bark especially on pine trees. Larger colonies live in the wood of ailing trees. Sometimes the nest begins in a ready made cavity like a rot hole. The workers divide it up and adapt it for their use with partitions of chewed wood and saliva. Later they dig tunnels and chambers into the wood where it is softened and eventually build a spongy network of chambers. The nest is made partly of tunnels in sound wood and partly of material reconstituted from wood powder and saliva. When this species nests among stones it builds cells entirely of sawdust and saliva (Soulié 1961). Tropical species of *Crematogaster* build this sort of nest too, in beetle holes, knots and cankers. *C. striatula* of West Africa uses carton to divide a preformed cavity and to make an entrance hole smaller (Strickland 1951a).

Other species of *Crematogaster* build nests on the outside of trees at heights of 5 metres and more. These are often in the shape of a giant egg, impaled on branches at a fork or flattened against the trunk on one side. *C. ledouxi* in south-east Asia builds a nest like this 175 mm. high and 130 mm. in diameter. It is not pure carton but has an addition of soil in it. There are many entrance holes, each sheltered above by a porch-like flake. Inside the nest is made of layer upon layer of inter-connecting cells each 0·5-1·5 cm. in diameter. The nest starts as a single flake, like those that overhang the doors of a mature nest. The flake is built over a small dimple on the bark of a tree. The nest grows by adding on flakes over and round the original one so that branches are gradually enveloped. In the finished nest the flakes are very firmly joined. The nest of *C. vandeli* looks the same but the earliest stage of the nest is a small cell bitten out of the trunk of the tree (Soulié 1961).

Crematogaster depressa and *buchneri* in Africa (Strickland 1951a) and *C. skouensis* in Asia (Soulié 1961) make nests up to 100 by 30 by 25 cm. of pure carton. The carton is dark and after it has dried for four to five days very hard. It is probably made of wood. *C. peringueyi* will accept any sort of fibre in captivity provided it is wet (Skaife 1961). Pure carton nests are also made by the addition of flake on flake (Ledoux 1958). *Crematogaster africana* has this sort of head-shaped nest, but also keeps scale insects in the hollow trunk of *Canthium* and other trees (Strickland 1951a). One of these large nests probably takes 20 years in building, and increases in size discontinuously two or three times a year (Ledoux 1958) probably after rain (Skaife 1961). Each year the nest increases about 4-8 cm. in length and perhaps 1 cm. in diameter. This is probably not enough to house the natural increase of the colony and new nests are founded, making the colony a polydomous one.

When a new branch nest is built first of all a large number of workers assemble at some distance from the mother nest. They spread a layer of carton over some 8-15 sq. cm. of bark so that all the fissures of the bark are filled. Then some workers turn from spreading carton to building out projecting flakes which mark the beginnings of 2-4 cells. The flakes which will form the floors and ceilings grow at the same rate at first but the upper one eventually outgrows the lower and forms a projecting porch. Several little groups of cells arise in this way, and meeting as they grow join together to make a single nest 4-5 cm. thick at its centre,

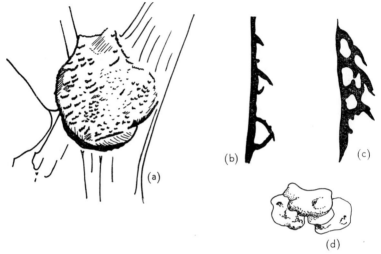

FIG. 4·11 (a) nest of an African *Crematogaster*, (b)-(d) texture of similar nest (b) first scales, (c) cells formed, (d) surface view. (b-d after Ledoux 1958)

where there are two or three layers of cells. There is only a single layer of cells at the edge. The whole mass at this stage might measure 25 by 10 by 15 cm., and its shape varies according to its position, lung-like and pendant below a branch, hemispherical in a fork or half-cylindrical against the trunk. Later brood is moved in from the mother nest. Young queens do not work carton in this way and it is possible that they enter a queenless branch nest which then becomes independent (Ledoux 1958, Soulié 1961).

4·5 Silk nests

A different solution to the problem of building a nest in trees has been found by *Oecophylla*. The ants in this genus, which is closely related to *Camponotus*, are spread in numerous subspecies from Queensland to West Africa. The African species are often referred to as *O. longinoda* and the rest to *O. smaragdina*, but the differences are not in fact very great. *Oecophylla* builds its nests from leaves, fastened together with silk to make pendulous bag-like nests. Some other less well-known ants also use silk in building. The silk that all these ants use is not produced by the workers but comes from the larval gland which generally provides silk for the cocoon. *Oecophylla* and species of *Polyrachis* which make silk nests do not spin cocoons at pupation, although most of the Formicinae do so (Wheeler 1915).

Some species of *Polyrachis* use silk to reinforce the walls of the earthen cells in their nests. When larvae of species which have cocoons spin

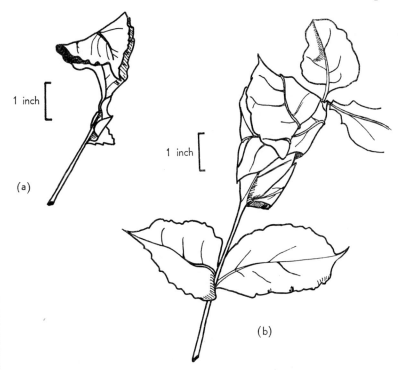

1 inch

1 inch

(a)

(b)

Fig. 4·12 Leaf nests of *Oecophylla longinoda* (a) formed by rolling up a single leaf, (b) formed by fastening several leaves together.

they are usually partly earthed up by workers. This evidently gives the mature larva an anchorage for the first threads of silk and allows it to draw out threads from its gland. Perhaps the mixture of silk with earth in *P. gagates* and in young colonies of *P. laboriosa* arose from this habit. Older colonies of *P. laboriosa* extend their nests into trees where they build bags of loosely felted silk in which dead leaves are entangled. Some other *Polyrachis* species build flatter earth and silk cells on the underside of leaves (Wheeler 1915, Ledoux 1958).

Oecophylla nests are not made in this simple fashion. Instead it draws living leaves together and uses larval silk to secure them, and to seal up the chinks between them. As the leaves die the ants make new nests in

fresh leaves, and they also quickly repair rents in their leaf nests. It is a
fairly simple matter therefore to watch how nests are built.

The first sign that a new nest is to be built is the assembly of 30 to 40
workers at the tips of branches. There is a good deal of excited running
about until one ant, holding on to a leaf with its hind feet, stretches out
to touch a neighbouring leaf with its forelegs or its antennae. It grips
the other leaf and begins to pull it (Ledoux 1949). *O. longinoda* recog-

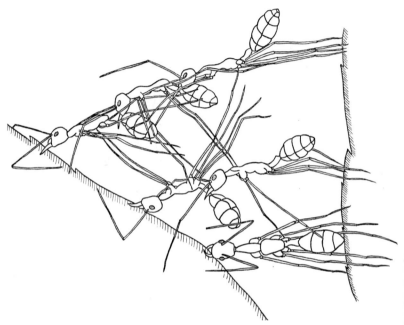

FIG. 4·13 *O. longinoda* workers pulling leaves together. (Ledoux 1949)

nises leaves by a chemical sense, for workers investigate and climb onto
leaves or pieces of paper treated with sap, but they simply attack or
ignore clean paper (Chauvin 1952). A worker which has bridged the
gap between two leaves attracts other workers, perhaps by its immo-
bility compared with other ants on the leaf. Some of its nestmates use
its body as a bridge to cross to the other leaf. In this way pairs of leaves
that can be drawn together are discovered.

Some hours, or even a day, later the ants reappear on both leaves,
bridge the gap and begin to draw the leaves together. Evidently the
earlier assembly on the leaves marked the leaves in some way (Chauvin
1952) or else the ants have learnt which leaves to use. About five ants
are employed in pulling the leaves and they take up various positions
on the leaf, but with their bodies more or less parallel to each other.
When the leaves which they are going to move are already quite close
together the ants keep all six feet on one of the leaves and seize the

other in their jaws. However if the leaves are further apart than 8-10 mm. they keep only the hind four or the last pair of feet on the leaf. Each effort the ants make to pull the leaves brings them about 2 mm. closer, and each movement allows more ants to span the narrowing gap. When the leaves have curved edges the distance between them is often still too great for a single ant to bridge. In this case chains of 2 to 5 workers are formed, each ant holding with its jaws the petiole of the next ant in the chain. Chains start when an ant reaches out and grabs the petiole of a neighbour obliquely. Then its own petiole is gripped by a third ant. In a chain any ant which is hanging free, without its

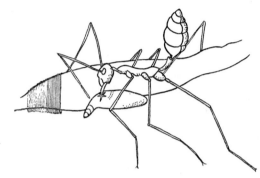

FIG. 4·14 *O. longinoda* worker using a larva to fasten two leaves together. (Ledoux 1949)

legs attached to a leaf, can do nothing but passively transmit forces applied to it by the other ants. There is no joint between the jaws and the petiole which could be used to pull leaves together. As the leaves get nearer and nearer to each other the ants walk backwards over the leaf, and they stop pulling as soon as the leaves touch and merely hold them together. This first phase of pulling leaves together lasts 1 to 3 hours.

At about the time that the leaves touch a few large workers appear each with a half-grown larva in its jaws. The larvae are held about one third of the way back from their head end with their backs towards the worker's body. In the nests the larvae lie belly up so that these larvae must have been turned over when they were picked up. The worker grips its larva hard enough to dimple its surface. When workers are simply carrying larvae from nest to nest they do not carry them in this way. The worker walks about the leaf edge with its larva until it finds a stretch free of ants. Then it touches the larva with its antennae. The larva thrusts out its head segments until it touches a leaf with them. As soon as it has touched one of the leaves the worker moves it across to the other leaf and so on, backwards and forwards from leaf to leaf, so that a zigzag of silk is laid between the leaves. The zigzag is so close set that adjacent threads of silk stick together to form a continuous sheet between the leaves. Each sheet of silk covers about 1 cm. of the edges of the leaves.

The workers who have been holding the leaves together release them now; no doubt they sense that the tension pulling the leaves apart has disappeared. Later other weavers work over the sheets of silk again, closing the gaps where ants were standing before. Larvae and plant-lice are then moved into the new nest (Ledoux 1949).

Another way in which *O. longinoda* builds nests is by using only a single leaf instead of a pair of leaves. In these nests the tip of the leaf is bent back over the blade like the fingers of a clenched fist (figure 4·11). The ants which bend it into this shape are not, as one might expect, attracted to the leaf tip; they start to pull at all parts of the leaf margin, perhaps after failing to reach a nearby leaf. Some ants do not keep on pulling but let go and move to another part of the leaf or go right away. Ants which change their position on the leaf are very likely to move to places where the leaf is already bent at the edge—one can show this by bending the leaf. As a result the ants become concentrated at places where other ants are having some success in bending up the leaf margin. In practice this means they collect between the veins and, above all, at the tip. Parallel teams of ants form, and chains of ants, which move backwards towards the base of the leaf as it rolls up (Ledoux 1949).

In these ways *Oecophylla* is able to make its nests from a wide variety of leaves including pinnate palms, the paired ovate leaflets of *Bauhinia* and the large stiff leaves of *Citrus*. In Zanzibar for instance nests have been found on 89 species of tree, all evergreen, some of them by no means specialised as ant-plants (Way 1954a). Even on an evergreen tree leaves wither and as this happens the ants build new nests to re-place the old. Each colony possesses up to 150 nests which may be spread over 12 trees. One side of a large tree is usually more intensively used than the others, but the preference changes with the season. It is not clear whether this is because of the direction of the wind (Way 1954a) or of the sun (Vanderplank 1960). Both change their position with the seasons in the tropics.

Oecophylla builds its nests in a way that cannot easily be brought into line with the methods ants use to build nests of earth or of carton. Obviously the nests are made by building walls, not by digging holes, but this seems only to be a formal resemblance. The strong dragging movements that *Oecophylla* uses to pull leaves together seems to have more in common with the transport of prey than with nest building. However until we know more details of how other ants build nests, for instance how they remove obstructions from their excavations, it is futile to look for the origins of *Oecophylla's* behaviour.

5 — How ants get their food

The diet of ants, like their earth nests, seems in the first place to have been an inheritance from wasp-like solitary ancestors. Unfortunately the wasps which seem most likely to be related to the ancestors of ants have become parasites in the nests of other solitary bees and wasps so that their feeding habits do not throw much light on how the ancestors of ants caught their food. From what we know about present-day ants, we should expect their ancestors to have caught insect prey which they carried home to feed their brood. Their taste in prey was probably rather catholic, and they may have used their stings to overpower prey larger than themselves. They almost certainly supplemented this with whatever sugary fluids they could find, either nectar and sap or the excretions of plant-feeding insects. Some Tiphiid wasps like *Myrmosia* are suspected of collecting honeydew, and their family probably lies close to the ants in evolution (Krombein 1939).

Many ants have kept this wide range of diet till the present time. In particular the most primitive forms in the Myrmeciinae and Ponerinae are conservatives as far as their food is concerned. *Myrmecia gulosa* workers collect nectar, and only hunt insects at times of year when there is brood in their nests (Haskins and Haskins 1950). This is very like the habits of solitary wasps which feed on nectar themselves, but collect and paralyse insects for their young. Not all ants which have a varied diet are primitive however. Wood-ants take a variety of foods which are in order of importance: honeydew from plant-lice (62%), insect prey (33%), sap and resin (4·5%), fungi and carrion (0·3%), seeds (0·2%). The importance of each sort of food varies with the time of year. Sap is most important early in the year when insects are not plentiful (Wellenstein 1952). Honeydew is collected more in late summer than in spring (Ayre 1959, Vowles 1955a). A wood-ant's diet contains all the items which become important in the diet of more specialised feeders. A diet like this is characteristic of many thoroughly successful ants in the Myrmicinae, Dolichoderinae and Formicinae. Ants which live in this way often lack any special adaptations to predatory habits. Most Ponerinae and Dorylinae feed almost entirely on insects.

However *Anomma nigricans* is often seen chewing the oily pericarp of palm nuts, and the common and successful *Brachyponera senaarensis* collects seeds and stores them (Bequaert 1912, Arnold 1915).

5·0·1 Specialised diets

In some ants the range of food is much less. The Myrmicine tribe Dacetini feed only on small soft-bodied insects, and predominantly on two types of Collembola or springtail (Wilson 1953b). Millipedes are the speciality of *Myopias,* woodlice of *Leptogenys triloba* (Wilson 1959c). Many other insects which are not restricted as much as this probably in fact depend on other social insects for their prey. This is particularly true in tropical forests where the concentrated colonies of termites support large colonies of predaceous ants, just as they support the large insectivorous mammals. Most of the large Ponerine ants raid termite nests; *Megaponera* and *Paltothyreus* in Africa, *Dinoponera* in South America and *Lobopelta* throughout the Old World tropics. The Cerapachyini (Wilson 1958b) and perhaps *Aenictus* among Dorylinæ (Sudd 1960c) specialise in raiding, not termites, but the nests of other ants.

Many other small subterranean ants are said to live by stealing the brood of larger ants from their nests. *Solenopsis fugax* builds its nests under stones and these may communicate by very fine passages with the nests of other ants, or even be built in the walls between the chambers of a larger ant. In these cases *S. fugax* steals the brood of the large ant for food (Forel 1928). Forel coined the name lestobiosis for the supposed life of brigandage which *S. fugax* leads, but he had to admit that its nest could also be found far away from any other ants' nest. As *S. fugax* carries its prey to its nest in small unidentifiable pieces no-one has been able to find out how important ant brood is in its diet, but it certainly cultures aphids below ground (Hölldobler 1928). Most of the other ants which are said to be lestobiotic are found well away from the nests of other ants too. Eighteen out of twenty-four nests of *Monomorium algiricum* were independent for instance (Bernard 1955). Even *Carebara,* which is usually thought to be an obligate thief of termites, has been found away from termite nests (Arnold 1915) and it will not eat fungus from termite nests in captivity, though it does eat termites (Lowe 1948). Of course the habits, and the occurrence even, of any subterranean ant are always a matter of doubt. *Stigmatomma pallipes* is usually reported from woody areas with moist soil but it has once been taken in the prairies of Kansas. It may well blanket the whole of the U.S. and south Canada but only be obvious where it nests near the surface (Creighton 1950). Equally 'thief-ants' may be very common in soil, but are only caught by ant-hunters who are digging in the nests of other species.

At the other extreme some ants rely almost entirely on honeydew for their food, others on seeds, and the Attini on the fungus they grow in their nests. These are highly specialised habits.

5·1 The search for food

The behaviour of ants collecting food can be divided into searching for food and handling it once it has been found. How much food an ant can collect depends not just on how quickly it can find food but on how much time it has to spend capturing it and carrying it to its nest. Some ants probably keep the time they spend in searching and in transport as small as possible by living near their food. Rotting wood provides a very easy way of doing this, especially in tropical forests where different species of ant specialise in living in wood at different stages of decay (Wilson 1959c). Nothing is known of how these ants catch food. Many of them have a restricted range of prey, and perhaps they have orientations which confine their hunting to places where their prey is plentiful.

Large colonies of ants face quite different problems for they are often forced to search over large areas. Ten acres in Maryland supported 73 nests of *Formica exsectoides*. Each nest occupied about 1·4 sq. yards and contained on average 200,000 ants. A total of several million ants spread out over the 10 acres. Their nests took up only 0·2% of the total area and they had to search the remaining 99·8% (Cory and Haviland 1938). In Yorkshire *Formica fusca* travels 26 feet from its nest in search of food, *Myrmica scabrinodis* 20 feet and *Lasius niger* 10 feet (Pickles 1935). The areas searched by different colonies of the same species fit together like the pieces of a jig-saw puzzle, though the areas searched by different species may overlap (Brian 1955, Talbot 1943). The foraging area of ants may be as small as 2·32 square metres in *Myrmica ruginodis* (Brian 1955), rising through 5,000 square metres in *Formica nigricans* (Wellenstein 1952) to perhaps as much as 2,000,000 square metres in *Myrmecia gulosa* (Haskins and Haskins 1950).

Of course only a small part of this area is really searched for food. Ants do not get a panoramic view of their foraging range. Each ant finds the food which lies within a short distance of its path through the range. Ants do not as a rule smell food from a distance of more than a few millimetres and they are not attracted to traps baited with food (Walker 1957). Wood-ants, which have rather good eyesight, are attracted to moving prey from distances up to 9 or 10 cm. only (Stäger 1930, Otto 1958). The path of an ant through the range seems to be decided by two things. First in many species individual ants return again and again to the same spot as long as they continue to find food there; second in some species an ant which has found food can direct its nestmates there too. Both these habits concentrate the ants in some parts of their range whilst other parts, often less productive, are left unsearched. (At the same time ants may explore new territory, and *Solenopsis saevissima* actually lays trails into extensions made to its foraging area in laboratory colonies (Wilson 1962a). This recalls the 'exploratory' behaviour of the cockroach *Blattella germanica*, which is increased by additions or alterations to the apparatus in which it is kept (Darchen

1952, 1955).) The *Myrmecias* of Australia show this tendency to revisit spots where they have found food. This seems to be a case of individual learning and there is no reason to think that *Myrmecia* workers can communicate their finds to others (Haskins and Haskins 1950). Fidelity to feeding sites is striking in wood-ants, and here too it seems to be due to learning, although the matter is complicated by the routes which all *Formica* workers use near the nest. Fidelity leads to 'partition of foraging grounds' (Dobrzanska 1958), and has been contrasted with the recruitment of workers to finds of food that is common in small ants in several subfamilies. The contrast is misleading. It is true that wood-ants do not seem to be able to direct other ants to finds of food, except from a very short distance. On the other hand 'partition of foraging grounds' may, and probably does, occur in ants which recruit nestmates from the nest.

The next sections describe some varied foraging methods in detail.

5·1·1 *The foraging of wood-ants*

Wood-ants are a group of species of *Formica* distributed through all the northern parts of the world. Unfortunately their systematics have been confused for many years. In Europe attempts to place all wood-ants either in *Formica rufa*, the red wood-ant, or *F. pratensis*, the meadow-ant with more black on it, were unsuccessful because colour and habits often did not vary in parallel with other characters that might be used to identify the ants. As a result many ants seemed to be intermediate in form or habits between *F. rufa* and *F. pratensis*. Affairs were made worse by the habit of describing these forms as if they were actually hybrids between the two supposed species. These were given names such as *F. rufa rufo-pratensis major* (Gösswald 1943). In America similar confusion followed when wood-ants were assigned either to *F. rufa* (mound-builders) or *F. truncicola* (nesting in tree-stumps), although the rules of zoological nomenclature were followed in the New World. No real solution to the difficulties of describing wood-ants has been found. The European forms are now placed in half a dozen species (Yarrow 1955), the American in rather more (Creighton 1950). It is still far from certain that the differences in the habits of say *Formica rufa* and *F. lugubris* in Germany (Gösswald 1943) are the same as the differences between the ants called by the same names in England. It is usually impossible to tell what species is meant when older workers refer to *Formica rufa* or *F. pratensis*. I have used the term wood-ant whenever there is doubt, to avoid the clumsy phrase 'member of the *Formica rufa*-group'.

Wood-ants build large nests which are easily found. Tens of thousands of workers leave these nests at rates as high as 50 a minute (Holt, 1955) and forage along definite and obvious routes. Because they are easily watched and also because of their importance in controlling the numbers of insect pests in forests, we know more about how wood-ants forage than we do of any other ants.

The different species of wood-ant all forage in much the same way but there are differences between them in the importance of honeydew and insects in their diets. In Germany *Formica rufa* lives mainly by hunting and only visits about a third of the trees in the neighbourhood of its nest in order to collect honeydew. It has no very definite routes. *Formica nigricans* is much less predatory, and has a small number of very clear narrow routes, which are sometimes excavated or even subterranean. The other wood-ants (*F. lugubris, polyctena* and *aquilonia*) which have several nests to each colony, have routes running to other nests as

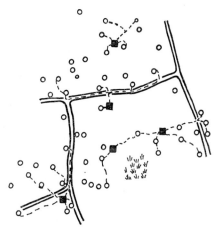

o   Trees
– – –   Ants' routes
■   Nests

FIG. 5·1 The routes of four wood-ant nests in Scotland. (After Driver 1935)

well as to trees. The number of routes in a colony of *F. lugubris* can be as high as twelve, whereas *F. nigricans* may only have one. A route may be 200 metres long and all the routes are kept cleared of twigs and leaves (Gösswald 1943).

Although the routes lead to trees, not all the ants on them collect honeydew or even reach the trees. In *F. aquilonia* the number of ants moving outwards from the nest on a route gets less as one goes further from the nest. This is because there is a steady leakage of outgoing ants from the route. The leakage is something like 0·5% per foot of route: that means that out of every 200 ants which enter any foot-long stretch of route, only 199 are still on the route at the end of the stretch. There is a balancing infiltration of returning ants to swell the number of returning ants on the route as one approaches the nest. Ants which filter out of the route in this way evidently wander about between the routes hunting, for the number of foraging ants becomes less the further from a route (Holt 1955). In ants which live in denser forest than the Scottish pine-woods where *F. aquilonia* is found the larger number of trees makes this effect less clear. The general effect is that hunters leave the routes, but not until they have been guided by them into certain sectors round the nest. At a radius of 9 metres only 16% of sample areas of 1 square metre contain more than 7 ants (Schwenke 1957).

The routes are more or less permanent and remain the same for a year or more (Chauvin 1962). We do not know how these routes arise or how the ants follow them. Interruption experiments do not necessarily disorientate the ant (Stäger 1930), though scraping away the soil on the route is said to do so (Forel 1928). This makes it unlikely that the routes are scent trails, at least scent trails of the usual type.

It is fairly old knowledge that individual wood-ants are to some extent faithful to particular routes or even to particular trees at the end of routes. Ants marked on trees or on routes are later caught again at the same place (Ökland 1938, Dobrzanska 1958). The significance of this can only be assessed if we are told how many marked ants were found on other routes. Other workers have released hundreds of marked ants on one route and found none or only two or three ever on another route (Kiil 1934, Otto 1958). It seems likely that each ant learns a route, perhaps as a light-compass response. The memory lasts some days, for ants which are not released till five days after they were captured still are faithful to the route on which they were caught (Kiil 1934). Training to a light-compass direction can persist this long (Jander 1957). In all these experiments ants were caught and marked perhaps 30-100 metres from the nest. When returning foragers of *F. aquilonia* were marked at the edge of a nest which only had two routes a quite different picture appeared. Fidelity was far from obvious and ants which entered the nest from the east were almost as likely to leave it by the west route as by the east. The small bias in favour of the east which was found was less than might easily appear by chance if ants showed no fidelity at all (Holt 1955). Probably this contradiction of older work is explained by a difference between honeydew collectors and hunters. Probably hunters are far less faithful to the route than the collectors of honeydew. The bias of ants which entered from the east in favour of leaving the nest again by the east would be explained if one ant in twenty were faithful. With a leakage rate of 0·5% per foot only one ant in 22 would still be on the route at a distance of 300 feet, the distance at which ants that have proved faithful have been marked. Nearer to the nest these faithful ants were swamped by the large numbers of hunters whose fidelity has not been investigated.

A number of other ants seem to forage in the same sort of way as wood-ants with permanent routes. Some examples are *Oecophylla longinoda* (Way 1954a), *Formica subintegra* (Talbot and Kennedy 1940) and *Messor* (Goetsch 1929). It would be useful to have more information about the route systems of these ants.

5·1·2 Foraging by groups—the use of language

The foraging method of a good many small ants is strikingly different from that of the wood-ants. Both the ants themselves and their nest are rather inconspicuous in the ordinary way, but large numbers of ants come out of the nest to carry away pieces of food. At first sight it seems as if the ants have a strong sense of smell and are attracted to the food. In fact their sense of smell cannot detect the food from more than a centimetre or so. Before they discover the food only a small number of ants leave the nest to forage—about 5 a minute in *Monomorium pharaonis* (Sudd 1960a), fewer in *Myrmica rubra*. These scouts do not as a rule look any different from the other workers in the nest but they are probably drawn from the older workers (Weir 1958, Wilson 1962a) and they are usually darker coloured, and often more battered, in consequence. Because they leave the nest so infrequently the scouts are sometimes said to forage independently. If their paths are recorded however they usually have their first sections in common. In *Monomorium pharaonis* all scouts leave the nest along definite routes which they follow more slowly and hesitantly than ants on true scent trails. The scouts leak from these routes, in a way rather as *Formica aquilonia* does, and search for food between the routes. There is no evidence that the routes develop from scent trails, but scent trails do follow routes for a reason which will be plain in a moment (Sudd 1960a). *Myrmica ruginodis* (Brian 1955) and *M. rubra*, as well as *Pheidole crassinoda* (Sudd 1960b) scouts have routes of this kind.

The behaviour of a scout that has found food varies somewhat from species to species. In species which drag prey to their nest whole (*Myrmica rubra*, *Pheidole megacephala* and *P. crassinoda*), the scout first of all tries to drag the food home itself. If it cannot it returns to the nest laying a scent trail as it goes. In other species which dismember large prey (*Monomorium pharonis*) and also sometimes in species which usually drag the prey whole, the scout often feeds before returning to the nest. Older, more experienced scouts of *Myrmica rubra* are more likely to return without feeding than young ones (Heyde 1924). A *Monomorium* scout can follow a fairly direct line home for about two metres. Its orientation during the homeward trip is impaired either by placing it on a clean surface or by moving it to a different part of its range. Probably it uses both chemical and visual clues in its navigation. It always joins an established route for the last part of its return so that part of a route is always included in the trail it lays (Sudd 1960a). When the scout enters its nest it rushes about, bumping into other workers and sometimes beating them with its antennae or legs (Eidmann 1927a, Goetsch 1934, Heyde 1924). After this many of the workers in the nest, and occasionally the queens too, leave the nest and rush out to follow the scent trail. This was once thought to be a direct effect of the excited movements of the scout and was one of the most convincing examples of the 'antennal language' of ants. The discovery of the dances of the honeybee, which are also gestures though more specific in their form and message, seemed to confirm this idea. The same 'alarm' effect can be produced by blowing into an artificial nest of *Solenopsis saevissima* the secretion of Dufour's gland. At least in *S. saevissima* the same substance sends workers out of the nest to a trail and guides them on the trail itself (Wilson 1962a). The movements of the scout are not essential to

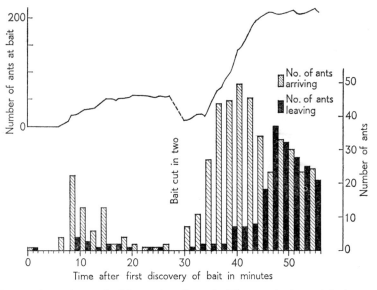

FIG. 5·2 Recruitment in *Monomorium pharaonis*. The prey had a cuticle the ants could not penetrate, no fed ants returned to the nest and no recruits left it. After the prey was cut ants fed and recruits came. (Sudd 1960a)

recruitment, which involves the chemical rather than the antennal language.

Once outside the nest the recruited workers follow the scent trail. There are many differences between species in how closely the trail is followed and in how far from the nest it can guide recruits. These depend on the amount and volatility of the trail substance in any species, and on how sensitive to it the ant is. *Monomorium pharaonis* can follow a trail in nature for up to two metres and keeps within 2-3 mm. of the centre of the trail (Sudd 1960a). *Solenopsis saevissima's* trails are kept short by the evaporation of the scent so that, on glass, trails are never more than 50 cm. long. In nature the speed at which the scout runs as it lays the trail and so the length of the trail may be increased by the use of alternative orientations. Long trails can also be laid by several ants in relay fashion (Wilson 1962a). In *Pheidole crassinoda* recruits do not follow the trail at all closely but they still reach the food. In this ant the scout uses visual navigation to return to the nest. Its path and the trail it lays are therefore more or less straight. It may be that once a recruit has picked up the line of the trail it can continue on that line, relying on its own light-compass, and only checking with the trail at intervals (Sudd 1960b). In *Myrmica rubra* there is very little doubt that the trail gives almost no guidance as to direction, and recruits give the impression that they are searching independently for the food (Eidmann 1927a). So we have a range of effectiveness of the trail in guiding foragers. In *Monomorium pharaonis* guidance is close, in *Myrmica rubra* it is hardly detectable. Perhaps the end of the series is an ant like *Formica fusca* which has recruitment but does not lay scent trails at all.

The number of recruits which respond to a single scout can be very few in *Monomorium pharaonis* or up to 50 in *Myrmica rubra*. In both species the number depends to some extent on the degree of excitement of the colony; for instance *M. pharaonis* recruits come to food in far greater numbers if they have previously been excited by a find of food, even if this happened 50 minutes earlier (Sudd 1960a). In laboratory experiments the number of workers that come out of the nest is in proportion to the amount of Dufour's gland secretion blown into the nest (Wilson 1962a). As one might expect the number of ants at a food find goes up very fast at first and then levels off to a figure which represents roughly the number which can conveniently feed at once. It does not seem to be true that the first scouts recruit just enough ants for the size of the food. In *Pheidole crassinoda* the number of ants that leave the nest is three or four times the number which eventually combine to drag the prey to the nest. Each returning scout recruits a small number of workers. In *Monomorium pharaonis* the number of scouts returning to the nest represents the number that have fed and thus the number of vacant places at the food. In *Pheidole crassinoda* the scouts that return are those which have been unable to move the prey. They therefore represent roughly the weight of the prey.

Behaviour like this is shown by most of the ants which can lay scent trails (chapter 3). It allows a colony to exploit new sources of food rapidly. If the number of ants from one colony builds up fast enough other colonies and other species can be excluded from the food, all of which is monopolised by the one colony (Brian 1955, Assmuth 1907).

5·1·3 Other uses of scent trails

Probably scent trails are used most to guide recruits to food, but this is not the only way in which they can be used. The African *Megaponera foetans* is one of the best known of the large Ponerine ants which raid termites. These large black ants move rather slowly over the ground in forests, in little bands of up to a hundred. This has earned them the popular name of company-ant, presumably as a diminutive of army-ant. They follow each other deliberately in file, with all the hesitations one associates with ants following a scent trail. An early account of this ant was given by David Livingstone who accidently disorientated a returning band by emptying his washing water onto the 'path by which a regiment had passed by before I began my toilet, and when they returned they were totally at a loss to find the way home'. Livingstone's view was that the column was led by an ant that knew the way, but this is only partly confirmed by later work. If the leading ant is taken away during the outward journey the following ants lose their way when they reach the spot where their leader was caught. Ants taken from the column and replaced further back on the line of march can follow it to the point that the leader reached (Collart 1925). When the leader is replaced the march begins again. The band is said to be going to a particular termitary, as it passes some without raiding them (Collart 1927). (This is very inconclusive evidence as we shall see in discussing slave-making ants.) When the ants are returning from the raid, taking away the leader does not upset the column. On the other hand disturbing the soil over which they pass does disorientate them (Collart 1927, Livingstone 1857). Apparently the leader finds its way to a termites' nest and lays some sort of scent trail as it goes. On the way back each individual ant either follows a scent trail which the band laid on the outward journey, or finds its way by clues of some other kind on the soil surface. No-one has done any critical experiments on this quite common ant.

5·1·4 *Driver-ants*

Doryline ants also raid in bands but their bands are much larger than those of *Megaponera*. The subfamily is found throughout the tropics as driver-ants (especially *Anomma*) in Africa and the Old World and army-ants (*Eciton*) in the New. *Neivamyrmex* reaches as far north as 45° in the Mississippi valley and equally far south of the equator in Patagonia (Schneirla 1958). Colonies of Dorylinae, unlike those of many predaceous ants, are very large and have no fixed nest site. They practise a sort of large-scale group raid which probably catches or chases away all the insect life of their immediate district. The first signs that a raid is coming are the excited insects which crawl out of the bush and climb up plants and up the walls of houses. In deep forest *Eciton* raids in the New World are also betrayed by the calls of ant birds, and the buzz of parasitic flies which lay their eggs on the ants' prey as it is carried back to the temporary nest. The raid itself in a species like *Eciton burchelli* or *Anomma nigricans* appears as a line of ants advancing in a front, up to 25 metres wide in *Eciton* and 15 metres wide in *Anomma*. The speed of advance is only about 20 metres an hour. The slowness is not due to sluggish movement on the part of the ants; on the contrary they move at a medium pace for ants. Each ant of the front moves forward only a few centimetres at a time and then turns back into the main line of ants. Interruption experiments show that the ants lay scent on the ground as they advance, and because of the large number of ants and their arrangement in a line the ground becomes fairly evenly coated with scent. Ants move forward rather readily over 'mastered' ground which has been coated in this way, but they will only move a short distance into unmastered ground before they turn back. This causes the front to roll forwards slowly, and the ants which make up the front

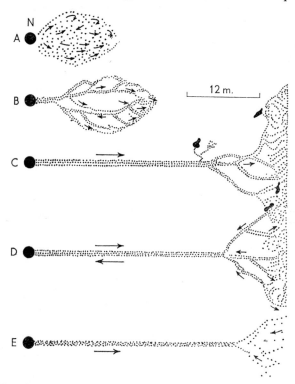

FIG. 5·3 Development of a raid of *Anomma wilverthi*. (A) The swarm leaves the nest, (B) a system of branching trails forms behind the advancing swarm, (C) raid at its height, ants pouring from nest to swarm, (D) workers begin to return with prey, (E) after a raid the swarm returns to the nest. (Raignier and van Boven 1954)

are always falling back and being replaced by other ants which come forward from behind. The front advances more rapidly where prey is being found, or the going is easy, so that it is deflected into smooth and productive directions. Behind the front, ants leaving it or coming to it are not evenly spread out. They form a system of columns branching towards the front and coalescing towards the nest, like a tree with its root at the nest and its crown at the advancing front. Ants which raid in this way are called swarm raiders, examples are *Eciton burchelli* (Schneirla 1956a, 1957a), *Anomma wilverthi* and *A. nigricans* (Raignier and van Boven 1955).

Eciton hamatum on the other hand does not have a wide front. Its front is broken into a number of small columns, each with a front about 25 cm. wide, advancing in the same way as the wider fronts of *E. burchelli* (Schneirla 1933a). In Africa small species of *Aenictus* raid in the same way. Their little columns, with fronts 2·5 cm. wide thrust into the underground nests of other ants and termites. When they enter a

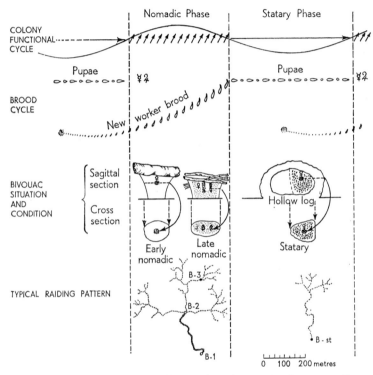

FIG. 5·4 The phases of *Eciton* raiding cycles. Arrows in the upper diagram represent emigrations. (Schneirla 1957a)

nest of *Pheidole*, the raided workers rush out madly like *Formica fusca* workers attacked by *Formica sanguinea* (Weber 1943, Sudd 1960c). Many other species raid entirely beneath the surface of the soil. Examples of these are *Nomamyrmex crassicornis* and *opaciventris* (Schneirla 1958) and *Dorylus fulvus*. All these species seem to be column raiders, though not all column raiders are subterranean. Probably column raiding allows ants to search crevices and in particular the nests of other ants. Swarm raiders on the other hand seem to drive everything and catch everything.

Anomma, *Eciton* and *Neivamyrmex* have a curious rhythm in their hunting activity. This takes its most regular form in *Eciton hamatum* and some other species (Schneirla 1933a, 1956a). Two patterns of raiding alternate. In one pattern, the statary phase, a nest is kept in the same place night after night, and each day's raids return to it in the evening. The statary phase lasts about 20 days in *E. hamatum*, and begins when all the brood is in the pupal stage, although the queen lays an enormous batch of eggs later in the phase. Each colony has a single queen and so the brood are in large batches all of much the same age. At the end of the 20 days all the pupae become adults more or less simultaneously, and the sudden addition of tens of thousands of highly active callow workers precipitates the nomadic phase. After a few days the callows become less active but by then the growing brood of the next batch are active larvae and this maintains the activity of the colony. In the nomadic phase very large raids are staged each day, often several at once in different directions. The raids all cease at dusk, as they do in the statary phase. Instead of remaining in the previous night's nest however, the ants which are not raiding, with their queen, brood and guests, follow up along the line of one of the day's raids for up to 200 metres. Somewhere along this line a bivouac is formed (section 4·0·1). This too is deserted the following evening. When the larvae spin cocoons before they pupate the next statary phase begins. The spinning movements of the larvae and later the oviposition of the queen result in slight increases in raiding activity during the statary phase. Thus the rhythmic pattern of hunting depends on the stimulation which the colony receives from its brood. The timing of the changes in the condition, and stimulative powers of the brood depend in turn on the rhythmic production of masses of eggs by the queen. The queen's reproductive rhythm may be innate, but it is reinforced by the increase in the amount of food the queen gets after pupation has removed the tens of thousands of hungry larval mouths (Schneirla 1957b). In other species the broods may develop less synchronously (Rettenmeyer 1963a).

The African *Anomma wilverthi* has a much less regular pattern. These ants are all eyeless and they raid by night and by day. The temporary nest is often subterranean, and the colony may remain in it from 6 to 60 days. What corresponds to the statary phase can therefore be either longer or shorter than in *Eciton*. Because of the prolonged statary phase it has been possible to see how a raid starts in *Anomma*; in other ways *Anomma* is harder to watch than *Eciton*, they are much more aggressive for one thing. A swarm first appears when very active ants begin to stream out of the nest openings and run wildly about in all directions. Eventually the swarm sets off in the direction where there have been most active ants. This is influenced by the tracks of previous raids, so that swarms tend to go in the same direction on successive days. Once the raid has started it may go on through light and dark for as long as 20 hours, though 8 to 11 is more usual. The traffic columns behind the raid front are very dense and about 3 mm. wide in *A. wilverthi*, a little less in *A. nigricans*. On average there are about 5 ants per sq. cm. on the columns, but in places there may be 16. As their length ranges from

2·5 to 12 mm. some ants are running over the bodies of others in the thickest parts. Although the front moves at about the same speed as in *Eciton burchelli*—20 metres an hour—movement in the columns is 3 or 4 cm. per second, about 9 times the speed of the front. As a support column can take over 10 hours to pass it is easy to calculate how many ants take part in a raid. A column 3 cm. wide which took 10 hours to pass at a speed of 100 metres an hour would cover 300,000 sq. cm. If there were 5 ants to the sq. cm. it would contain about one and a half million ants. About 22% of the ants are carrying prey so that some 300,000 insects might be caught. Many raids are larger than this (Raignier and van Boven 1955). The columns often run in a furrow excavated by the ants which may be roofed over with crumbs of soil, or quite often by the arched bodies of large workers. Sometimes the column is enclosed within a wall of large workers instead of being excavated. If this living wall is broken, which takes a considerable amount of force, the ants inside the column surge out like water from a burst pipe. This 'pressure' can be applied to the base of the swarm front and is responsible for the forward movement of the raid. Raids have a tendency to continue in one direction even in the eyeless *Anomma*. It may be that some undiscovered orientation to wind or slope keeps their movement more or less straight.

The nomadic phase of *Anomma wilverthi* is a continuous migration in column which lasts for 1½ to 4 days, not a series of evening migrations as in *Eciton*. The migration often follows the track of an earlier raid, but it does not start in the same way as a raid. Instead it begins as a column of ants rolling forwards like a swarm, and later ants carrying pupae join in. The speed of migration is about 30 metres an hour—faster than in a raid. Migration does not occur until the brood has already pupated; *Anomma* larvae do not spin cocoons.

Anomma and *Eciton* share the same pattern of hunting; but their isolation in different hemispheres has resulted in differences in behaviour as well as in anatomy. We do not know how many other Dorylines are nomadic or how many have alternating statary and nomadic phases. *Dorylus* and *Aenictus* species seem to appear first in one place and then in another as though they shifted their nests. *Aenictus eugine* has been seen carrying brood and males with it (Brauns 1901) but its statary phase seems to be prolonged (Schneirla 1965). Nomadic habits and group raiding go together outside the Dorylinae too. The Ponerine *Leptogenys diminuta* and perhaps *Megaponera foetans* and Cerapachyinae too seem to have driver-ant ways of hunting (Wilson 1958c). The social insects on which these large Ponerines prey live in colonies. Each colony provides a concentration of prey in one spot, but the spots are some way apart. A nomadic way of hunting is particularly suitable for this kind of prey. Possibly the habits of *Eciton* and *Anomma*, which take all sorts of prey, are a development from this. However the migrations of *Eciton* do not depend on the way the prey is distributed, but are related to the reproductive rhythm of the queen and of the colony as a whole.

5·2 Slave raids

Some ants—the best known are *Formica sanguinea* and *Polyergus rufescens* —make group raids from which they bring back the pupae of other species of ant. Some of these are eaten but the rest emerge in their captors' nest and take part in the social life there, especially in rearing the brood of the captor. This slavery is a sort of parasitism and is the subject of section 6·5·3. At present we are concerned with how the slaves are obtained, for this has much in common with food collection.

Polyergus rufescens raids are made by a compact phalanx of ants which is 1-3 metres long and 10-21 cm. wide (Huber 1810, Dobrzanski and Dobrzanska 1960). It was once supposed that the phalanx was led by a few experienced ants which had already located suitable nests of the slave, usually *Formica fusca*. This is almost certainly not right. In the first place the 'leaders' of the phalanx are always being replaced by ants which overtake them from behind, so that the front of the phalanx rolls forward like the front of a Doryline raid (Forel 1928). Although single ants can be found exploring the ground before raids are made they are not scouts of any kind. In fact if they are all captured a raid still takes place (Dobrzanski and Dobrzanska 1960). When a laboratory colony of *P. rufescens* was placed in a garden it began to make raids into places where there were no *Formica fusca* colonies, and it would raid artificial colonies of *F. fusca* which had only just been set out, and so could not have been known to any of the raiders (Emery 1915). This seems to make it pretty certain that a *Polyergus* raid, like those of driver-ants, scouts as it goes.

Polyergus raids start rather like driver raids too. They raid only in the afternoon. The first sign that there is going to be a raid is when a few very active and excited ants appear and run over the top of the nest. These ants are not scouts, and they are essential to the raid, for if they are captured there is no raid. More and more ants join these active workers on the nest roof and form a milling crowd. Suddenly the crowd forms itself into a phalanx and shoots away at a speed of about 100 metres an hour (Emery 1915, Wheeler 1910, Dobrzanski and Dobrzanska 1960). The track of the phalanx, though not perhaps the tracks of individual workers, is fairly straight, but it can bend to follow a path or a branch (Emery 1915). When the front of the phalanx finds a nest of *F. fusca* the ants plunge in, digging away soil if necessary, and come out in a few minutes with *F. fusca* pupae. The attacked workers mostly run away, carrying with them enough of their brood to restock a nest, and few of them are hurt. About two out of every three sorties fail to find any nest to raid, and when the raiders have found a nest they may reraid it on several successive days (Forel 1920). On perhaps the third day of this series of raids, part of the phalanx may turn off to the side and discover a new nest (Dobrzanski and Dobrzanska 1960). The raids of the American species of *Polyergus* are very much like those of *P. rufescens*, though some of them seem to kill more of the *F. fusca* workers (Wheeler 1910).

If the raids of *Polyergus* are less organised than older stories supposed, what must be said of *Formica sanguinea* which was always thought to be less efficient as a raider? *F. sanguinea* is less dependent than *Polyergus* on its slaves for food and nursery care and a good proportion of colonies in some districts have no slaves at all. The unfortunately named *F. aserva* does sometimes have them (Creighton 1950). Some colonies of *F. sanguinea* only make two or three raids in a season whilst *Polyergus* colonies can make 44 raids in 30 days (Forel 1920). The raids of *F. sanguinea* seem to have an almost accidental air. No swarm leaves the nest, instead a dispersed band builds up near a *F. fusca* nest as raiders arrive singly or in small groups. *F. sanguinea* and its races hunt along fairly definite routes but these are much wider than the roads of wood-ants, and can be up to 8 feet across. The density of ants on these of course is low. Some ants travelling outwards on these routes find food and return home with it. Others press past the ends of the routes into new country. If one of these explorers stumbles on the nest of another species of ant it usually retreats, but if it has the company of a number of its nest-mates they will begin to attack the nest (Dobrzanski 1961). This seems to be how stories of this ant's hesitation and of its waiting for reinforcements arose. *F. sanguinea* does not send for reinforcements in any way (Dobrzanski 1961) though there is a good deal of excitement of one ant by another in the raiding band itself (Talbot and Kennedy 1937). Because they raid as individuals and not in a phalanx *F. sanguinea* workers appear to surround the nest of their victims by stealth rather than to make a frontal attack like *Polyergus*.

Although some colonies raid rather rarely others do so regularly, up to twice a day, with a midday pause between in *F. subintegra*, an American race (Talbot and Kennedy 1937). Like *P. rufescens, Formica sanguinea* only raids in late summer after its sexuals have flown. Any nest of *F. fusca* that is near enough to a *F. sanguinea* route to be found by a fair number of ants may be raided. Artificial nests of *F. fusca* almost always attract a raid if they are well sited. In nature about one raid in three succeeds in collecting pupae (Dobrzanski 1961).

It is possible that *F. sanguinea* raids the nests of other ants primarily for food, as indeed Darwin suggested in his speculations on how the habit evolved (Dobrzanski 1961). No-one seems to have prepared a detailed diet sheet for *F. sanguinea*. It certainly raids the nests of a good many species of ants as well as *F. fusca*, even those of quite different subfamilies (Brown 1958). *F. fusca* however is particularly often exploited because it more often flees when attacked (Wallis 1963). Very large nests of *F. sanguinea* are aggressive, and can attack the nests of ants more able to defend themselves such as *F. rufa* and *Lasius niger*. Pupae from these species are less likely to survive in a *F. sanguinea* nest, and in any case the survival of captured pupae is always less in a large nest than in a small one. This may be because there are more meat-hungry workers in a large nest (Dobrzanski 1961).

Several other ants are thought to make slave raids, but their habits have not always been seen in the field. No doubt some of them move only at night or below the soil. *Harpagoxenus sublaevis* and *H. americanus* are found with slaves of *Leptothorax* species in their nests. In the laboratory these species send small bands—a dozen workers in *H. sublaevis* and half a dozen in *H. americanus*—to collect pupae (Viehmeyer 1921, Creighton 1950). It would be only by good luck that anyone would see this in the wild. Another ant *Rossomyrmex* is rather rare in mixed nests with *Proformica nasuta* near the Caspian. It raids in the evening and night towards the end of the hot arid summer of the steppes. Ants move to the site of a raid not in a phalanx but in pairs, one ant carrying another in the way wood-ants do. Some 40 metres from their own nest they stop and each bearer puts down its passenger. All of them then search for the moundless inconspicuous nest of *Proformica*. Apparently they often fail to find one (Arnoldi 1932).

Finding two species in the same nest does not mean that one is a slave raider. Apart from those species like *Lasius umbratus* which are temporary social parasites (section 7·5) or like *Anergates* are permanent parasites (section 6·5·3), some ants like *Strongylognathus testaceus* keep slaves, but retain a slave queen to breed them. This is often thought to be a degenerate form of slave-keeping, and it is certainly true that other *Strogynlognathus* do raid. *S. huberi* will collect pupae in artificial nests (Forel 1928, Kutter 1920) and *S. rehbinderi* has been caught in the act of carrying *Tetramorium caespitum* pupae to its nest. Actually there are a number of ways in which mixed nests can arise apart from slave-raiding and these are discussed in other chapters. Slave-raiding very much resembles, and may have evolved from certain types of group hunting. Ants are often the worst enemies of other ants, and enslavement and predation may be pretty near relations.

5·3 Handling prey

We have just seen that ants do not have any exceptional power of finding food. They are not like some insects which locate prey from a distance or through half an inch of growing wood. The same is true of the way they handle prey once they have caught it. On the whole ants do not have the elaborate structure or behaviour for catching other insects which we find in praying mantids, ant-lions or spiders. Even the sting, which is used by solitary wasps for killing prey, is kept for their own defence by many ants, and modified into a squirt for this purpose in Dolichoderinae and Formicinae. Ants catch their prey with their mandibles but in the vast majority of species the mandibles are simply triangular in shape. A biologist who had never seen an ant before might deduce that it was a predator but would not be particularly impressed. The reason for the relatively harmless shape of the mandibles is that the mandibles are used for digging and for handling the brood as well as for catching and breaking up insect prey.

A marked exception to all this is the trap-jaw type of mandible, which occurs in many quite unrelated ants scattered through the whole family: *Odontomachus* and *Anochaetus* (Ponerinae), the tribe Dacetini (Myrmicinae) and *Myrmoteras* (Formicinae). This type of jaw is not a

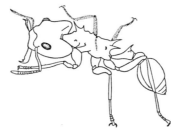

FIG. 5·5 *Daceton armigerum* in its stalking posture. (Wilson 1962b)

primitive feature, although primitive ants are hunters; it is a speciali-sation which has appeared several times. The habits of the Dacetini are known best (Brown and Wilson 1959). Primitive members of the tribe, like *Daceton armigerum*, forage on trees in the tropics. They stalk, and if necessary pursue, small insects up to about 8 mm. long. While they are doing this they are probably guided by short-range vision as they turn towards slight movements. As they turn they open their long mandibles to an angle of about 170°. They begin to approach the prey slowly and cautiously, and then their mandibles close with a convulsive snap that usually transfixes the prey and lifts it off its feet. It is not always neces-sary for the ant to sting its prey too. More specialised Dacetines forage on or below the soil and feed almost entirely on Collembola. They hunt in two ways. Some like *Strumigenys* still have long mandibles like *Dace-ton*. *Strumigenys louisae* can probably only recognise its prey when it is as close as 1 mm. It turns towards it with its mandibles held wide. The corners of the ant's labrum are pushed between the mandibles to hold them in this position against the pull of the muscles which close them. As soon as the long trigger hairs on the centre of the labrum touch the prey the labrum moves down and the mandibles are released to spring shut, piercing the prey.

Most other Dacetines have short mandibles—part of an evolutionary trend to foraging on the ground or below it. Other changes which go with this are a reduction in size, lighter colour, deep scrobes in which the antennae rest and a particularly bizarre sort of hairiness. There is also a difference in the ants' behaviour; active search over a large area gives place to intensive search where prey is common. The strike of the short mandibles of *Trichoscapa membranifera* does not do as much damage to the prey as it would in *Strumigenys*. Instead of merely lifting the prey *Trichoscapa* strikes, then holds the prey and almost always stings it. Both long and short mandibled forms have therefore behaviour which stops the Collembolan prey from using their tail-springs to leap away (Wilson 1953b).

The behaviour of all trap-jawed ants seems similar, though not all ants with long mandibles have a trap mechanism, *Belonopelta deletrix* is an example of one that has not (Wilson 1955). *Myrmoteras* has a true trap-jaw, with trigger hairs, and its proventricular valve is less complex than in most Formicinae because it is more carnivorous (Gregg 1954). Incidentally the tale that long-mandibled ants use their jaws for jumping (Wheeler 1910, 1922) is based on the recoil of an ant whose jaws fail to get a grip on a hard smooth surface, such as the glass tube it was caught in.

Outside these rather special cases we know very little about the way ants seize their prey or what senses they use when they do so. A good many small ants probably use a combination of touch and chemical sense (Vowles 1955a) but experiments which show this are very thin on the ground. *Formica polyctena* is attracted to moving prey from as far away as 10 cm. and will attack a moving stick half as often again as a dead insect. It does use a chemical sense as well as vision though, for moving insects or moving sticks smeared with insect blood are attacked even more often (Otto 1958). The differences between large and small ants are mainly due to the more effective eyes of large ants. Very large ants such as *Myrmecia* can evidently see well enough to attack entomologists from a good way off, and *Paltothyreus tarsatus* is attracted from a distance of several inches to strike at the moving feet of giant millipedes. Prey is often attacked or not according to the hunger of the ant; *Formica polyctena* is almost twice as likely to attack if it has not been fed for 24 hours (Otto 1958).

Prey is not bitten in any special way, though wood-ants have been said to seize caterpillars by the back of the neck (Wellenstein 1954). *Formica lugubris* and *Myrmica rubra* take their prey by any point where they can get a grip and this quite often means a leg, a wing, the mouthparts or the edge of an abdominal sclerite (Sudd 1965). As a result many smooth insects including ladybirds and other beetles are not captured by ants unless they are so inept as to have their wings or wingcases open (Wellenstein 1954). This, together with keeping still (in the ichneumon fly *Aphidius*) or pressing the body close to the floor and pulling in its legs (in the ladybird *Adalia*), protects many of the insects which eat aphids from the attacks of *Lasius niger*. The larva of the ladybird *Scymnus* exudes a waxy secretion to protect itself (Wichmann 1955).

Hairy caterpillars like *Zygaena filipendulae* are protected by their hairs. When an ant tries to grip them the hair comes away in the ant's jaws and it cannot get a grip. A more subtle defence is that of the beetle larva *Crioceris lillii*. This has the habit of smearing itself with its own faeces. *Lasius niger* and *Pheidole pallidula*, like a lot of other ants, cover sticky or offensive substances with earth, and they do this to the beetle larva instead of attacking it. Later however the weight of the earth may pull off the faecal camouflage, and unless the larva is able to replace it it may be attacked and eaten. Coverings such as the silk and leaf nests of bag-worm moths, and the froth of cuckoo-spit insects protect their owners from wood-ants by concealing the movements and chemical make up of the insect inside (Stäger 1929b). As we shall see, in aphids and in the guests of ants (section 6·5·1), attractive or repellent secretions can save insects from attack too.

Large insects can often escape from the grip of a single ant, but may be overpowered by a mass attack. *Lasius niger* (Pontin 1961) and *Pheidole crassinoda* (Sudd 1960b) can guide nestmates to help in an attack. As they have to return to the nest to do this they are not very successful with prey which runs quickly or jumps. Wood-ants are attracted to the struggles of prey which has been gripped by another ant, just as they are attracted to the movements of any object. This brings help to an ant which has, say caught a crane-fly by one leg. Other ants come and pull the prey down, held with its legs stretched in different directions (Sudd 1965). The stretching, or venom, soon kills the prey. *Oecophylla* is also said to stretch its prey to death (Hingston 1928, Gressit 1958), though it is not very clear how this kills an insect.

5·3·1 Transport

Once the prey has been found and captured it has to be moved to the nest. Liquids and soft foods, for instance rotting fruit, are swallowed by the ant and carried home in its crop. Filling the crop in this way takes several minutes, and the ant's gaster is usually swollen and translucent. Solid foods can be transported in two ways. Some ants, especially small ones, carry food home in small portions. When *Monomorium pharaonis* workers are feeding on a large insect they chew and tear off little pieces which they carry home in their mandibles. Probably they also fill their infrabuccal pockets with pulp and their crops with juices. Driver-ants feed in the same way. Many other ants do not cut up their prey before they move it. *Prenolepis longicornis* (Assmuth 1907) and *Pheidole megacephala*, which like *Monomorium pharaonis* live in houses, usually attempt to move the whole prey to their nest. Ants adopt several methods in carrying burdens in their jaws. They carry very light ones vertically between their mandibles and slightly heavier ones under their heads. To move loads which are heavier still they turn and walk backwards dragging the burden over the ground after them. *Pheidole crassinoda* and *Myrmica rubra* begin to do this with prey weighing 7 mg., about four times their own weight: *Formica lugubris* with prey of 12-15 mg., twice its own weight (Sudd 1965).

Wood-ants normally inspect the prey for a short time before they begin to move it. Prey which has already been inspected by one ant however may be carried home directly by another ant (Chauvin 1950). Ants which drag their prey whole stop dragging from time to time and crawl over the prey biting it and licking it (Otto 1958); this seems to be the same action as 'inspecting' the prey. *Myrmica rubra* workers spend about 11% of the time they are with prey in licking it, and *Formica lugubris* 24%. They are more likely to lick the prey if juices such as blood or gut contents are oozing from it. Probably the predatory behaviour of dragging prey can be outweighed by behaviour of licking sweet fluids, for the gut contents of hoverflies, containing nectar, are specially attractive. This has a bearing on the way ants treat aphids (section 5·4·2).

The ability to turn and drag prey is found in Ponerinae, Myrmicinae, Dolichoderinae and Formicinae, but is absent in Dorylinae and in ants like *Monomorium pharaonis* which move their prey in small pieces. The few ants that have been studied and which drag prey, orientate visually while they are doing it. Possibly some ants which do not drag prey are unable to orientate visually with enough accuracy. *Anomma* is in any case blind, and *M. pharaonis* normally navigates by scent trails. The desert ants, *Equesimessor*, which are nocturnal, carry seeds in a curious way by straddling them like a hobby horse (Bernard 1951b), and this may perhaps allow them to carry large burdens and follow scent trails at the same time.

Myrmica rubra and *Formica lugubris* have a number of ways of coping with snags and difficulties when they are moving their prey. In the first place it is not the weight of the prey alone which decides whether the ant should carry it or pull it. Changes in the gradient or the roughness of the route provoke changes from carrying to dragging and vice versa. Further when the prey an ant is dragging catches on a snag the ant begins to swing its body through angles up to 200° so that its pull is applied to the load from a new direction. Sometimes it also lets the prey go and then siezes it at a new point. These manoeuvres often free the prey from the snag (Chauvin 1950, Sudd 1960b, 1965).

Large prey or seeds are sometimes moved to the nest by groups of ants working together. Other ants are attracted by the movements of an ant which has a load, just as they are in the earlier stages of struggle. In *Messor structor* the captor readily gives up its prize to the newcomer and transport is more often on a relay principle (Goetsch 1929). These ants also deposit seeds on the way to the nest which are carried further by other ants from the nest. *Formica lugubris* and other wood-ants do not abandon their prey so easily so that groups of up to ten ants form round prey and try to move it. Ants come and go from the group all the time: 30 marked workers of *F. polyctena* were concerned in moving a caterpillar 15 metres in 3½ hours, but not one of them was with the prey all the time (Otto 1958). Groups work in the same way in *Myrmica rubra, Pheidole* spp. and in *Lasius niger*. Groups of these ants form in a different way by the recruitment of workers along scent trails. Transport by groups allows the ants to collect larger prey than one ant could

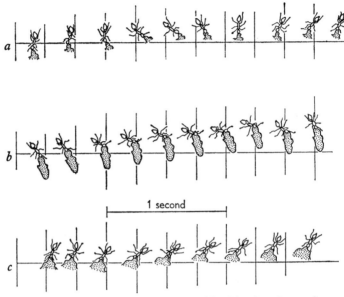

FIG. 5·6 Three examples of swings performed by *Myrmica rubra* workers pulling prey. Read each line from left to right. (Sudd 1965)

carry, and may help them to overpower struggling prey. They can only get these advantages if their efforts are applied in a reasonably efficient way, that is if they are co-ordinated. How this co-ordination comes about is considered in chapter 8.

5·4 The collection of honeydew

Collecting sugary fluids is a very ancient habit of ants as we have seen. Today many ants collect nectar and sap from flowers. *Lasius niger* (Grensted 1956, Smith and Harper 1957) and *Myrmica rubra* (Hölldobler 1938b, Felton 1958) visit a number of wild flowers, especially dandelion and some buttercups. Tropical plants attract ants to nectaries on their leaves which produce sweet secretions: *Crematogaster striatulus* feeds on the leaf nectaries of *Cola* and *Atopomyrmex moquerysi* takes nectar from several Anacardiaceae (Strickland 1951a). Ants also take the juices of plants. *Aphaenogaster testaceus* collects the wilted petals of *Cistus* flowers in the Alps and chews them (Stäger 1935b) and woodants collect resin from trees and chew the young growths in spring

(Wellenstein 1954) as *Camponotus herculeanus* does (Hölldobler 1938a). Some of the plants which shelter ants in their hollow stems produce growths which ants take, and which appear to be nutritious. No traces of any food except the gall-like growths from inside the stem of its host plant have been found in the infrabuccal pocket of *Viticola tessmanni*. The only other food it is known to eat is the eggs of its own queen (Bailey 1924).

Honeydew, which is much superior to all these plant products as a food, is the excretion of aphids, scale-insects and other Homoptera which feed on plants. There is no single name in English for all these small insects, but it will be convenient to follow the Germans in calling them plant-lice. Many plant-lice do not just insert their feeding bristles into the outer parts of plants; they tap the main food stream of the plant in the phloem. Their excretions when they are taking such a rich food contain many amino-acids, carbohydrates (Auclair 1963) and some lipids (Strong 1965), and can be a complete diet for ants that collect them. A large aphis like *Tuberolachnus salignus* can produce up to 1·7 cu. mm. of honeydew an hour (Mittler 1958). A colony of *Lasius fuliginosus* can collect about 6 kg. of honeydew from aphids in 100 days (Herzig 1938a) and *Formica nigricans* colonies can collect many times this amount (Wellenstein 1952). Honeydew-producing insects live in all parts of the world, aphids are found on the roots of plants even on the high plateau of Tibet (Eidmann 1927b). It is not surprising that very many ants feed on honeydew.

Some ants depend more on honeydew than others. At one end of the scale *Leptothorax* is said only to lick up fallen honeydew from the leaves of plants. At the other the tropical *Acropyga* are totally dependent on their own species of scale-insects, which are found nowhere but in the ants' nests (Bünzli 1935, Flanders 1957). Between these extremes ants like *Myrmica* take honeydew regularly in late summer, and species of *Lasius* take it even more, though both still hunt insect prey as well. Broadly speaking the proventricular valve, which prevents liquids in the crop from passing to the midgut, is best developed in the Formicinae (Eisner 1957) and it is in this subfamily that the ants most devoted to honeydew are found.

Some aphids, like *Forda formicaria*, are found only in the nests of ants, and some ants confine themselves to a small selection of plant-louse species, usually root-feeders, which live in the ants' nests. Other ants visit plant-lice in the open air on plants some distance from their nest. Wood-ants for instance visit 65 species of aphids and may travel 100 metres on their routes to them (Wellenstein 1952). Journeys to aphids are in fact guided by the same kinds of navigation as the ants use in hunting. *Lasius fuliginosus* lays scent trails to aphid colonies as freely as it does to any other food (Herzig 1938a) and the same is probably true of *Myrmica rubra*. Wood-ants use their ability to return to the same spot, but they also may remain overnight with their aphids on trees many yards from the nest (Ökland 1938). In spring *Lasius niger* sometimes stays out all night too (Eidmann 1927b); perhaps this is because honeydew is not produced very fast early in the year and the ants will not go home till they have a full crop (Herzig 1938a). At any rate in summer, when there are plenty of aphids, *L. niger* returns quickly to its nest as soon as it has filled its crop (Huber 1810, Banks 1958). *Lasius fuliginosus* workers (Herzig 1938a) and wood-ants (Otto 1958) on the other hand often give up their honeydew to nestmates they meet at the foot of the tree, so that it is carried home by a relay system.

5·4·1 How ants milk plant-lice

Ants can pass among aphids without disturbing them or provoking them to any of their defensive behaviour. When predators like ladybird larvae approach them on the other hand the aphids walk away from them, kick at them with their feet or drop from the plant. If the ladybird larva seizes an aphis it tries to pull itself free, and in the last resort daubs the secretions of its dorsal tubes, the siphunculi, over the attacker's head. The waxy secretion paralyses the larva for some minutes (Dixon 1958). Although some aphids like *Microlophium viciae* and *evansi* treat ants in the same way, *Aphis fabae* allows ants to visit it (Ibbotson and Kennedy 1959, Dixon 1958) (Plate 2b).

Huber (Huber 1810) described beautifully the way ants get honeydew from aphids. The honeydew is not produced continuously, and aphids which are not attended by ants throw the drop of liquid away from them with a flick of their third leg. Ants collect honeydew by touching the hind end of the aphis repeatedly with their antennae until a droplet appears. This time the aphis does not throw it away but holds it on the tip of its abdomen (Plate 2a). The ant sucks it up at once and goes to another aphis for more. Every point in this account has been confirmed since Huber's time and very little has been added to it. When there are no ants the aphis gets rid of the honeydew drop by kicking it away or by throwing it away with the cauda—an elongated point at the tip of its abdomen (Banks 1958). Some scale-insects which have short legs and no cauda can squirt honeydew about 5 mm. from their rectum (Gray 1962). But when an ant tickles it the plant-louse does not get rid of the droplet. Aphids which are attended by ants produce smaller droplets more often, and usually only when an ant touches them. *Aphis fabae* can suck a droplet back into its body until an ant comes for it (Banks 1958).

In short both ant and aphis show altered behaviour in each other's presence. The aphis retains its excretions, and the ant rarely attacks the aphis. We do not understand how this comes about. The way the ant tickles the aphis with its antennae looks the same as the way it begs food from a nestmate. It has in fact been suggested that there is enough resemblance between the front end of an ant and the hind end of an aphid for either to release the same begging behaviour in a hungry ant. The hind legs of the aphis represent the ant's antennae, its siphuncles the mandibles and its cauda, anus and perianal hairs the maxillo-labial tongue. Whilst a simple oval or round piece of wax is not tickled by ants, similar models with two bristle-like projections are (Kloft 1959). Unfortunately the 'tickling' of an aphis or of a nestmate is very like the antennal movements of ants feeding from a dish of syrup. No-one has made a study of the movements detailed enough to distinguish them. In the honeybee the smell of the head of another bee is the most important thing in releasing begging behaviour. The presence or absence of antennae does affect the likelihood of a bee begging from a severed

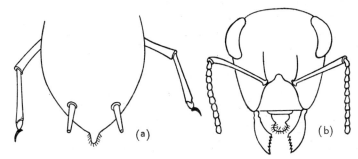

FIG. 5·7 (a) the abdomen of an aphid, (b) the head of an ant, showing similarity in features. (After Kloft 1959)

head of a bee, but they are most important in directing the begging to the right bit of the head. 'False antennae' made of wire are just as good for this purpose (Free 1956). It is quite likely that the geometry of the hind end of an aphis is as important in showing the ant where to suck. The resemblance between the head of an ant and the stern of an aphis can hardly be responsible for stopping the ant attacking the aphid, for ants attack objects which look much more like ants, including of course the heads of other ants. In any case siphuncles are missing in scales and Membracid bugs which ants also visit. The predatory behaviour of ants can often be inhibited by offering them a sweet substance: *Myrmica rubra* will stop in the middle of dragging home a hoverfly to suck up nectar oozing from the fly's mouth or anus (Sudd 1965). *Lasius niger* treats any small insect on which a drop of honey is placed as if it was an aphid, tickling it and returning later if it gets no response (Herzig 1938a). This seems more likely to be the basis of the change in the ants' behaviour.

5·4·2 Ants as herders of plant-lice

Aphids attended by ants thrive (Way 1963). A colony of aphids to which ants are admitted often grows nearly twice as fast as one from which they are excluded (Banks 1958), and will produce fewer winged forms (El-Ziady and Kennedy 1956). One reason for this may be that the ants drive away or destroy insects that eat aphids. When aphids on trees are isolated from wood-ants by grease bands on the trees their numbers fall, and the proportion of the number of predators to the number of aphids rises to 30%. When the bands are removed and ants can attend the aphids, aphid numbers go up to four times their previous number and their predators fall to 10% of the number of aphids (Wellenstein 1952). Aphid enemies only form 2·4% of the prey of wood-ants however and many of them are more or less protected from the attacks of ants (Wichmann 1955). Some predators of aphids are tolerated or even encouraged by ants. *Myrmecobosca mandibularis*, a parasite, is actually fed by the attendant *Lasius niger* and also milks the aphids itself (Pontin 1959). It is not at all a simple matter, for colonies of *Planococcoides njalensis*, a scale-insect, are more heavily parasitised when they are tended by ants. This may be because their colonies are then larger (Strickland 1951b).

Another benefit which, it has been thought, aphids derive from ants is the removal of honeydew. We have seen what trouble aphids take to fling away their excretion. Honeydew can cause the growth of sooty moulds, which may (Das 1959) or then again may not (Strickland 1951b) be harmful. The presence of honeydew can increase the number of predators too, for the hoverfly *Syrphus corollae* lays twice as many eggs on leaves contaminated with honeydew as on clean ones (Bombosch 1962). Washing the leaves every other day with distilled water gives the same benefit to aphids as putting ants with them (Bartlett 1961).

In general ants affect aphids they attend by stimulating their feeding (and therefore their honeydew production) (Banks and Nixon 1950) and reducing their tendency to wander and to produce winged forms (Banks 1958). Feeding seems to be linked antagonistically to dispersal in aphids (El-Ziady 1960).

Although these benefits to the aphids stem from the collection of honeydew by the ants, they are in a sense incidental. Wood-ants protect their aphids from predators at least partly because the movements of ants among the aphids simply disturbs parasites and predators. Ants which collect honeydew are often not interested in preying on other insects (Otto 1958). However the routes to the trees lead a certain number of their nestmates who do hunt to the trees, and these may attack any insect that moves. The hunters may even attack aphids, for *Lasius niger* carries many dead aphids into its nest (Pontin 1958).

Can it be true then to say, with Linnaeus, that aphids are ants' cows? Ants have been described not only as milking aphids and protecting them from attack. They have been said to herd them together in favourable sites above or below ground, to remove them from danger and carry them to new plants. They are also described building shelters over them, and collecting and storing eggs in winter to replace them on the food plants next spring.

Some of these claims were based on purely circumstantial evidence. Ants may be seen carrying aphids about at the same time that aphids appear on food plants, but the connection between these two observations is not what one might suppose. Sometimes the misunderstanding dates from a time before the life-cycles of aphids were understood. Young fundatrix females of *Aphis fabae* hatch from eggs in spring on their winter-host spindle-tree. Although it is difficult to find the eggs they are there through the winter, and fundatrices appear in equal numbers on twigs from which ants are excluded by grease-bands (Herzig 1938a). Far from placing aphids or their eggs on the plants in spring, ants prevent the escape of newly-hatched aphids from their nests (Eidmann 1927b). The ants do not carry aphids to their nest in hard weather in spring for aphids can be found on spindle even at temperatures below −1° (Herzig 1938a).

On the summer-host, bean or beet, summer colonies start when a winged aphis alights on a plant. It moves to the furled growing leaves and begins to feed and to produce young. As the plant grows the colony of aphids moves up to newer leaves. The adults on the other hand move to the undersides of leaves lower down the plant before they begin to reproduce. When the aphids are tended by *Lasius niger* this downward movement is delayed by about two weeks. As a result the aphis colonies are large and more compact (Banks 1958). There is no reason to think that ants herd the colonies together as sheep-dogs herd sheep. The excretory behaviour of aphids is altered by the presence of ants, and their dispersal may be affected too. Indeed if ants beg for food and then fail to collect it, perhaps because the colony is densely packed, the aphids become restless and may disperse more than if no ants were present (El-Ziady 1960).

Many ants do carry aphids away when they are disturbed. *Lasius brunneus*, which covers the bark of oaks with a sheet of carton, carries aphids with it into darker places if the covering is broken. A more curious example is that of the scale-insect *Hippeococcus* in Java, which is found with some *Dolichoderus* species. Young scales were found on twigs with the ants on many plants. When they were disturbed the ants tapped the scales with their antennae, and the scales climbed nimbly on to the ants' backs where they perched transversely and were carried away. Gravid female scales were found in the nests of the same ants. Oddly no-one has seen the ants collecting honeydew from the scales (Reyne 1954).

Very often the ants just seem to carry scales with them, and the results may not benefit either ant or scale. *Pseudococcus njalensis* is a sluggish scale which lives on cocoa. When 3,000 scales were released in a grove of cocoa trees only one succeeded in reaching a tree, from a distance of about 2 metres. Scales which were released on a felled tree where there were nests of *Crematogaster africana* appeared on 8 out of the 96 trees in the grove. This however was when the ants themselves were forced to disperse. Their effect in dispersing scales may have been no more directed than that of wind (Strickland 1951b, Cornwell 1956).

Sometimes transport seems to be methodical. The large *Stomaphis quercus* is always attended by *Lasius fuliginosus* and lives all the year round on oak trees. Its winter eggs are laid in crevices of the bark on the trunk of the tree up to 2 metres from the ground. In northern Italy the eggs hatch in mid-April and the young aphids are carried by ants towards the top of the tree 20 metres or more up. At this height the aphids thrive and produce a new generation viviparously. As soon as these daughter aphids are born they set off down the tree, stopping at

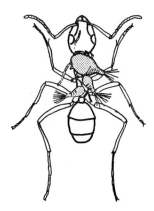

FIG. 5·8 *Dolichoderus gibbifer* carrying two first-stage and one second-stage *Hippeococcus* scale-insects. (After Reyne 1954)

intervals to feed. They reach the base of the tree in three to four weeks in the middle of June. After that they stay at the bottom of the tree feeding till autumn when males and females are produced which lay winter eggs. This farcical proceeding does seem to involve a movement of aphids in one direction and not a general dispersal. The author does not record what proportion of ants were carrying aphids up, perhaps some also moved them down, and the migration was less purposive than it appears. He thought that the aphids found better feeding conditions and produced better honeydew in spring on the ends of branches but that the climate near the ground was kinder to them in winter (Goidanich 1959).

A good many of the aphids which ants carry to their nests are dead (Pontin 1958, Strickland 1951a, Goidanich 1959) and are presumably eaten. Aphis eggs are found in the nests of ants in winter and *Lasius flavus* licks and cares for them as it does the eggs of its queen. There are no ants' eggs in the nest in winter. Yet these eggs do not belong to the aphids which *L. flavus* rears in its nests, in fact *Forda formicaria* and *Tetraneura ulmi*—two common aphids in ants' nests—overwinter as adult females, not as eggs at all (Muir 1959). The idea that the ants solicitously place the aphids on plants in spring is probably wrong too. Often the aphids actually have to escape from the ants which treat them as if they were their own brood. Even when they are turned out of the nest they have to find food plants for themselves. At least three species of aphids are involved in the case of *Lasius flavus*. Each has its own food plants, and the ants would have to identify the species of aphis and its food plant if they were to be any real help (Pontin 1960b).

Where there is an obligate relationship between ant and plant-louse, that is where each is found only in association with the other, matters may be different. For one thing if the plant-louse is only to be found in the nests of ants, a new ant colony can only get plant-lice from an older colony. In Surinam eleven species of scale-insect infest the roots of coffee trees. Five of them are only found in the nests of an ant, *Acropyga* (*Rhizomyrma*) *paramaribensis* or less often *R. rutgersi*. The ants' nests are at the roots of the trees. Coffee of course is not a native plant in the New World and both the ants and their scales seem to have moved to coffee from grasses and Cyperaceae which they still attack as well. Disturbed *Rhizomyrma* workers always pick up either ant brood or scales. Their need to do this is so strong that if there are neither brood or scales they will pick up soil instead. During the mating flights every winged female which leaves the nest is carrying an immature scale-insect. This is supposed either to form the stock of a new colony, or to be received with the fertilised queen into an established colony (Bünzli 1935).

5·4·3 Sheds for the ants' cattle

Last of all comes the story of the cattle-sheds which some ants build over plant-lice. *Lasius niger* (Muir 1959) and *L. neoniger* (Orlob 1963) dig little pits at the roots of plants and aphids live in them. *L. neoniger* at least does not put aphids in the pits but those that do get in flourish because they are protected from predators. *Formica nigricans* makes pits which only a few hoverfly larvae penetrate (Wellenstein 1952). *Formica exsectoides* digs at the roots of various trees and female tree-hoppers (Membracidae) enter them to lay their eggs. Later in the year the ants cover the pits with twigs and gravel so that they resemble a small *F. exsectoides* nest 4-5 cm. in diameter and 2-3 cm. high (Andrews 1929).

In the tropics ants build earthen shelters over plant-lice they visit. On cocoa 80% of colonies of the scale *Pseudococcus njalensis* are covered with shelters by *Crematogaster striatulus*. The doors in the shelters are large enough for *Crematogaster* workers but too small for some other tree ants like *Oecophylla* or for ladybird larvae. A midge larva does however get in and prey on the scales (Strickland 1951b). Apart from protecting the plant-lice from enemies the shelters keep out the weather too. This is important for even a light wind can stop *Tuberolachnus salignus* feeding and so reduce its honeydew output (Mittler 1958). *Crematogaster striatulus* builds over its scale-insect only in times of rain. During a dry period in Ghana there were only three sheds on 75 cocoa trees. As an experiment 15 trees were protected by little roofs of thatch. After a short period of rain 159 sheds were built on the 60 unprotected trees but there were none on the 50 colonies of scales on the roofed trees (Hanna et al. 1957). Perhaps the ants find the shelter as welcome as the scales do. *Oecophylla longinoda* does not feed from exposed colonies of scales during rain. It stays in its nest and feeds from the plant-lice that live there (Way 1954b).

In fact ants may build shelters round any rich source of food, such as a dish of syrup or a flower which produces a lot of nectar (Goetsch

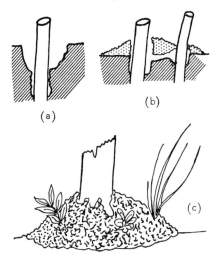

FIG. 5·9 Shelters round young trees made by *Formica exsectoides* and inhabited by leaf-hoppers: (a) pits, (b) later, covered with litter, (c) well covered in late season. (After Andrews 1929)

1953). It may be that at least some of the ants which are collecting honeydew are still able and inclined to undertake building as well. Building is often done by ants which are of an age to forage (chapter 8). Any place where ants congregate and stay for some time may be liable to be built up by the ants. The style of building seems to resemble that of the nest of each species, and rain promotes the construction of nests as well as cattle-sheds (section 4·4). This is not to say that the sheds do not protect plant-lice or ants; no doubt they do. But it does not seem that cattle-sheds are built as part of a special instinct.

The behaviour of ants to plant-lice resembles the way they behave to each other and to their brood. Aphids are in some way able to enter the food traffic which exists in ant colonies. They are in quite a different position from the many parasites and guests of ants however. The plant-lice are actually introducing food into the traffic from outside, the guests merely divert some of it through their own mouths. Though aphids will appear again in the next chapter their true place is among the sources of food.

5·5 Food in bad seasons: stores of seeds

Huber, writing of the nests of wood-ants, said that they built their mounds not only of twigs and leaves but also with seeds of wheat, oats and barley. He thought this gave rise to the ancient fable of the harvesting ant that stored corn for the winter, for he knew that northern ants are quiescent in winter and do not eat. (Huber 1810.) Huber lived in Switzerland: writers in the ancient Mediterranean world were well acquainted with the seed-collecting habits of harvesting ants. These ants depend on seeds for their food, at least at some times of the year, and they are typically inhabitants of lands with a hot dry season. Seeds are collected by ants in cooler parts of the world too, and there seem to be two reasons for collecting seeds.

Among the ants of northern Europe *Tetramorium caespitum, Myrmica rubra, M. lobicornis, Lasius fuliginosus, L. niger, Formica fusca, F. exsecta* and the wood-ants all collect seeds in summer in large quantities (Sernander 1904, Wellenstein 1952). Many of the seeds they collect have an oily seed-coat, an oily appendage, or there is an oily part of the flower or of the inflorescence. It is this oil body, or elaiosome, which attracts the ants to the seed. *Lasius niger* workers collected ten whole seeds of sweet violet within three minutes. In six minutes they only took seven out of ten seeds whose oily caruncle had been stripped off. Similar results followed the removal of the stalk and seed coat from primrose seeds (Sernander 1904). Wood-ants remove certain seeds which have been placed on one of their routes to their nest and eat them. Other seeds and glass beads they simply clear to one side (Stäger 1929a). They will collect and take to their nests glass beads smeared with some vegetable oils (Stäger 1935a). Oily seeds are eaten by some tropical ants which one thinks of as carnivorous: *Anomma nigricans* feeds on the pericarp of fallen oil-palm nuts and so does *Paltothyreus tarsatus*. Sernander argued at great length that many of these seeds are specially adapted for distribution by ants, just as others, like burrs, are distributed by birds and mammals. The oil-body is the principle adaptation he mentions, though the behaviour of the plant in exposing its seed or even in placing it on the ground could be important (Sernander 1904). The effects of ants on the distribution of plants are not very striking, even in deserts where seed-collecting ants are very common. Rodents have a more noticeable effect (Tevis 1958a). A further suggestion that ants collect the seeds of marigold and *Dimorphotheca* because of their resemblance to caterpillars does not fit what we know of the hunting methods of most ants. Even northern ants take some oilless seeds, like sweet pea, as well as oily ones.

In deserts, savannahs and Mediterranean lands seed-collecting ants take seeds including those of cereals. The most important of these true harvesting ants are *Messor* and *Monomorium* (*Holcomyrmex*) in the Old World, *Pogonomyrmex* and *Veromessor* in America, and species of *Pheidole* throughout the world. There is no doubt that *Messor* and *Pheidole* actually eat the whole of the grain of wheat, barley or rice in laboratory cultures; some Italian *Pheidole* even eat macaroni (Stäger 1929a, Delage 1962). There is no question of the ants only eating some oily titbit and leaving the seed viable. Most of these ants also eat insect and other flesh, and turn to seeds at seasons when insects are scarce (Arnold 1915, Stäger 1935c, Bequaert 1922b). In Chile *Solenopsis gayi* collects seeds in the deserts of the north but not in the forests to the south. The seed-collecting *Pogonomyrmex bispinosus* of the north is replaced by the insectivorous *P. laevigatus* in the south (Goetsch 1953). In deserts even seeds are scarce during drought and are collected in greater numbers after rain. In California after six years of drought *Veromessor pergandei* had 68% of its foragers laden with seeds, and the rest with fragments of insects, stones, rat and bat droppings and other rubbish, most of it quite inedible. After rain 92% of foragers carried seeds, 6·5% flowers and only 1% had insects (Tevis 1958b). The seed-collecting habit, characteristic of ants in the dry season in other places, allows desert ants to take advantage of the seed crop which follows rain in very severe climates.

The ants of these hot dry regions do not collect seeds for their oil content: they need the starch and other parts of the seed itself. Since some ants appear to prefer germinating seeds in the laboratory, it was once thought that they only used the starch after it had been malted. This would involve the conversion of the starch to sugars by allowing the seed to germinate and then drying it in the sun. This idea is incorrect. *Messor* often does not take germinated seeds at all (Delage 1962) and if it does take them this is merely because the husk is cracked (Goetsch 1928). *Messor structor* will feed on any seed it can open or which is given to it ready opened (Goetsch 1929). *Messor* collects seeds by a similar method to the foraging method of *Formica*. Ants learn to return to spots where thay have found seeds. Established nests have a system of routes which are cleared and sometimes partly excavated (Goetsch 1929). When an ant seizes a slippery or hard seed it brings the tip of its gaster forward to prevent the seed slipping and it may possibly mark it with a secretion at the same time (Goetsch 1928).

In its nest *M. structor* opens the seeds and chews them to a paste of starch and saliva; often several ants work at the same seed (Goetsch 1928). After *M. capitatus* workers have been chewing a seed no starch can be detected in their guts, but there is a lot in their infrabuccal sacs. The chewed paste on the other hand contains maltose, which is absent from crushed seeds which have not been chewed (Delage 1962). The crushed heads of *Messor* workers can digest starch to a reducing sugar (Goetsch 1930). The labial glands, and no other gland that opens on the head, secrete saliva containing an amylase and a maltase, which can in turn convert starch to maltose and maltose to glucose (Delage 1962). The seeds then are the source of sugars, which in other ants might be obtained from flowers or plant-lice. How much protein *Messor* needs in its diet, and whether it can also be obtained from seeds is not known.

What kind of seed is collected by desert ants depends on what sort of seeds they can get. In North Carolina *Pogonomyrmex badius* nests contain mainly seeds of grasses and Compositae (Wray 1938). In more extreme conditions in California *Veromessor pergandei* took seeds from eleven species of plant. Most seeds were either of a plantain or a *Pectocarya*, and these were the only seeds common enough to be seen in the soil. After rain the ants climbed the stems of ephemeral plants to collect seeds, even unripe ones. *Oenethra* became the most common and *Plantago* and *Pecto-carya* were neglected. Ants make little impression on the seeds resources of a desert. *Veromessor pergandei* collects about 15 million seeds an acre a year. In California the estimated seed production after rain is nearly 1,500 million seeds an acre. Even after six years of drought enough seeds at least of *Plantago* and *Pectocarya* remain on the sand. The ants collect no seeds from below the surface (Tevis 1958b).

5·5·1 *Stores of liquids*

Seeds can be collected, prepared and stored in much the same way as insect prey. They provide a reserve of food for many ants, especially in the Myrmicinae, which either feed on insects themselves at other times, or which have near relations that do so. Some Formicine ants can store liquid foods instead. Ants never store food in liquid form in cells of any kind, as bees do. Instead they keep it in the bodies of certain workers who are specialised for this and who are called repletes. The gaster of a replete is many times enlarged by the volume of liquid in its crop. In most subfamilies of ants food is held in the crop, and not allowed to pass into the intestine, by the contraction of muscles in the stomodaeal valve. In some Myrmicinae, like *Pogonomyrmex*, which take little or no liquid food, this valve is poorly developed. In Dolichoderinae and Formicinae the valve is not held closed by the active contraction of muscles. The pressure of fluid in the crop itself keeps the valve closed, and there are special muscles to open the valve by distorting it. In the best developed examples (Formicinae) a special arrangement of 'sepals' allows a very high rate of flow when the valve is open, in spite of its automatic nature. Valves of this kind can be kept closed almost indefinitely without any expense of energy (Eisner 1957, Eisner and Brown 1958).

A good many ants which feed on honeydew fill their crops pretty full, and workers of for instance *Lasius niger* returning to the nest sometimes have large and translucent gasters. True repletes are characteristic, like true harvesting ants, of places where there is a hot dry season. Thus *Prenolepis imparis* has a curious distribution, living on heavy soils in North America and in the Balkans (Wheeler 1930). It never forages above ground in summer, but feeds its brood on stores of fruit-juices which it collects in autumn and winter, even during periods of frost. In winter 80% of its worker force are in a replete condition but by the end of summer the proportion of repletes has dropped to 67% (Talbot 1943).

The food stored in repletes can be passed to the rest of the colony. *Proformica nasuta* lives in east Europe and south Russia in steppe conditions where there is a hot dry summer. It is also found less commonly in the Mediterranean lands. Its workers range from 3 to 7 mm. in length but only the larger workers become replete. When the ants are kept in the laboratory at 20° food passes from workers to repletes, but at a higher temperature, 30°, when worker needs are higher there is an overall transfer of food from the repletes to the rest of the colony (Stumper 1961).

In American deserts *Myrmecocystis* also has repletes whose gasters are swollen to five or eight times their original size (Wheeler 1910). The repletes live in the depths of the nest as much as 5 metres below the surface; they can move only with difficulty and usually hang from the roofs of the deep chambers. Contrary to an old tale they can climb back up again if they fall off. Often however they would be quite unable to crawl through the small tunnels which lead from chamber to chamber so that they are in fact prisoners (Creighton and Crandall 1954).

Repletes are anatomically simply ordinary workers, often of the larger sort, whose gaster is enlarged by the stretching of the membrane between the plates. In *Proformica nasuta* some large workers were readier to take up honey than others and this probably inclines them to become repletes (Stumper 1961). *Myrmecocystus* workers must, it is said, begin to overfeed when they are still callows (Wheeler 1910), and this may mean that some change, either of elasticity or of growth, is necessary in their cuticle.

5·5·2   *The cultivation of fungi*

Storing food in nests is a poor substitute for actually producing it there. As we saw, some ants are able to live entirely on the honeydew produced by plant-lice which live in the ants' nests. This allows them to live an entirely subterranean life in places where conditions above ground are too hot, too cold or too dry to suit them. Another way of producing food inside the nest itself is by the culture of fungi. However this habit has so far at least had a limited success, mostly in climates already favourable to ants, and only those in the New World at that.

Because the air in them is usually moist all ants' nests are liable to grow fungi. No doubt most of these moulds are harmful or at least inconvenient to the ants. Their growth is prevented by hygienic measures which the ants take: licking brood and eggs, removing dead ants and the remains of prey and so on. Some ants have pure cultures of certain fungi in their nests. The carton of the nests of *Lasius fuliginosus* is riddled by the fungus *Cladosporium myrmecophilum*, and that of *L. umbratus* by

Hormiscum pithyophilum which is usually found on pine leaves (Elliot 1915). As the carton is made from wood it is only to be expected that it should be invaded by some of the fungi which feed on wood. In these cases it is possible that the fungus strengthens the carton but unlikely that it provides the ants with food.

Ants in the New World tribe Attini depend for their food on fungi which grow in their nests. The habit is shared with some families of termites and with the ambrosia beetles (Wheeler 1907). Many Attini also collect fruit and will feed on dead insects or on honeydew. Each species of ant has its own species of fungus and will not readily accept the fungus of other species in the laboratory (Goetsch 1939). Fungi from other genera of ants are never accepted (Wheeler 1907).

The fungus grows on 'gardens' which the ants build from various objects which they carry in from outside. They are not therefore totally independent of the outside world. In *Atta*, the largest forms, the garden is made of pieces of leaf. The ants go out of the nests in crowds by day, along routes up to a kilometre long, which lead partly over the ground partly along branches and creepers. They prefer to collect leaves from trees in forest edges and clearings, and also of course in plantations. Both scent and light-compass navigation is used on the routes. (Goetsch 1939.) On the trees the workers, which vary considerably in size, cut more or less circular pieces out of leaves with their long, scissor-like mandibles. They do this by turning around one leg like a compass, so that a disc of leaf in proportion to each worker's size is cut. These pieces are of course easily carried by one ant, though some pieces change owner-ship on relay principles, like the seeds of *Messor* (Lutz 1927, Eidmann 1938).

Inside the nest the foragers may drop their leaves. Other workers then continue the treatment which makes them suitable for use in the fungus garden. Sometimes the forager does this itself. First of all the leaf is thoroughly scraped and licked. This may remove foreign fungi which would otherwise infect the gardens. Next the leaf may be cut up if it is large. After this the main preparation begins. The ant repeatedly cuts the leaf in half, keeping only one half each time, until it has a piece no bigger than its own head. The rejected halves are taken in charge by other workers. After this the small piece of leaf is crimped round the edges by the mandibles, and both its surfaces are scarified. It is now quite limp and can be rolled into a ball. The ant carries the ball of kneaded leaf to the fungus beds, jabs it in with a sharp movement of its head and firms it well with its forelegs (Wheeler 1907). Older accounts suggest that the ants work over the fungus bed and weed out foreign species. This does not seem to be necessary and the ants may in fact have rendered the compost unsuitable for foreign species in some way (Goetsch 1953). In ants' nests the fungus produces no spores and only spreads vegetatively. At the tips of its hyphae small swellings usually called kohl-rabi form. They are found on the earliest fungus beds before any workers have cultivated the gardens (Huber 1905). It is these on which the larvae are fed.

The fungus culture is not acquired as an accidental infection. When the queens of *Atta sexdens* leave the nest for their mating flight they carry pellets in their infrabuccal pockets. The pellets are made up of a mixture of bleached leaves, cuticular spines from the bodies of workers and queen ants (but with no larval spines) and fungus mycelium. This is evidently the combings from their own bodies and those of their nestmates (von Ihering 1898, Huber 1905). *Atta cephalotes* and *Acromyrmex octospinosus* females carry similar pellets (Weber 1937). New colonies are formed by single queens each of which crawls to any cavity it can find in bare ground. The queen digs a hole barely larger than her own body and seals herself in completely with soil (von Ihering 1898). Inside the nest she spits out the infrabuccal pellet, which begins to grow. She tends it by pulling out small tufts of fungus and applying them to the tip of her gaster where they absorb a yellowish liquid. The tufts are then replaced in the growing fungus garden, which may reach a size of 10 mm. by the tenth day after the mating flight. The queen also lays eggs and she places some of them on the fungus where they hatch. She breaks other eggs and adds them to the fungus garden or feeds them to the young larvae. She eats some of the eggs herself but does not feed fungus to her larvae. Workers emerge from the first pupae three to five weeks after the mating flight. All this time the ants and the fungus live on material which comes from the queen's body as eggs or faeces. No leaves are added to the garden until the new workers begin to forage in another nine days or so. By this time the fungus garden may be 2·5 cm. in diameter (Huber 1905). The first workers are often too small to cut leaves and only carry in fragments of dead fallen leaves (Weber 1937). Unfertilised queens will carry out the procedures for founding a colony even if they have not flown and have not been fertilised. If they are taken from the nest when they are newly hatched they may have no fungus in their infrabuccal pouch. In this case they collect and tend a small heap of sand grains (Weber 1937).

The first workers immediately begin to care for the larvae and the queen does not tend them herself any more. She does continue to deposit her faeces in the garden. The young workers do so too, and as they deposit them around the edge of it the garden grows into a cup shape (Huber 1905).

Not all the Attine ants collect leaves in this way. The colonies of other forms are often smaller than those of *Atta sexdens* and *A. cephalotes*, and some of them spread further from the equator. The Attini are thought on anatomical grounds to have evolved from another specialised group of Myrmicine ants, the Dacetini. This tribe as we have seen is a highly predatory one. This makes it interesting to see that *Cyphomyrmex* and *Apterostigma* collect not leaves but caterpillar droppings as a substrate for their fungi, and that they also incorporate pieces of insect skeleton in their fungus garden. This probably supports it and lets in air. *Cyphomyrmex costatus* colonies contain less than 100 workers, each only about 2mm. long (Weber 1957). Some species of *Apterostigma* also incorporate wood-dust in their gardens, which are single and may be suspended in a cavity in a rotten log. The garden is held together in a bag of fungal mycelium and it is sometimes suggested that the ants weave this themselves. Although *Moellerius* and *Acromyrmex* cut leaves for their fungus, other genera may simply collect fallen ones, like the first workers of *Atta sexdens*. *Trachymyrmex septentrionalis* cuts leaves, *T. turrifex* and *T. hartmanni* pick up fallen petals and leaves (Wheeler 1907, Weber 1958).

All Attine ants seem to manure their fungus gardens with their faeces. Probably the fungi they culture first grew on ant faeces on an ant midden near the nest. Later the ants came to crop it as a food. A further evolutionary step was to supplement their own droppings with those of caterpillars, often bulky and plentiful in forests. Finally the caterpillars were excluded from the food chain in the case of *Atta* when the ants collected leaves directly (Weber 1958). This interesting history of elimination of the middleman has enabled the Attini to become independent of other insects for their food. Like seed-eating ants, which are also more or less independent of other insects, some of them have become characteristic of American deserts. Their finest development, and probably their place of origin however is in tropical forest, where soil conditions and temperatures are perhaps nearer to the requirements of the fungus.

6 — The traffic in food

The amount of food each worker ant can collect is grossly in excess of its own needs. Most of what it collects is in fact transferred in one way or another to a nestmate. How soon this happens depends on the species of ant. *Atta* workers have very small crops, and if they are fed syrup they must share it or vomit it to waste; repletes of other species of course can retain large crops full for months. The result of this traffic in food is, overall, a flow from the foragers to all the members of the colony that cannot or do not forage. These are the domestic workers, the queens, young male and female adults and, above all, the larvae. The flow is not all one way; foragers feed each other and foragers may be fed by domestic workers. Indeed experiments with syrup marked with radioactive substances show that all possible combinations of feeder and fed occur—even eggs and pupae acquire some radioactivity by being licked by the workers (Gösswald and Kloft 1960). It is only the balance of the flow which is towards the nurses and larvae, at least in a normal colony. If the colony is starved things are different and the nurses may eat the brood, which amounts to a reversal of the flow. Various names have been given to the food traffic. The term trophallaxis has been stretched to cover almost all social contacts between ants (Le Masne 1953). 'Food-exchange' seems to have a flavour of reciprocity and simultaneity which is misleading. 'Food-sharing' and 'Food-traffic' are suitably neutral.

6·1 Food-traffic among workers

A forager that has got a load of food rarely does more than bring it into the nest. She may even be relieved of her load outside the nest. In *Myrmecia* of Australia foragers may bring pieces of insect right to the larvae (Haskins and Haskins 1950), and the same may happen in very small colonies of other ants. As a rule food which foragers bring in is first passed from mouth to mouth among a good many workers. When a forager of *Formica polyctena* feeds on radioactive syrup it retains most of the syrup in its crop; only 20% has passed to the ant's midgut after three or four hours. If it is put with other workers it will be able to feed eight to ten from its crop, and in a colony about 80 ants might become radioactive in a few hours. More of the food is passed into the midgut by the ants which the forager has fed: only 20% of it is still in the crop after 2½ hours. Their blood becomes radioactive and so does the labial gland in the thorax (Gösswald and Kloft 1960). The picture is much the same in all species of ant which take a good deal of liquid food: wood-ants, *Camponotus ligniperda* (Gösswald and Kloft 1956), *Formica fusca* and *pallidefulva* and *Crematogaster lineolata* (Wilson and Eisner

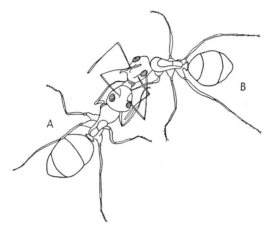

FIG. 6·1 Two workers of *Formica fusca* sharing food. (Wallis 1962a)

1957). In other ants which take solid food such as seeds (*Pogonomyrmex badius* Wilson and Eisner 1957) or flesh (*Solenopsis saevissima* Wilson and Eisner 1957, Ponerinae Gösswald and Kloft 1958), the flow of syrup is slow and radioactivity does not spread beyond a few workers if at all. These differences are partly related to differences in the anatomy of the proventricular valve (section 5·5·1). Probably solid foods are also handled by a large number of workers before they reach the larvae, but it is more difficult to demonstrate this.

The way in which liquid food is passed from one worker to another has often been described, but there are frequent contradictions in detail. More recent work has cleared up this difficulty. A *Formica fusca* worker which is receiving food from a nestmate lifts its head and the forepart of its body so that its forelegs are off the ground. Its mandibles are closed and its palps directed backwards, but its antennae are folded forwards so that their tips converge on the head of the ant which is giving it food. It often strokes the other ant's head as it feeds. The ant which is giving food on the other hand raises its head only a little and its antennae are folded back at right angles to its head. Its mandibles are opened wide and a drop of liquid appears on its extended tongue

(Wallis 1962a). This much is common to most descriptions, at least in Myrmicinae, Dolichoderinae and Formicinae. More advanced Ponerines, such as *Ponera edouardi* (Le Masne 1952), *Euponera* sp. and *Odontomachus* sp. feed in the same way and so does *Myrmecia regularis* (Haskins and Whelden 1954). In all these however food-sharing is rather irregular in occurrence, and the ants' behaviour lacks the slickness one finds in higher ants. It is rather as if the routine leading to food-sharing is not fully worked out. A number of Ponerine ants have never been seen sharing food, even by people making an extensive study of them (Haskins and Whelden 1954). Probably no Doryline and few other flesh-eating ants show much food-sharing of this kind (Wilson and Eisner 1957). However the amount of food-sharing depends very much on how the colony is fed, so that negative evidence is a bit unreliable.

A moment ago the word routine was used to describe the food sharing of the higher ants. In fact this particular piece of behaviour is much more stereotyped than many items of worker ant behaviour. The preliminaries which lead up to the point where one ant regurgitates a drop of food and the other sucks it up are long and recall the courtship which is often a preliminary to mating in other animals. In a courtship one can usually discern a series of gestures which are made by the male and the female, often alternately and in a definite order. These result in the movements of mating being performed, and performed at the right time and place by both male and female. However attempts to find this sort of regularity in the food-sharing of worker ants have usually run on to rocks. Most people from Huber on, have thought that the antennal strokes the acceptor gives the donor induce it to regurgitate food. The almost frenzied way an acceptor strokes an unwilling donor which is beginning to move away would certainly incline any observer to think this. The excesses of some believers in 'antennal language' led other people to discount the effect of antennal stimulation on the donor, while they admitted its role in alining the acceptor and guiding it to the donor's mouthparts. After all similar movements are made when an ant is feeding from sugar syrup in a dish. According to this view food-sharing starts when a would-be donor offers food to an acceptor, by regurgitating a drop of food onto its own mouthparts (Vowles 1955a).

In fact food-sharing can be initiated either by the donor or the acceptor according to circumstances. *Formica sanguinea* workers that have been left for some time without food in small jars of dry air are more than usually inclined to accept food. If they are returned to a well-fed colony they go round begging food from the other ants. In these conditions 90% of all food-sharing incidents are started by acceptors. On the other hand a forager returning to a well-fed colony is more inclined to give food than its nestmates are to accept it. The forager goes round offering food and most of the (rather few) acts of food-sharing are started by the donor (Wallis 1961). This state of things is by no means peculiar to *Formica*; a two-edged system like this is necessary to explain the sharing of food in small groups of *Monomorium pharaonis* and other ants too.

Either acceptor or donor may stroke its partner with its antennae or even with its forelegs. The amount of gesticulation in fact measures the inclination of the ant to give or accept food. Ants which have been desiccated, and so are inclined to accept food, stroke donors more with their antennae the longer they have been desiccated; stroking with the forelegs in particular is a sign of strong inclination to accept food. In *Formica fusca* and *F. sanguinea* antennal stroking is more common in ants strongly inclined to give food to others. The stroking does have its effect on the other partner however, for a reluctant donor or acceptor may be brought to the point by persistent strokes from its partner (Wallis 1961).

Probably then antennal gestures serve basically to locate the acceptor and the donor correctly, so that they can pass a drop of food between their mouthparts. This, it may be remembered, is the conclusion we came to on their role when aphids feed ants. Here too the aphids sometimes produce a drop for the ant before, other times after it has touched them. No doubt, as often happens, other functions have been added to this in the course of evolution, and the gestures also give one ant an indication of the other's inclinations. This ancillary role is confirmed by the fact that ants whose antennae have been removed can still accept food from their nestmates, as Reaumur seems to have been the first to show (Huber 1810). Antennaless ants however are fed less often than normal or blinded ants, and are less successful in feeding (Wallis 1961).

6·1·1 Food-traffic and the recognition of companions

In honeybees food-sharing between workers produces a uniform odour for all the bees in a colony. Each colony has collected nectar from a slightly different range of flowers and so the odour characterises the colony and is possessed by all its members. Bees of 'strange' odour are attacked (Kalmus and Ribbands 1952). In ants too colony members are recognised by smell. Ants which enter a colony are examined and licked. Both aliens and nestmates may be threatened by ants, which open their mandibles wide, but aliens, and nestmates which have been kept apart from the nest for some time, are threatened most. The threat may, but need not, be followed by an actual attack on aliens. Their legs are seized and they are dragged about. The victim usually submits and escapes when it can. Certain ants like *Formica fusca* are more timid and most likely to flee. Other ants like *Formica sanguinea* may actually take the offensive in a strange colony (Wallis 1962b, 1963).

Early experimenters gathered a good deal of evidence that ants were accepted as nestmates or attacked on the basis of their smell. For instance chloroformed ants, which could give no cues by antennal language, were accepted by their nestmates. Ants smeared with the blood of foreign ants of the same species were attacked whenever they moved, but foreign ants were accepted if they were washed and then smeared with the blood of ants of the colony. This showed that there was a superficial difference between ants from different colonies which could easily be removed or overlain. The superficial difference however was somehow regenerated, for if friendly ants were washed their own colony would not accept them again until they had been kept in isolation for some days (Bethe 1898). Antennae were involved in the recognition of friend and foe for workers from the same, usually peaceful, colony of *Myrmica ruginodis* attacked one another fiercely after their antennae were cut off. In other ants cutting off their antennae made them unusually peaceful and *Formica sanguinea* and *nigricans, Camponotus ligniperdus* and *Lasius niger* could all be kept in a single nest (Forel 1928). *Formica sanguinea* is sometimes made more aggressive by having its antennae removed (Wallis 1961), so obviously this is not a simple matter of reflex attack.

The difference in an ant's behaviour to friends and to strangers only affects the social relations between worker and worker, and to a smaller extent worker and queen. The relations between worker and larvae, which date back to the relation between mother and offspring in the days before ants were social, are not affected. Larvae are usually accept-able whatever their origin. Not only larvae from other colonies of the same species, but even those of other species are often accepted. *Myrmica rubra* workers accept and rear *Anergates atratulus* larvae with their own brood. *Tetramorium caespitum, Leptothorax nylanderi* and *Solenopsis fugax* will accept *Anergates* larvae if they have no brood of their own (Plateaux 1960 a, b and c). Pupae and even freshly emerged workers are some-times not attacked by other species (Fielde 1904), though each species probably has a preference for its own pupae over those of other species (Forel 1920).

These early experiments seem to have been bedevilled by the idea that ants recognised fellow-members of their colony by some individual characteristic. Even when it was realised that a colony odour was the deciding feature, the odour was thought of as a personal characteristic and not as derived from social life in the colony. Species and colony characteristics were confused to some extent as well. A complicated set of odours was postulated to explain the results of experiments in which different colonies were mixed together (Fielde 1904, 1905). Each ant was supposed to possess at least two odours. One was a characteristic of its species and normally prevented mature ants of different species being formed into a single nest. Newly emerged workers could however be placed together and in the mixed colony that resulted both species lived together peaceably. If the two species were then separated and reared apart for some months, very equivocal results could be obtained by reuniting them. In some cases the species fought, this was thought to show that they had forgotten the odour of the other species. In other cases it was possible to reunite the two species. Naturally this showed that they remembered each other's odour. The parade of the care which was needed to reunite the two does throw a good deal of doubt on the importance of this result. It seems very reasonable to suppose that ants recognise their own species partly by its odour. It is equally reasonable to suppose that other characteristics too are important, such as shape and movement. No doubt all these signs by which species can be recognised are part of the genetic inheritance of the species.

Unfortunately this idea of a genetic origin was extended to the odours which characterise colonies as well. Since colonies that had once been split could not always be reunited it seemed that colony odour could change. This was supposed to be because each ant had a 'progressive odour' which altered with its age (Fielde 1905). The hostility between different colonies of the same species must therefore depend on their having a different age structure among their workers.

It seems far more likely that the colony odour changes because of differences in diet. A better indication of whether two ants accept each other as members of the same colony is the extent to which they feed one another. Two parts of a colony of *Formica polyctena* have been kept apart for as long as four months. As long as the diet of the two halves was the same they exchanged food freely when they were reunited. The amount of food-sharing could be very much reduced by adding spruce bark extract to one diet and fruit juice to the other. Differences in the sort of nesting material they were given also altered the freedom of food-sharing between them (Lange 1960). Short periods of isolation are not always effective with this species. Groups which had been isolated for 22 days and given food flavoured with pine oil, did not share food more among themselves than with other ants which had not received pine oil in their food (Otto 1958). It would be a mistake to press the analogy between bees and ants too closely. In the single species of the honeybee, colony differences which arise from differences in diet are very important. But the diet of an ant colony is quite different from that of bees. In many species the food consists of many varieties of insect, each variety having one supposes, its own flavour. No-one knows to what extent these flavours could be incorporated in a colony odour, or how far they could be made common to all the ants in a colony. Certainly in carnivorous ants radioactivity is communicated only slowly through the colony. No hostility seems to exist within the colony however. In species, like wood-ants, which take honeydew from plant-lice feeding on a small number of species of tree one might expect that colony distinctions would be blurred because the diet of different colonies is less distinct. This does seem to be the case. Experiments with radioactive syrup have shown that there is a lot of food-exchange between neighbouring nests of *Formica polyctena* (Chauvin, Courtois and Lecomte 1961); *Lasius minutus* gave similar results (Kannowski 1959a). Visitors from other nests have been seen in *Formica opaciventris* (Scherba 1964).

6·1·2 Channels of food-traffic among workers

The traffic in food among workers shares the food through the colony. The speed of flow of the traffic is altered by the number of foragers coming home, and by the amount of food they bring in (which affects their inclination to feed other ants). It is also altered by the hunger of the colony (which affects the inclination of ants in the nest to accept food) (Wallis 1961). Probably, though there is no direct evidence for this, the 'hunger' of the nurse workers (and therefore their readiness to take food) depends on the number and size of the larvae they have fed. There is not a mere diffusion of food through the colony but a definite flow from fed ants to hungry ones; that is an overall flow towards the queen and the larvae which are the main consumers of food. The more food they eat the more the flow will be tilted in their direction.

This gradient of hunger is not the only thing that influences the flow, although it fixes its general direction. There are also, so to speak, a number of eddies. Well fed workers of *Formica polyctena* will feed other workers that have been in contact with a queen twice as often as they feed those that have not. This is not merely because the queen takes food from workers and so makes them hungrier, for contact with a dead queen is just as effective (Lange 1958). When *Lasius flavus* workers are fed with poisoned syrup the whole colony is not, as a rule, poisoned. If some workers are given poisoned syrup and others syrup containing a dye, it seems that each worker passes syrup on to a 'clique' of workers. Some workers are found dead, but not dyed, while coloured workers survive (Goetsch 1941). In *Formica polyctena* workers which have been fed with radioactive syrup on a route 50 metres from the nest do not pass radioactivity on, to workers which are using other routes (Chauvin, Courtois and Lecomte 1962). The exact significance of these eddies in the flow is not known. They show at least that there are restrictions on the flow of food, perhaps simply because an ant is more likely to meet and feed some of its nestmates than others.

6·2 Care of eggs and young larvae

The young of ants are entirely dependent on the care of the workers (or of the mother queen in newly founded colonies) and neither eggs or larvae can survive without the continual attention of workers. In some, though far from all, ants the pupae are less dependent, and may be able to dispense with the workers' care though usually they do receive it.

Queen ants lay their eggs one at a time, and in an established colony the eggs they lay are usually collected by a worker immediately. In fact the queen is actually 'delivered' by a worker which seizes the egg as soon as it appears from the queen's body. In other cases the queen simply raises her abdomen and extrudes her sting, if she has one, and the egg drops or is rubbed off onto the ground. The queen's eggs may be produced in a rapid succession, but in *Eciton* (Schneirla 1956) and in

Myrmica ruginodis (Brian 1957b) egg production is periodic. *Eciton* queens lay a massive batch of eggs every three weeks and *M. ruginodis* two batches a year. In most ants the eggs are collected into piles by the workers and adhere to each other in clumps. Those of *Myrmecia regularis*

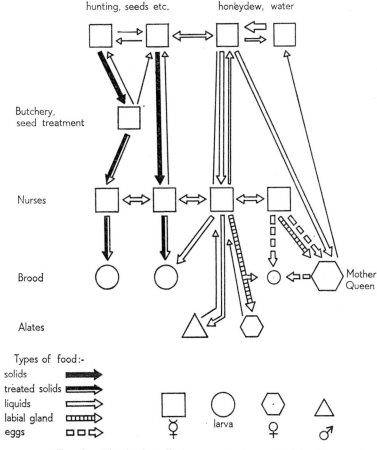

FIG. 6·2 The food-traffic in an ant colony. (Original)

however remain single (Haskins and Haskins 1955). *Prenolepis longicornis,* a crevice-nesting house-ant, is said not to form piles. Instead its workers carry the egg clumps around (Assmuth 1907). This may be an adaptation to crevice life, but it is hard to be sure what undisturbed workers do. The eggs in the pile are turned over all the time by nurse workers so that first one and then another is at the surface and probably all the eggs are licked. Eggs which are not licked, or which are kept without workers either dry up or go mouldy. Although eggs can become radioactive by being licked by radioactive workers (Gösswald and Kloft 1960) it is unlikely that eggs are 'fed' by workers in this way. The supposed growth of eggs is probably only the change in the eggs' shape as the elongated larvae develop inside. Worker ants use their mandibles for handling eggs, and species which have 'trap-jaw' mandibles may have a pad half-way down their mandibles where they hold eggs (Forel 1928).

Hatching takes place without any help from the workers. In fact they do not even detect it and the first-stage larvae stay in the egg pile and are licked and manipulated like eggs. At this stage they live by eating the other eggs in the pile (Brian 1953, Freeland 1958, Weir 1959b). Perhaps the eggs which Huber and Forel supposed to grow were in fact first-stage larvae.

6·3 Care of older larvae

After their first moult larvae respond when the workers touch them by bending themselves to their ventral side (Le Masne 1953, Weir 1959b). The workers collect larvae of this size into separate piles of larvae. Many larvae have hooked hairs which hold the pile together. The behaviour of workers which concentrate the larvae in this way is opposed by a tendency to disperse the larvae so that the workers have access to them all. In a large undivided artificial nest the more workers are supplied the larger the area of floor covered by the larval pile becomes. The area does not increase as fast as the area the increasing number of workers needs, if each is to have access to the larvae. Where there are almost as many workers as larvae therefore, many workers are partly denied access to the larvae, and cannot make their full contribution to caring for them. In a nest divided into many cells the larvae are more dispersed. Two hundred larvae, which could just be packed into one of the cells, were spread over two cells by 25 workers, over 4 cells by 50 and over 8 cells by 100 workers. Two hundred workers did not disperse the larvae even more in proportion (Brian 1956). The dispersal of larvae is necessary so that workers can lavish attention on them all. These attentions include licking the larvae, feeding them and assisting them in their moults, in spinning a cocoon, and in the case of pupae, helping them from the cocoon. It is not necessary for the workers to remove the faeces of the larvae, except when they are about to become pupae. The midgut of ant larvae, as in wasps and bees, does not open into the hindgut until this time.

6·3·1 Feeding the larvae: solid foods

The larvae of ants are usually barely capable of movement and the nurse workers have to bring the food to them. The food is of three sorts, and the amount the larvae gets of each sort depends on the habits of the species of ant and on the age of the larva. The first sort of food consists of fairly large pieces of insect prey. These are not usually fed to the youngest larvae. In some Ponerine ants like *Pachycondyla* pieces of meat are simply placed among the larger larvae. The larvae, which have elongated bodies, thrust their heads into the pieces of meat to eat them. Their skins have rough tubercles on them which give them enough grip of the ground to thrust in this way (Wheeler 1910). Other carnivorous ants lay pieces of insect on the upturned ventral side of their larvae. The Dacetine *Smithistruma* however places its larvae on top of the whole, dead Collembola which it carries home. Its larvae have long sclerotised mandibles which allow them to feed in this way (Wheeler and Wheeler 1954).

Very often insect meat is prepared by the workers before they give it to the larvae. Some workers of *Formica polyctena* specialise in this butchers' work, just before they begin to hunt. The prey is skinned and well soaked in saliva (Otto 1958). It is difficult to say whether the workers merely cut the food (Le Masne 1953) or whether they chew it over ('malaxation') before they let the larvae have it. Malaxation cannot be told from rather clumsy cutting up. It is rather as if one customer blamed the butcher for using a blunt cleaver while another praised him for beating the steak well. Seed-eating ants like *Messor* and *Pogonomyrmex* certainly chew seeds before they give them to their larvae, but they also let them have whole cracked seeds. The larvae thrust their heads into the seeds rather like a *Pachycondyla* larvae eating an insect (Goetsch 1953).

Doryline ants apparently feed their larvae with large pieces of insect and also with the contents of the infrabuccal pocket (Wheeler & Bailey 1925). Probably a good many of the ants that were described as piecemeal collectors of food in chapter 5 also use the contents of the pouch as food for their young. The Pseudomyrmicine ants are most given to this habit. Their larvae have a curious pocket on their thoraxes, which is formed by the bases of their rudimentary legs. This is filled with food, perhaps as an adaptation to life in stems where the larvae and their food have no floor to lie on. The contents of this thoracic pouch or trophophylax are bits of insect, spores and plant hairs. These seem to be the groomings from the surface of worker and larval ants. Pseudomyrmicines have been graphically described as 'combining the contents of dust-bin and garbage can and serving up the mixture as food for their young'. The larvae of *Pseudomyrma* from live acacia twigs and thorns have little but Beltian bodies in their pockets and are evidently fed on them (Wheeler & Bailey 1925). Fungus-growing ants feed their young on the kohl-rabi growths of the fungus.

6·3·2 *Liquid foods*

The second sort of food is the liquid which worker ants feed from their mouthparts to the larvae. In *Iridomyrmex* the larvae lie, like those of most ants, on their backs or sides. A nurse worker may approach them from any direction. She opens her mandibles and places her tongue (i.e. maxillo-labial organ) over the slightly extruded mouthparts of the larvae. A drop of fluid appears on the worker's tongue and disappears into the larva's mouth (Newell 1909). In *Formica polyctena* and probably in other ants as well, larvae which are destined to become queens and the queens themselves are not fed with the contents of the workers' crops, although these contain honeydew which is probably an adequate diet. When single workers were fed with syrup containing radio-active phosphorus the radioactivity spread quickly through the other workers in the colony. Queens and larvae were seen to be fed by radioactive workers but they did not become radioactive at first. It was only a day or two after the workers had been given the syrup that any activity appeared among queens and larvae. This is explained by the way the radioactivity spread through the bodies of workers that fed on the syrup. Three hours after feeding all the radioactivity was still in the worker's crop. Twenty-six hours after the feed it had spread to the whole of the gaster and to parts of the thorax. The labial gland in particular was very active. Apparently the food passed to queens and to sexual brood by 'regurgitation' does not come from the crop at all. It is an elaborated product of the labial gland and presumably is a more concentrated diet, perhaps enriched by extra protein. Males however are fed from the crop: as their testes are fully developed in the pupa thay have little need of protein when they are adult (Gösswald and Kloft 1958, 1960).

Probably even highly carnivorous ants like *Myrmecia* feed water to their larvae by regurgitation (Freeland 1958). Where honeydew is the basis of the larval food however it may contain more water than the larvae need. In some wasps the workers remove a watery fluid which the larvae produce when they are touched. Many ants do not do this or do not do so in response to being touched (Le Masne 1953). Unlike wasps, whose paper nest would be damaged by water (Brian and Brian 1952), ants in earth nests have no need to collect this excretion. Some ants are said to give their larvae fluids which they produce from their anus (Torassian 1959, 1960, 1961). One cannot be sure that this fluid is not broken eggs.

6·3·3 *Eggs as a larval food*

Perhaps the most important food many larvae receive may prove to be eggs laid by the nurse workers. The fertility of workers has been known for some time and also the fact that the workers eat their own eggs. It is now clear that the production of eggs by workers is a regular channel in many species for the refinement of food which is brought into the nest. Worker ants produce from this diet a rich output of yolky eggs which they feed to the brood, and to the queen. Young larvae in the first stage evidently eat nothing but eggs from the pile in which they still lie. In the same way queens of *Myrmica* eat eggs from the pile and

depend on doing this for their survival and for full egg production
(Weir 1959a), and *Myrmecia forceps* queens never eat anything but eggs
(Freeland 1958). Clearly the queens cannot survive by eating their
own eggs, and this arrangement is dependent on the dilution of the egg
pile by fairly large quantities of workers' eggs, which are usually infertile (Brian 1953).

Egg consumption is not limited to almost incidental scrumping of
this kind. Workers actually place eggs on the mouthparts of larvae.
The eggs *Myrmecia forceps* workers lay are soft-shelled and the workers
burst the eggs before they feed them to larvae (Freeland 1958). *Myrmica*
workers deliver themselves of their own eggs and either feed them
straightaway to larvae or place them in the egg pile. Other workers
take them from there and feed them to larvae (Brian 1953). Workers'
eggs are more elongated than the queen's in this species (Weir 1959a).
Leptothorax tuberum workers do not lay eggs until they have been de-
prived of their queen for some days, and not then if they are occasionally
fed by workers that have had access to a queen (Bier 1954). Presumably
worker eggs are not an important food of larvae in this species.

6·3·4 *The distribution of food to larvae*

In artificial colonies the workers can be seen going over the larvae
and placing food on their mouthparts. Often they put an egg or insect
piece on several larvae in succession (Brian 1953). The conclusion that
larvae are fed by 'test-feeding', and that a worker may revisit a larva
and offer it food before it is ready for it (Brian 1956), may perhaps be
true only in the special conditions of laboratory cultures. Just as in
some conditions food-sharing between workers is initiated by donors
and in others by acceptors, so 'test-feeding' may occur in experiments
where plenty of food is given. When a worker touches it a larva lifts its
head, but it can also 'solicit' from the worker by raising its head
spontaneously (Le Masne 1953). There is no real evidence that this
makes the worker feed it however.

Workers do not in any case simply go round the larvae in rotation.
Large third-stage larvae are fed more often than small ones of the same
stage. When ten small larvae and four or more large ones (of about
three times the weight) are cultured with four workers the small larvae
fail to gain weight. This must be because food is given to large larvae in
preference to small ones and because four large larvae fully engage
four workers. When similar groups of larvae are tended by ten workers
the small larvae do gain a little. Large larvae not only attract more
than their share of the feeding, in proportion either to their number or
their weight. They actually stimulate the workers to feed them, for the
gain in weight of the *groups* of larvae tended by ten workers increases as
the number of large larvae in the group increases. All this increase,
and more, however goes to the large larvae. Although the total gain of
the group is more, the gain in weight of the small larvae is actually less.

When groups all of small larvae are cultured the gain in weight of the group is shared more equally, and each larva's share gets less as the number in the group is increased (Brian 1957a). These results show that the workers are actually stimulated in some ways by large larvae. The larger weight-gain of large larvae might be explained if they were always ready to accept food, when a worker 'test-fed' them. It is hard to see how this could inhibit the feeding of smaller larvae.

The effect of this way of distributing food to larvae is that the larger and faster-growing larvae are 'brought-on'. Smaller larvae gain little weight unless worker attention is very plentiful; they do not die as a rule and usually stand starvation well. Adult queens also compete with larvae for the attention of workers. When a queen is present the weight-gain of small larvae is even further reduced. The queen also attacks larvae as the scars on their bodies show (Brian and Hibble 1963).

6·3·5 Food-exchange

There is very little to be said for the view that larvae offer workers something in exchange for feeding and other attentions. Among social wasps the larvae often produce a drop of clear liquid when a worker touches them. This has been seen as in some way a reward for feeding the larva, for the worker eagerly sucks it up. It is hard nowadays to see why a reward should have been thought necessary. Feeding larvae is almost certainly an instinctive activity, and most instinctive behaviour is 'self-rewarding'. It almost seems as if there was a confusion between this sort of behaviour and some kind of learning. The fluid wasp larvae produce is not in the least attractive to the workers except in the context of contact with a larva. They will not drink fluid which has been collected from larvae (Brian and Brian 1952). Although the circulation of chemical messages round the colony is an important way in which the colony's activities are co-ordinated food 'exchange' does not provide the ties, almost of self-interest, which early students seem to have believed in (Wheeler 1928).

6·4 Care of pupae

The pupae are usually placed in a different part of the nest from the eggs and larvae; commonly in a warm but dry part. As a result the brood is often sorted into three classes: eggs and first-stage larvae, larger larvae and pupae. In a nest of *Lasius alienus* which had sixteen cells only four cells contained worker pupae, and these were at depths from six to twelve inches. All the larvae were collected in another chamber at a depth of twelve inches, there were a queen and some callow workers in a cell at twelve inches and some queen pupae in a cell at thirteen inches (Headley 1941). This sort of arrangement is a common experience of collectors. The position of the larvae is probably simply the cell which has the preferred temperature and humidity of the nurse workers (Peakin 1960). Whether the position of the pupae represents the choice of some other group is not known.

The actual transformation of a larva to a pupae does not require much assistance from the workers. In Ponerinae and Myrmicinae the larval midgut and its contents are eaten by the workers and may actually be pulled from the body of the prepupa (the transforming larva) by a worker (Le Masne 1953). The larvae can however pass this meconium without any help from workers. Formicine workers do not eat the meconium.

Larvae that spin cocoons, that is most Ponerinae and Formicinae (Wheeler 1915), need to be banked with earth so that they can attach the first threads of the cocoon to something firm. Possibily the incipient spinning movements which *Formica fusca* larvae make are a stimulus to the workers to do this (Wallis 1960). How the larvae of *Eciton* spin cocoons even in a statary bivouac is not known; it seems unlikely they can be earthed up.

In the actual movements of spinning the larva moves alternately in a bending movement towards its ventral side which runs threads along its body and a swinging movement which loops threads over these from side to side. Each cycle of these two movements lasts about a minute. Then the larva turns through an angle of anything from 22° to 110° (mean angle 55-66°) and begins another spinning cycle. Altogether spinning takes 16-20 hours and consists of about 60 cycles (Wallis 1960). When the pupal stage is completed the callow workers are normally removed from their cocoons by workers. If they are not freed from them in this way many fail to escape from the pupal skin. *Myrmecia* workers emerge from the pupa inside the cocoon and get no help from workers (Le Masne 1953).

6·5   Guests and exploiters of the food traffic

Although the traffic in food generally flows towards the queen and her brood there are animals which live in ant colonies by diverting part of this flow to their own mouths. Some of them only divert a small proportion of the food and do little harm to the ant colony. Others, especially the parasitic ants, divert so much of the flow that they cripple or even destroy the colony. Some of these exploiters of ants take a toll of the food before it has reached the ants' nest; others, and these are the more interesting kind, take part in the traffic inside the nest. A good deal of paper has been used in distinguishing different sorts of relationship between ants and their guests or exploiters, and the taste of some workers produced a large vocabulary of names for them. *Synechthrans* are always treated with hostility by the ants and usually they, in turn, prey on the ants. A second class is formed of *Synoeketes* which provoke no response in the ants at all—they are either ignored or tolerated. The last class of *Symphiles* are received amicably by the ants (Wheeler 1910).

This is not really a good way of looking at ant guests because we need to be able to recognise amicability and hostility in the ants when we see it. These are very anthropomorphic terms and in any case the ants may be variable or inconsistent in their responses. The beetle *Atemeles pubicollis* lives in summer in the nests of wood-ants without being attacked. In autumn the ants become more aggressive to it and it leaves their nest and spends the winter in a *Myrmica* nest. The *Myrmica* colony tolerates it in winter but it is driven out again in spring (Hölldobler 1941).

There are really two important ways that the guests interact with the behaviour of the ants: they avoid attack and they get food. As they do these two things in quite independent ways it is not possible to make a satisfactory classification of ant guests. Many guests which are never attacked by ants take part in the traffic in food on the same terms as ants do. Others, equally 'welcome' to the ants like some species of *Paussus*, feed on ant larvae. Among the guests that avoid attack by stealth some are fed by the ants, some are predators and others merely scavengers.

6·5·1 Tolerance of guests

Ants do not usually tolerate intruders into their nests. They usually attack them and often kill them, overpowering them by large numbers called up by alarm scents or other signals. Even members of other colonies of the same species are attacked. It seems strange that various Collembola, crickets, cockroaches, mites and, above all, beetles can live in ants' nests. They use three methods to achieve this: protective shapes and armour, mimicry and glandular secretions (Wasmann 1903). All these methods are used not only by guests inside the nest but by insects that associate with ants outside their nests as well, for instance by aphids and their predators (section 5·4·2). Ants are unable to capture or harm animals covered with smooth, hard, rounded shields. Many other guests simply avoid contact with the ants.

A more interesting way in which guests avoid attacks is by some degree of mimicry of their ant hosts. Many insects and spiders resemble ants and presumably gain some protection against other predators. For instance the hard stinging *Pseudomyrma elongata* is imitated by a black variety of the jumping spider *Synemosyma smithi* and a variety of the same spider imitates the orange and black *Ps. pallida*. Both ants are also imitated by a Lygaeid bug *Pamphatus* (Myers and Salt 1926). In this case it is not clear whether the mimic deceives the ants (which have good eyesight) or predators such as birds and reptiles. When a mimic lives inside the ants' nest we might suppose that its mimicry is directed at the ants themselves. Some of the ant-like features of ant guests —narrow head, long legs, swollen abdomen with a slender base, lack of wings, pigment or eyes—are 'pseudomyrmecoid'. That is they

resemble ants because both they and the ants are adapted for life underground. Some of these features are characteristics not just of ants but of
soil- or cave-dwelling animals in general (Heikertinger 1927). Mimicry
which deceives in the darkness of the nest is more likely to involve
things which look trivial in the light of day. The beetle *Mimeciton pulex*
superficially does not resemble its host *Neivamyrmex nigrescens* for it is
pale red while the ant is black (Wasmann 1903). Its antennae however
are modified so as to resemble those of *Neivamyrmex nigrescens*, and in the

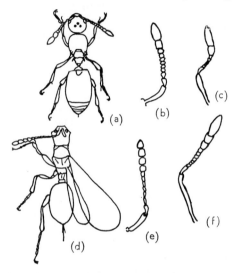

FIG. 6·3 Guests which are mimics of their ant hosts: (a) the wasp *Solenopsia
imitatrix*, (b) its antenna, (c) antenna of its host *Solenopsis fugax*, (d) the
wasp *Tetramopria aurocincta*, (e) its antenna, (f) antenna of its host
Tetramorium caespitum. (All after Wasmann 1899)

same way the antennae of *Dorylostethus wasmanni* look like those of
Dorylus helvolus. Both the antenna and the forelegs of the Proctotrupid
wasp *Solenopsia imitatrix* have the same proportions as those of its host
Solenopsis fugax, and *Ecitopria crassicornis* resembles *Eciton praedator*, and
Tetramopria aurocincta Tetramorium caespitum in the same way (Wasmann
1899). These are evidently the sort of feature which might deceive an
ant in the dark of its nest; they suggest that other things than a strange
scent may arouse ants' suspicions. The cricket *Myrmecophila acervorum*
does not look in the least like an ant to our eyes, but it is protected by
its movements. When it is placed in an artificial nest with ants its
movements at first are very slow but it gradually 'thaws' and begins to
behave as an ant among ants. In a colony of *Formica fusca* its movements
are lively, but it is said to alter them and move more slowly if it is transferred to a *Myrmica* nest. A cricket which had been accepted for a long
time as a member of a *Camponotus herculeanus* colony was immediately

attacked when the colony was illuminated, either because this altered its behaviour or because its mimicry was no longer deceptive (Höll-dobler 1953). Injured crickets too are attacked and eaten by the ants (Wheeler 1910). The larva of a hoverfly *Microdon* is protected partly by its smoothness and hard cuticle (Wheeler 1910), it also resembles in shape and texture the scale-insect, *Pseudococcus*, on which it feeds in the nests of *Solenopsis saevissima* (Borgmeier 1953). Perhaps some other predators mimic other guests instead of the ants themselves.

The last means by which guests protect themselves from attack is by using the secretions of special glands to turn aside the ants' aggression. These glands are of two kinds: one which attracts the ants and one which repels them. *Lomechusa strumosa*, a beetle guest of *Formica sanguinea*, possesses 'alarm glands' concealed under the fourth dorsal plate of its back. The glands have a reservoir which opens just in front of this plate. When an ant threatens to attack it the beetle raises its abdomen and squirts the contents of the reservoir at the ant. It can direct the spray to right or left into the ant's face. This makes the ant run away. The secretion is poisonous and ants put in a tube in which ten *Lomechusa* have been shaken will die in 20 to 30 minutes (Jordan 1913). Fifty years ago the investigator of this beetle said that the secretion smelt like amyl acetate or perhaps methyl heptenone. Although he favoured the former it is interesting that methyl hepten-one is a component of the repellant glands of *Tapinoma nigerrimum* (section 2·1·4). Clearly *Lomechusa* deserves chemical study.

Lomechusa also has tufts of golden-yellow hairs or trichomes on its first five abdominal segments. On the cuticle between the hairs many single-celled glands open. The trichomes are exceptionally attractive to ants. A *Formica sanguinea* worker has been seen not just licking them, but with the tuft stuffed right into its mouth, and it stayed like this for 15 minutes. The ants also lick the rest of the beetle's cuticle in a less abandoned way (Jordan 1913). Similar trichomes are found on other Staphylinid beetles and on the wasp *Tetramopria*. The trichomes are said to taste sweet to man. There is little doubt that sweet fluids im-mediately reduce the aggressiveness of many ants to their prey, and as we have seen this may be the basis of the behaviour of ants to aphids (section 5·4). The trichomes are also said to have an attractant scent which draws ants from a distance (Wheeler 1910). If this is so it is not clear what advantage the beetle gets from it.

Lycaenid caterpillars which are attended by ants often have attract-ant and repellant glands. The dorsal glands, and sometimes labral glands too, are supposed to attract ants from a distance. This would be advantageous as some of the caterpillars need to be taken by ants and carried into the nest to complete their life-cycle. When a *Myrmica rubra* worker finds a fourth-stage larva of the blue butterfly *Maculinea agrion* it spends up to an hour licking the caterpillar's dorsal gland. After this the butterfly suddenly hunches up its thoracic segments and the ant carries it to the nest as if it was retrieving a larva. It may be that the hunched shape plays a part in deceiving the ant though one would think that some chemical sense would be involved too. In the nest the caterpillar eats ant larvae (Hinton 1951).

These cases where the guest produces a fluid which is attractive to ants and which they feed on remind us of the relation of ants and plant-lice. Plant-lice too produce both attractive and repellant secretions. In the past some of the guests of ants have been thought of as if they yielded food to the ants. Obviously a guest which obtains all its food from the ants cannot make any contribution in quantity to the ants' diet. It is possible that it could give the ants essential vitamins which they were unable to synthesise for themselves, but there is no evidence that they do this. Even the blue butterflies have stopped feeding on thyme when they are adopted by ants. Plant-lice are quite different, for they are able to tap a diet so rich that they can produce quantities of honeydew. For this reason they stand in a very special relationship to ants.

6·5·2 The food of ant guests

Some of the animals which are found in or near ants' nests are probably attracted by the physical conditions like higher temperature, greater aeration of the soil and altered plant growth near the nest (Ayre 1958b). Some may actually be attracted to the ants. The wood-louse *Platyarthrus hoffmanseggi*, which is found in the nests of most species of European ants is said to be attracted to formic acid (Brooks 1942). This could not help it to find the nests of for instance *Myrmica rubra*, where it is common, as this ant does not produce formic acid. *Platyarthrus* feeds on the cast out infrabuccal pellets and other rubbish in the nest, or more probably on mould on them. It is also said to leave the nests of *Lasius niger* at night to feed on honeydew (Eidmann 1927b). Many of the guests which avoid contact with ants feed as scavengers like this. Some others feed in a similar kind of way, but do not avoid ants. The mite *Laelaps oophilus* is said to lick the coat of saliva on the ants' eggs (Wasmann 1897a) and *Pachylaelaps* the surface of the ants themselves (Hölldolber 1928). The beetle *Thorictus foreli* is supposed to live by biting holes in the antenna of its host *Myrmecocystus viaticus* and sucking out the blood (Wasmann 1898). It would be hard to verify any of these statements.

A more interesting way in which guests can get food is by tapping the traffic in food. It is probably a more efficient way too from the guest's point of view, for it eliminates the ant from the food-chain. Where the host ant feeds most on solid foods, the guest can feed on this inside or outside the nest just as a scavenger does. If it is true that there is very little sharing of liquid foods among Doryline ants (Wilson & Eisner 1957), the very large number of guests these ants have must live either in this way or by eating the brood (Rettenmeyer 1963b). The

African fly *Bengalia* feeds on the burdens of worker ants outside the nest. It walks near columns of driver-ants, and when it is approached by an ant it flies a few feet away and returns a moment later. When it encounters an ant a little way from the main column it attacks it and seizes the prey or brood which the ant is carrying and pulls it. The ant does not attack the fly, it only pulls back so that there is a miniature tug-of-war between the two insects. The ant wins the tug-of-war and

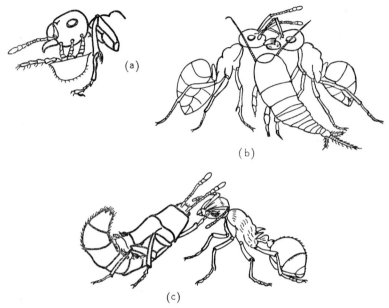

FIG. 6·4 How guests obtain regurgitated food from ants: (a) *Antennophorus* below the head of *Lasius umbratus* tickling its mouthparts, (b) *Atelura* stealing from the drop one ant offers a nestmate, (c) *Atemeles* tickles a *Myrmica* worker with its forefoot. (a and b after Janet, c after Wheeler 1910)

the fly flies off, but the prey or brood has been sucked dry. *Bengalia* also attacks other ants like *Pheidole crassinoda* near their nests in the same way. Its method of predation takes advantage of the behaviour of ants carrying burdens.

Inside the nests of ants that share liquid foods by regurgitation other insects take advantage of the food-sharing behaviour of the ants. When a colony of *Formica sanguinea* was fed sugar marked with a radioactive substance both the adults and larvae of the guest beetle *Lomechusa strumosa* became radioactive. Even larvae which had not eaten ant larvae were radioactive. The beetles had been fed with the crop contents of the ants and not with the secretion of the labial gland (Gösswald and Kloft 1960). Earlier experiments with dyes (Wasmann 1897b) suggested that only large larvae and adults of *Lomechusa* were fed by ants and that the smaller larvae ate the eggs and larvae of the ants.

The guests get liquid foods from the ants in a number of ways. The silverfish *Atelura* steals part of the drop of food which one ant is regurgitating to another; it cannot make an ant produce a drop to order (Janet 1897b). Other guests may feed by theft in this way, but they can also induce the ant to regurgitate for them. The mite *Antennophorus foreli* sits under the head of its host, *Lasius niger*, and strokes the ant's cheeks with its long first legs until the ant produces a drop of food (Wasmann 1902). The ant *Formicoxenus nitidulus* can feed from the mouth of its host, a wood-ant much larger than itself, from below too (Stäger 1924). Some of the other guests that feed in this way are more nearly the size of an ant. Among beetles *Claviger testaceus* uses its antennae to stimulate the ant, *Atemeles* and other Staphylinidae use their forelegs (Janet 1897b). The wasp *Solenopsia* uses its ant-like antennae but not, it is said in the same sort of movements as ants use (Hölldobler 1928). Since there is a good deal of doubt what part the antennal movements of ants play in the sharing of food (sections 2·5·3, 6·1) it is difficult to say how important these differences are.

What is certain however is that some ant guests represent suitable objects to be fed by ants. In other words they are able to release behaviour which is normally applied to other ants or to ant larvae. Whether ants more often treat guests as fellow workers or as larvae is hard to say for we do not usually know enough details of ant behaviour to characterise their treatment of guests. In any case the ants need not behave consistently in this respect, and the guests no doubt exploit the releasing mechanisms appropriate to either pattern. A cut-off abdomen of *Claviger testaceus* was kept on the brood pile of *Solenopsis fugax* (Hölldobler 1928). *Atemeles pubicollis* is tolerated in spring and summer in the nests of wood-ants, which rear their sexual brood at this time and whose nest contains no larvae in winter. The beetle spends winter in the nest of a *Myrmica* species which does have diapause larvae in it in winter (Hölldobler 1941). It seems more reasonable to suppose that it is tolerated as a brood substitute than as if it was a worker ant. Although *Formica sanguinea* treats *Lomechusa strumosa* larvae in some respects like larvae, burying them in soil when they pupate (Hölldobler 1948), it feeds them crop contents as it does worker ants, not labial gland secretion (Gösswald and Kloft 1960), and does not give them any preferential treatment compared with its fellow workers. The deception can be practised not only on ants but also on aphids, which feed certain flies (Herzig 1938) and possibly *Platyarthrus hoffmanseggi* (Eidmann 1927b) as well as ants.

The relation of guests to their ant hosts is simply based on the exploitation by the guest of the behaviour associated with the food traffic. There is no reason to speak of a special 'Instinct of Symphily' (Hölldobler 1948). Different species of ant have their own species of guest, and this no doubt shows that the guest is adapted to that particular ant.

The adaptation need not leave the guest incapable of living with other ants; it may simply prevent it from taking up residence with them. *Claviger testaceus* normally lives in the colonies of *Lasius* especially *Lasius flavus*, *niger* and *alienus*. If it is introduced into nests of *Tetramorium caespitum* or *Solenopsis fugax* it is accepted and fed. *Solenopsis fugax* does not normally have even a similar species of beetle in its nests, but it will feed *Claviger* in preference to its own wasp guest *Solenopsia* (Hölldobler 1928, 1948). *Lomechusa strumosa* is accepted by wood-ants as well as by its normal host and *Atemeles* from *Myrmica* nests may be taken over by *Formica exsecta*. *Dinarda dentata* from nests of *Formica sanguinea* is usually attacked and killed by wood-ants but may be accepted by *Formica fusca*. *Dinarda märkeli* (from wood-ants) was attacked and killed when it was introduced to a colony of *Formica sanguinea*. This particular colony seemed to learn from this experience to detect the deception of *Dinarda* species, for it killed its own *D. dentata* too (Wasmann 1908, Hölldobler 1948). If guests can be interchanged between species of ant in this way it is not because the association between host and guest species dates from before the separation of the different ant species. It is the behaviour which the guest exploits that is ancient, not the association itself.

6·5·3 Parasitic ants

If beetles or even mites can enter an ant colony and join in the food-traffic we might expect that other species of ants would also be parasitic. In fact about one sixth of all European species of ants are parasitic to some extent. Over the whole world the proportion may be less, for this sort of parasitism is possibly an adaptation for survival, and more particularly colony foundation, in cold climates (Gösswald 1938b, 1950). Parasitic forms are found in all the main groups of ants, and host and parasite are usually rather closely related (Brown 1955).

The parasitism of one ant on another is slightly different from the parasitism of a beetle on an ant. Whilst parasitic beetles offer themselves as substitute ant workers or larvae, individual for individual, parasitic ants are themselves social and replace the whole reproductive unit of the host colony. Usually the parasitic relationship begins when a newly fertilised parasite queen enters a host colony and diverts the food flow to herself and, subsequently, to her brood. To do this as a rule she has to displace the original host queen. This is an important difference from the parasitism of ant colonies by other sorts of insects, which usually only divert a part of the food flow, though in some cases enough to reduce the size or fertility of the ants' progeny (Wheeler 1910).

In some ants like *Epimyrma gösswaldi*, the parasite queen destroys its host queen and is fed preferentially by the host workers though only with crop contents. In *Formica sanguinea* the workers readily obtain food from the host or slave *Formica fusca* workers and presumably feed it to their brood (Gösswald and Kloft 1960). *Polyergus rufescens* workers on the other hand play only a small part in food traffic (Gösswald and

Kloft 1960, Beck 1961). Presumably their queen and brood are fed almost entirely by their hosts. The queen of *Anergates atratulus*, unlike *Epimyrma gösswaldi*, receives labial gland secretion from her hosts (Gösswald and Kloft 1960). Other species of parasitic ants are found in colonies which contain a host queen as well. *Strongylognathus testaceus* keeps a queen of *Tetramorium caespitum* alive, and allows her to have worker progeny which is reared by the host workers. No host queens or males are produced (Gösswald 1938b). *Strumigenys xenos* may live in the same way (Brown 1955). The queen of *Lasius umbratus* does not kill the *L. niger* queen in the colony she invades. The parasite queen is so much more attractive to the host workers that the host queen is deserted and eventually killed by her own workers (Gösswald 1938b).

Sometimes the parasitism is only temporary. One way this occurs is when the parasitism is a temporary expedient for the foundation of a new colony (section 7·5). *Anergates atratulus* is a short-lived parasite and is able to produce its own sexual generation before the now queenless host colony dies out. The parasitism can become permanent in three ways, which maintain the numbers of host workers after their colony has been taken over. *Epimyrma gösswaldi* has hosts in which the workers become fertile after their queen has been destroyed and their eggs are reared to maintain the worker force. *Tetramorium caespitum* retains its queen after it has been invaded by *Strongylognathus testaceus*. In both cases only workers are produced. The last method of maintaining workers numbers is by slavery (Gösswald 1938b).

7 — Colony reproduction and the life of winged ants

Not all the larvae in an ant colony develop in the same way. Most of them turn into wingless, more or less sterile workers. But some, which presumably get a larger share of the colony's food supply, grow more rapidly than the others and do not pupate when they reach the size at which worker larvae turn into pupae. Instead they continue growing, turn into large sized pupae and eventually emerge as winged, potent males or females (Brian 1957c). Their sex depends on whether the egg cell from which they developed was fertilised by a sperm from the store in their mother's spermatheca or not. Fertilised eggs grow up to be females, unfertilised ones become males. After the females have mated with males they can lay eggs of both types. The females either found new colonies or, by being adopted into an established colony, they can supplement or replace an older queen. In either case the life of an ant female is a play in three acts: the production and liberation of the winged ants, mating, and the foundation of a new colony or the rejuvenation of an old one. The males only appear in the first two acts for they die after mating.

7·1 The liberation of the winged forms

In temperate lands most ants produce their sexual forms at the end of the fat season when food has been plentiful. Earlier in summer all the larvae turn into workers. The mating flight is therefore usually late in the year, and the newly fertilised queens hibernate at once and do not begin laying eggs till next spring. The first workers appear in the same summer. *Manica rubida* however lays eggs which produce workers the same year, and in *Lasius niger* and a few other species eggs are sometimes laid in the same year as the mating flight, but no workers emerge until the winter is over (Eidmann 1926). In the southern hemisphere the appearance of winged ants bears the same relation to the seasons. The Australian Myrmeciinae (Wheeler 1916, Clark 1951) and the South African *Anoplolepis custodiens* (Steyn 1954) fly in January. Ants of deserts and steppes do not fly in late summer, when the queens would be exposed to hot dry weather in the time when they are founding colonies. The flight is delayed till spring. Males and females of *Messor* species may fly in autumn in southern Europe (Goetsch 1930), but in Hungary (Andrasfalvy 1961) and in Central Asia (Kuznetzov-Ugamsky 1927) their flights are in spring. The sexual forms mature in the nests in autumn on the harvest of seeds, but spend the winter there as adults. *Prenolepis imparis* in America (Talbot 1943) and in Hungary (Andrasfalvy 1961) also keeps its winged forms in the nest till spring. Spring flights occur in *Cataglyphis* and in desert species of *Camponotus*; the autumn flying *Lasius*, *Myrmica* and *Formica* are absent from Central Asia (Kuznetzov-Ugamsky 1927). Wood-ants are exceptional in producing a sexual brood in summer—as early as May—from eggs laid in the same New Year (Gösswald and Bier 1954). In Siberia however their flights are spread over a longer period (Marikovsky 1961).

In the tropics the time when the sexuals are liberated may be related to the seasons in the same sort of way. *Eciton burchelli* and *hamatum* produce one of their many cyclic broods each year which consists entirely of sexuals. This happens at the start of the dry season in Panama (Schneirla and Brown 1952). *Oecophylla longinoda* produces sexuals throughout the year in West African forest conditions, but they are slightly more common just after the end of the rains in November (Ledoux 1949).

7·2 The mating flight

The wings which the sexuals of most species of ants possess earn them the name of 'alates', and suggest that they are 'destined to change their residence' (Huber 1810), that is to disperse the species. In fact however in many species they only fly a short distance and the female does not fly at all after she has mated, so that the flight produces very little dispersal (Wilson 1957). Rare finds of colonies of ants established far from the normal range of their species—an American prairie ant in Hawaii and a desert ant in Massachusetts (Wheeler 1910)—may show that occasionally females may be carried long distances by winds. But even in *Tetramorium caespitum*, which mates high in the air, the females usually fall within 100 metres of their parent nest (Poldi 1963).

Probably the most important function of the mating flight is to make matings between partners from different nests more likely. Mating outside the colony is promoted by two features of many mating flights. The first is the synchronisation, during the mating season, of flights from different nests over a large or small area. The synchronisation is probably achieved by the dependence of the time of flight on an unknown change in weather. Huber himself suggested that a temperature of 15-16° Réaumur—about 20°C—was necessary before *Lasius niger* would swarm (Huber 1810). *Myrmica fracticornis* is said to respond to decreasing light in evening, *Tapinoma sessile* and *Dolichoderus* species to temperature (Kannowski 1959b). Other species like *Formica sanguinea subintegra* (Kennedy and Talbot 1940) and *Myrmecia forficata* (Clark 1951) fly in the morning. Some of the problems involved here can be solved by collecting data about the time and date of flights and relating these to weather. Experiments on the ants' behaviour are badly needed too. No-one has boxed in the mounds of a species like *Lasius flavus* and varied the temperature and other conditions in the box near the time of the mating flight. The workers are said to prevent the alates from leaving the nest before the flight but it is hard to judge how important this is, or whether it is the workers who control the start and rate of the flight. In some ants like *Myrmica fracticornis* and *Formica fusca* the alates leave the nest rather slowly, from about 3 each minute, in others like *Lasius minutus* and *L. speculiventris* the rate is hundreds in a minute (Kannowski 1959b).

However the flights are started there is no doubt that sometimes flights of a particular species occur at the same time over a wide area. On August 8th 1915 for instance sexuals of *Lasius niger* were in flight over most of England (Donisthorpe 1927). These widespread flights are not of any particular significance in themselves, except that they show that whatever stimuli start the flights off can be spread over wide areas too. It is of course extremely unlikely that an ant from Northumberland will mate with one from Lincolnshire.

The second feature of the flights that assists mating between nests is that the alate ants form swarms. These are almost always formed as a result of orientated flight by the ants, and ants from different nests can probably join the same swarm. The swarms are like those of midges and mayflies and have nothing whatever in common with the 'swarms' of the honeybee which consist of workers following an old mated queen. Nor, for that matter have they much in common, in many ants, with the supposed mating habits of honeybees.

Swarms of *Myrmica ruginodis* form at particular mating stations which are often also used at other times by other species of *Myrmica*. A mating station is usually a bare flat surface near to a vertical feature: for example a path which runs by a house or a tree (Brian and Brian 1955). Bare patches also mark the mating stations of *Pheidole sitarches*, and although the swarms which form over bare patches may be blown away by wind they return to their former position (Wilson 1957). Other ants, including several American mountain species (Chapman 1957) and among British species *Myrmica scabrinodis*, *M. lobicornis*, *M. sulcinodis*, *M. ruginodis* and *Leptothorax acervorum* (Collingwood 1958) seem to form swarms on mountain tops. The swarms are formed on calm days when there can be no question of their being blown there. Swarms of *Lasius niger* on the other hand may form large clouds because they are not attracted to landmarks like this. They are attracted to light (Polimanti 1911) and this may cause them to fly upwards.

The ants in the swarm are mostly males which fly round and round,
· returning to the swarm if they happen to leave it. Almost all sexuals,
particularly the males, have eyes with more facets than their workers
have, and their orientation to the swarm is almost certainly visual.
Myrmica ruginodis males remain at the mating station for days on end,
walking about and hiding in crevices at night. They fly in a swarm
when weather conditions are suitable. The females on the other hand
come to the mating station, mate and leave at once to start colonies
(Brian and Brian 1955). In *Pheidole sitarches* the females fly through the
swarm of males in slow even circles (Wilson 1957), and the European
P. pallidula, a form of the widespread *P. megacephala*, swarms in the same
way (Goetsch 1953). The males seize passing females and the pair drop
to the ground at once where they mate. Wood-ants do not seem even to
form their pairs in the air. The males of *Formica lugubris* fly over landmarks—one was a heap of sawdust—on which the females crawl and
occasionally take to the wing. The males pounce on the females and
they mate on the ground or on the tips of plants (Donisthorpe 1927,
Gösswald and Schmidt 1960). *Camponotus ligniperdus* (Viehmeyer 1908),
Myrmecia sanguinea (Wheeler 1916) and *Formica opaciventris* (Scherba
1958) seem to be similar to wood-ants in mating habits. This sort of
mating also characterises many ants of steppe and desert (Kuznetzov-
Ugamsky 1927, Forel 1928, Marikovsky 1960).

The older view that most ants mated in mid-air (Huber 1810) is
probably only true of some ants in which the female is large in comparison with the male. In the genus *Lasius* species like *L. niger* and
L. flavus have large females and when the male seizes the female in the
air the pair does not fall to the ground (Forel 1928, Eidmann 1931). The
pairs of *Lasius fuliginosus*, whose female is small, fall to earth and mate
on twigs and bushes (Donisthorpe 1927). In this species, as in *Myrmica*,
not only would the female not be able to carry the weight of the male
in flight, but the male may be unable to develop enough thrust to
insert his genitalia into the female unless he can hold on to the ground.
The male genitalia of ants lack the grappling hooks which are found in
some aerial maters. The females of *Tetramorium caespitum* are also much
larger than the males. The mating flight starts when the alates leave
the nests and climb plants or pebbles to take flight. After the flight no
pairs of ants *in copula* fall to the ground, only mated females. It seems
that this species must mate fairly high in the air (Poldi 1963). Naturally
we have little opportunity to observe them there.

In some species there seems to be no mating flight though both sexes
have wings. The small *Monomorium floricola* nests in old pupal cases of
moths and other small crevices. When the sexual brood emerges from
pupae the whole colony, including old mated queens, is thrown into
great excitement. The young winged females race about the nest
chased by the males. A female stops running when a male strokes her
head with his antennae. Then the male climbs sideways on her petiole

and begins to rub her abdomen with his genitalia until they mate
(Barth 1953). Many other crevice-nesters, including *Monomorium
pharaonis*, also mate in the nest. In *Lasius* males and females do not seem
to attempt to mate before flying, and probably neither sex will show the
behaviour of mating until they have flown. *Harpagoxenus americanus*
sexuals will not mate until they have flown and are said to refuse partners from their own nest even then (Wesson 1939). Both these habits
promote outbreeding.

In some species of ant one or other sex is wingless or has short wings
and cannot fly. This necessarily alters the way they mate. *Anergates
atratulus*, the workerless parasite of *Tetramorium caespitum*, has a 'pupoid'
male which is not only wingless but can hardly walk because of his
distorted gaster. Mating takes place inside the host nest between
brothers and sisters, and the females fly after mating (Donisthorpe
1927). Some other ants which are social parasites also have wingless or
worker-like males; *Formicoxenus*, *Symmyrmica* and a sprinkling of independent species have them too. *Ponera edouardi* has both normal winged
males and wingless one as well, though in Algeria this species does not
seem to produce the worker-like (ergatoid) form of male. The ergatoid
male is paler than the other castes of the ant and is much longer lived
than most males. It does not leave the nest and is fed by the workers,
as well as eating scraps of prey. Like the male of *Anergates* the ergatoid
male of *P. edouardi* mates in the nest, but it has never been seen to mate
with queens, only with workers. In laboratory nests in fact it will only
mate with callow workers or with workers which are still inside the cocoons, and it cannot tell worker cocoons from male ones. No-one knows
whether it really behaves like this in wild nests. The workers of *P. edouardi* do lay eggs, but these do not usually develop (Le Masne 1948).

Females with reduced wings or no wings at all are found in many of
the lower ants, especially *Myrmecias* and in all Doryline ants. The
queens of at least some *Myrmecias* forage when they are founding a new
nest, and so they have no need of the protein store the wing muscles
provide (Haskins and Haskins 1955). Doryline ants form new colonies
by colony division and they also need no protein store. While some
Myrmecias like *M. sanguinea* (Wheeler 1916) and *M. forficata* (Haskins
& Haskins 1955, Clarke 1951) have females with fully developed wings,
others like *M. pulchra* have wingless ergatoid females which mate on the
ground near the nest (Clark 1951). The females of *M. regularis* have
short wings which break off before they leave the nest. The males are
winged and fly well. The dealated females which are found in the nest
have not mated, will not lay eggs and keep their wing muscles fully
developed until they die. They do however wander about outside the
nest and are probably fertilised by the low flying ranging males (as *M.
tarsatus* is); after this they found nests on their own (Haskins & Haskins
1955). The queens of some large ponerine ants including *Megaponera
foetans* are wingless and ergatoid (Arnold 1915).

The Dorylinae have sexual castes which are so different from their workers that they were originally placed in different genera. The male is a large winged insect with large compound eyes, hook-like mandibles and an enormous abdomen and genitalia. The males fly to lights and are familiar as 'sausage-flies' in West Africa. Linnaeus called them wasps in his genus *Vespa* and Fabricius later moved them to a new genus *Dorylus*. Meanwhile the workers had been collected from raiding columns, without of course any sexuals. The workers are a different shape and colour from the males and they are blind; many of them were described as species of *Anomma*. The females—there is only one in each colony of a million or more workers—were found later. They are always wingless, but their thoraxes are not like a worker's and they have large abdomens, even before their ovaries start developing. They were placed in the genus *Dichthadia*. It was nearly the end of the nineteenth century before anyone showed the true relations of these supposed genera. *Dorylus* is now the generic name but *Anomma* lives on as a subgeneric name. *Dichthadia* lives on too in the name Dichthadiagyne sometimes used to describe the female, which is neither simply a wingless female or an ergatoid form. In the same way the males are sometimes called Dorylaners.

We do not know how the winged Doryline males find and fertilise the wingless queens. In *Eciton* and *Anomma* at least, new colonies are formed by colony division and the queens never leave the protection of their workers (Schneirla 1956b, Raignier and van Boven 1955). In *Anomma* the males try to fly as soon as they emerge from their pupal stage, and as in most ants, they are held back by the workers. There is no evidence for the belief that the workers drive the males out of the nests. They will only fly by night and the fact that they are so common at house lights suggests that they can fly quite a distance (Raignier and van Boven 1955). They evidently have some special orientations at this time. Professor J. E. Webb once showed me how a number of males of a small *Dorylus* species having entered a closed room through a letter box, all came to rest in a small box of dry sand in one corner of the room. The males all fly clumsily and also crawl on the floor forcing their way into crevices. Whether this represents their behaviour searching for the excavations of a statary phase nest, or merely the way they hide in the day-time one cannot say. Perhaps the most curious fact about Doryline males is that old males with their wings torn off are sometimes found crawling among the workers on a raiding column. Probably after a dispersal flight the males fall to the ground and either find their way to a Doryline colony or are captured by raiders and taken there. A winged male of *Neivamyrmex* has been found mating with a young female in a temporary nest (Creighton 1950). No-one has placed males in raiding columns to see how the workers treat them. If males get to nests by either of these methods they would be unlikely to meet an unfertilised female, which are only to be found in newly divided colonies (which are smaller than normal ones) or for a very short time in colonies on the point of dividing. It may be that Doryline queens need to mate several times in their lives because of the number of worker-producing eggs they lay (Raignier and van Boven 1955) but there is no evidence for this. All other female ants seem to mate only once. The large number of males which Dorylines produce has been ascribed to the large proportion of queens which have run out of sperm and can only lay unfertilised, haploid male-producing eggs. If this is so there must be a large-scale conversion of haploid eggs to workers.

7·3 The act of mating

Few details of the act of mating in ants are known. The male *Myrmica rubra* seizes the female by the body with his legs, and the pair spirals down to the ground. He inserts the inner valves (*sagittae*) of his genital armature into her vagina. This must almost certainly require the co-operation of the female for the male cannot penetrate her vagina until she has bent her sting sharply upwards. The remaining valves (*volsellae* and *stipites*) of the male's genitalia are not inserted in the female but remain outside gripping the base of her sting. The male then lets go with his legs and if the female walks he may be tipped onto his back and dragged behind her (Clausen 1938, Forbes 1952). Probably this somewhat bare story lacks a good many details especially of the female's behaviour. The female of *Monomorium floricola* is said to stop when the male touches her with his antennae (Barth 1953). There can be little doubt that other ants too have some sort of precopulatory behaviour, which may never be seen if it occurs in the air or as the pair sink to the ground.

It is not clear whether males can mate with more than one female, or females with more than one male. *Pheidole sitarches* males will not mate a second time, but if they become separated from the females before they have mated they return to the swarm (Wilson 1957). Usually a female which has mated simply walks steadily to shelter and begins to excavate a nest (Wilson 1957, Brian and Brian 1955). It has been said that several males grab a single female *Lasius niger* and mate with her in turn (Forel 1928). This cannot be seen however as mating usually occurs high in the air; a female with several males on her might well be borne to the ground and in such an abnormal case it is possible she may mate more than once. Several males pounce on the female of *Myrmecia sanguinea* and all of them fall to the ground in a struggling mass. Only one of the males fertilises the queen, the rest return to the swarm (Clark 1951). In Britain wood-ant females only mate once, in Siberia both male and female mate several times but in Tientsin the female frequently bites off the male's gaster as he mates with her (Marikovsky 1961).

Interspecies crossing between ants is probably rare, for the features of the mating flight which synchronise it in different nests of the same species prevent flights of two different species occurring at the same time. In the laboratory the closely related wood-ant species will cross. *Formica polyctena* and *rufa* mate as readily as two *rufa* but this cannot happen in the wild because *polyctena* flies earlier in the year than *rufa*. *F. polyctena* will also mate with *F. nigricans*. *F. rufa* and *lugubris* will not cross because the male will not mount the female, and crosses between *rufa* and *nigricans* are hard to obtain (Gösswald and Schmidt 1960). Older systematists thought that ants which seemed to be intermediate between two species were the progeny of interspecific crosses, especially in wood-ants (see section 5·1·1) (Forel 1920, Donisthorpe 1927, Yarrow 1955). It is unlikely that this is so. The 'intermediates' arose either from bad taxonomy or from some peculiarity of evolution in ants; either way their systematics are certainly very difficult.

Alate ants provide food for many predatory animals as soon as they have left their parent nest. The flying swarms are attacked by all sorts of bird, and many animals, including ants, attack them when they fall to the ground. In any case the males do not survive long, but some of the females succeed in finding a safe enough place to begin a new nest.

7·4 The behaviour of females after fertilisation

When the female has mated on the ground, as species of *Pheidole*, *Myrmica* and *Formica* do, the female walks away and finds a place to make a new nest. We do not know how far she may walk to find one. Females which mate high in the air may fly afterwards or at least control their descent. Female *Lasius niger* and *Lasius flavus* land on bare soil more than they would be expected to by chance. Nests in shaded positions are less likely to succeed than nests in full sun (Pontin 1960a). *Pogonomyrmex barbatus* females prefer to dig their first nests in soft ground round puddles, and they may be so crowded together in such places that their burrows touch (Wheeler 1917b). *Tetramorium caespitum* females also prefer sunny spots and avoid shade (Poldi 1963). Temperature make a good deal of difference to the early nest, for a *Lasius niger* queen takes twice as long to rear her larvae at 20° as she does at 28° (Goetsch and Käthner 1937, Gösswald 1938a).

In the three to five days which follow her mating the female ant loses her wings. In *Myrmecia regularis* and exceptionally in *Formica lugubris* and *polyctena* she may lose them before she mates (Haskins and Haskins 1955, Gösswald and Schmidt 1960). Unmated female *Formica* all cast their wings at once if they are treated with carbon dioxide or with nitrogen. This suggests that the products of metabolism in the flight may lead to wing-fall (Gösswald and Schmidt 1960). It is sometimes said that cutting off the wings of an unmated female will release all the behaviour she usually shows only after she has mated (Wheeler 1910); this may sometimes be the case but it is dangerous to describe the behaviour of mated females from experiments on unmated ones. Shortly after she has lost her wings the female's wing muscles begin to degenerate and are replaced by strings of cells rich in fat and in protein (Janet 1906, 1907 a and b). The queen draws on these cells as a reserve of food while she is founding her colony. How she founds the colony is bound up with the amount of her reserves. Some species have queens which can rear a few workers without feeding and without the aid of workers. In other species the queen must be assisted and fed by workers of her own or another species.

7·4·1 *Independent foundation by isolated queens*

In species whose queens are large in relation to the workers, the queen usually brings up her first brood in complete isolation, often completely sealed in a cell in the earth or under bark, and with no workers to help her. Female *Tetramorium caespitum*, captured after they have mated, can be isolated in laboratory nests, and provided they are kept at 20-28° and in saturated air, they will raise a few workers in 6-8 weeks. During these weeks the female's weight falls from 10·8 mg. to 5·2 mg. In terms of dry weight the loss is 3·3 mg., made up of about 2 mg. of fat and 1·3 mg. of protein. Altogether 73% of the total fat and 61% of all the protein the queen started with is used up (Poldi 1963). Similar results are obtained from *Lasius flavus* (Peakin, 1965). These materials are used to produce eggs and to feed the larvae until they pupate. How the queen transfers the materials to them is a matter of behaviour.

During the 60 days or so taken to rear her first daughter workers the queen lays 250-300 eggs. The fate of most of these eggs can be guessed from the small number of larvae that result. On about the tenth day after the queen starts her colony there may be as many as 70 eggs in the nest. The largest number of larvae occurs 10 days later but only reaches about 18. Clearly three quarters of the eggs are eaten. The queen does not eat eggs in *T. caespitum* so it must be that the larvae do. There is no evidence whether the queen gives any other forms of food to her brood. About one larva in fifty develops rapidly and becomes a worker (Poldi 1963), the remaining larvae stay in a shrivelled state until the new workers bring more food into the colony (Brian 1957a).

This type of colony foundation by an isolated female living on her own reserves is perhaps the most characteristic way ants found colonies. It is different for example from the ways wasps found theirs. In the past the vast majority of ants have been thought to found their colonies in this way. Certainly among European ants it is the normal way of founding colonies in *Lasius flavus* and *niger*, *Formica fusca* and its relations, *Camponotus aethiops*, *ligniperdus* and *herculeanus*, *Tapinoma erraticum*, *Tetramorium caespitum*, *Solenopsis fugax* (Hölldobler 1938a), and *Messor* species and is one of the ways in which *Myrmica* can found colonies. A *Camponotus ligniperdus* female can produce her first worker pupa in about 8½ months (overwinter) and the first adult worker in about 11 months. She will probably rear only about a dozen workers by herself (Eidmann 1926). *Messor structor* can rear as many as 48-81 workers in isolation. Even an old queen which has been in her daughter colony for a year or two is still able to rear workers on her reserves (Meyer 1927).

The queens of our common black and yellow wasps also found their colonies without the help of workers, but they leave the nest and hunt for food for their brood themselves. The primitive Australian ants, *Myrmecia*, may do so too. *Myrmecia regularis* for instance founds colonies by single females but the female, which loses her wings before mating, forages for herself. Presumably her wing muscles are not large enough to provide for her young (Haskins and Haskins 1955). A claim has been made that *Myrmica rubra* queens also forage for themselves at this time (Hölldobler 1938a), but this was based on the inability of captured queens to found colonies unless they were provided with food. The queens in these experiments may well have been of the smaller type (microgynes) which are unable to found colonies without the help of workers (Brian and Brian 1955).

7·4·2 Foundation with the help of workers

Most queen ants however are unable to forage for themselves and those which have not sufficient reserves to see them through the foundation of their colony must get help. One way of doing this would be for several mated queens of the same species to set up house together. The combined reserves of several queens might provide enough food, in the form of eggs, to raise workers. This has been called foundation by alliance (Viehmeyer 1908, Forel 1928). In laboratory experiments pairs of *Camponotus vagans* (Stumper 1962) or of *Lasius flavus* (Waloff 1957) can raise more workers than single females do. In the field two or more queens of the same species are sometimes found together. It is said to be normal in *Pachysima aethiops* (Bequaert 1922). There is not much evidence to show that this is an important way of founding colonies.

It is much commoner for the queen to receive the help of workers of her own species. One way of doing this is by colony division. In *Eciton* species as soon as daughter queens emerge from their cocoons the colony shows signs of an impending split, and the workers group themselves round one or other queen. Eventually the queens part company each one taking a part of the workers and brood with her (Schneirla 1956a). The African Doryline *Anomma wilverthi* splits its colony in the same way, except that all the young queens—up to 56 of them—are killed save one (Raignier 1959). The queens of *Carebara vidua* in Africa are much larger than their workers and sometimes take workers tangled in the hairs on their feet with them on their mating flight. Since such a large queen must have enough reserves to raise workers it was suggested that she would be unable to feed the tiny larvae herself—she is 24 mm. long, a full-grown worker about 2 mm. (Arnold 1915). The

Malayan species *C. lignata* can be found in incipient nests of a queen, brood and callow workers only. In an artificial nest a queen reared 16 workers unaided in 40 days. Her eggs formed a pile on the ventral side of her gaster, which she kept turned forward between her legs. Presumably the larvae fed on the pile (Lowe 1948).

Many ants which regularly have more than one queen in each colony form branch colonies and these may sometimes become independent of the mother colony. This probably happens in wood-ants, in *Monomorium pharaonis* (Peacock et al. 1955) and in other ants as well. The queens in a nest which divides in this way are not always young newly mated ones, so that it is rather a different sort of division from those which have just been mentioned. It quite often happens that some of these branch nests are formed without queens at all. These queenless offshoots may adopt a young queen of their own species after her mating flight and become independent in that way. Many ants like *Myrmica ruginodis* produce two sizes of queen. The large form or macrogyne can found colonies independently; the small or microgyne form is not able to do this, but can be adopted into an older colony (Brian and Brian 1955). Adoption of this sort also goes on in *Crematogaster skouensis* and *vandeli* (Soulié 1962) and in *Dolichoderus quadrimaculatus* (Torassian 1960). Wood ants are also able to make their branch nests independent, but this will be discussed in relation to the next method of colony foundation.

7·5 Temporary social parasitism

A queen who is adopted into an existing nest of her own species can do nothing to extend the range of the species into new territory, for she can only go where nests already exist. A queen that cannot found a colony for herself can however move into places where there are no nests of her own species if she is adopted by another, related species. The workers of the host species provide food and care for her larvae. Later the intruding queen's daughter workers take the nest over, or the queen, with or without workers, may continue to live as a parasite in a 'mixed nest'. Apart from permanently parasitic ants like *Anergates atratulus* the first species whose queens were shown to begin their colonies in the nests of other ants was the American *Formica difficilis*. In late summer several types of mixed colony can be found. Some consist of a small number, 10-30, of workers of *Formica nitidiventris* and one or two queens of *F. difficilis*. Colonies which seem to be further on in their development have only one *F. difficilis* queen, a few *F. difficilis* pupae or workers and up to ten *F. nitidiventris* workers. Colonies with simply a *F. difficilis* queen and her first progeny are not found, nor are colonies with queens of both species. Medium sized colonies of *F. difficilis* often show the distinctive features of a former nest of *F. nitidiventris*, and very rarely a few *F. nitidiventris* workers (Wheeler 1904). In laboratory experiments small groups of *F. nitidiventris* workers accept and care for *F. difficilis* queens but other species of *Formica* will not (Wheeler 1906a). The inference is that *Formica difficilis* queens fairly often found colonies in small, perhaps queenless, nests of *F. nitidiventris*. There is a good deal of evidence that other ants in the *Formica microgyna* group (to which *F. difficilis* belongs), and some in the *F. rufa* and *F. exsecta* groups too, are also 'Temporary Social Parasites'. Their hosts

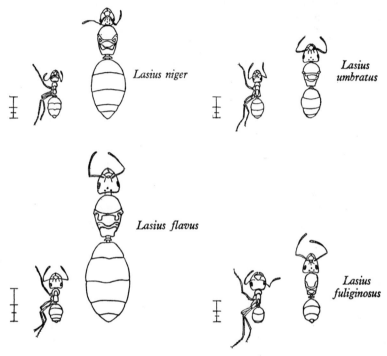

FIG. 7·1 The relative sizes of queen and worker in four species of *Lasius*. *L. niger* and *L. flavus* found colonies independently, *L. umbratus* and *L. fuliginosus* are Temporary Social Parasites. (Eidmann 1926)

are usually members of the *F. fusca* or *F. pallidefulva* groups, most of which can found nests independently (Creighton 1950). The females of Temporary Social Parasites are usually small, and often have long hairs on their bodies, like the American *F. ciliata* and *criniventris*.

There is some evidence that wood-ants themselves can be Temporary Social Parasites, starting their colonies in nests of *Formica fusca* and its relations. Wood-ant queens never lay eggs if they are isolated after they have mated; they usually die (Wasmann 1908). Single wood-ant queens with incipient colonies are never found in the wild. Small nests with perhaps one wood-ant queen, 150 wood-ant workers and 50 *F. fusca* workers are found, but not very commonly (Donisthorpe 1911).

Similar nests of *F. exsecta* with *F. fusca* (Wasmann 1908) and *F. ulkei* with *fusca* (Creighton 1950) have been found too. Although the idea that these species are 'normally' (Wheeler 1910) Temporary Social Parasites became widespread, the evidence for this is circumstantial and hard to find, compared with say the case of *Lasius umbratus*. All the evidence is that the adoption of a wood-ant or *exsecta*-group queen by other ants is rare. The nests of *F. exsecta* (Wasmann 1908) and of *F. ulkei* (Scherba 1958) occur in clusters (formed by colony division) with the occasional single nest, always in the middle of an area inhabited by the *Formica fusca* group. Probably most of the queens that succeed in establishing themselves in colonies are adopted into colonies of their own species, only a small proportion go into those of a temporary host. When single wood-ant queens (usually *F. polyctena*) are added to groups of other wood-ant species or of *F. fusca*-group ants they are killed unless the group is small (tens of workers) and queenless. Queens of *F. rufa* may be adopted by weak *F. fusca* colonies which have queens, and in this case the *F. fusca* is later found dead (Gösswald 1952).

As a rule the queens of Temporary Social Parasites are smaller than the queens of related species that found colonies independently. This feature has given its name to the *Formica microgyna* group, all of which are thought to be Temporary Social Parasites. It is also true in the genus *Lasius*, where *L. niger, alienus, brunneus* and *flavus*, with all their New World relations and subspecies have large queens which found colonies on their own. *Lasius umbratus* and *fuliginosus* on the other hand have smaller queens, relative to the size of their workers, and are Temporary Social Parasites. Temporary Social Parasitism may be an adaptation to colony foundation in cold climates (Gösswald 1938b) but our knowledge of colony foundation in tropical ants is insufficient to say whether fewer ants there are parasites. It is interesting that *Camponotus chilensis* is said to found nests independently in the warmer north of Chile, but to be a parasite in the south (Goetsch and Käthner 1937).

7·5·1 *Invasion of the host nest*

To establish herself as a Temporary Social Parasite a queen needs to find and enter a host nest, to avoid being killed or expelled by the host workers and to establish herself, and eventually her brood as part of the colony. Not a great deal is known about how she does any of these, but relatively least is known about the first. Wood-ant queens have been seen accosting *Formica fusca* workers outside a nest before going into it. Naturally no more was seen of these queens (Donisthorpe 1911) and no mixed nest resulted (Gösswald 1952). A little more is known of the habits of *Lasius umbratus* queens. After her mating flight the queen breaks off her wings and runs about on the ground. If she finds a nest of *Lasius niger* she sticks her head in at an entrance hole and then pulls it out again. She may do this up to six times before she comes out with a *L. niger* worker in her jaws. The head of a *L. umbratus* queen is too large for a *niger* worker to grasp. She then digs a shallow hole in the ground where she eats the *niger* worker. This is quite different from the nesting behaviour of a *niger* queen, which digs fast and hard at once (Gösswald 1938b). After a mating flight large numbers of *L. umbratus* queens can be found on the ground and half of them may carry or be eating *niger* workers (Donisthorpe 1927). After this presumably the *umbratus* queen enters a nest of *L. niger*. What their peculiar habit of catching and eating a *niger* worker means we do not know. It is unlikely that it gives them the 'species smell' if any, of *niger*. If it did it might not help them to enter a *niger* nest for *niger* queens themselves are attacked if they enter a strange nest (Gösswald 1938b). The behaviour of a *L. umbratus* queen differs from that of *L. niger* in the way she searches for a nest. A queen of *L. niger* may have her standards by which she chooses or rejects possible places for her burrow. The queen of *L. umbratus* has to find a place where *L. niger* is. As we shall see her behaviour inside a host nest is submissive and quite different from her predatory behaviour outside it (Hölldobler 1955). Eating a *niger* worker may be the stimulus that brings this change about, for it shows the queen as clearly as possible that she has found a *niger* nest. A *Harpagoxenus americanus* queen also begins by capturing a worker of her host species *Leptothorax curvispinosus*. She does not eat it but lets it go again. The escaped ant goes back into its own nest in a highly alarmed state and the alarm spreads to other members of the colony. In the confusion the *Harpagoxenus* queen slips into the colony (Wesson 1939).

Lasius umbratus seems to be obliged to start colonies in the nests of *Lasius niger*. A colony of *L. umbratus* will not accept a queen of its own species, as wood-ant colonies do. *Lasius fuliginosus* too seems to be an obligate parasite (or hyper-parasite) of *L. umbratus* (Donisthorpe and Crawley 1911). It is to be expected that they should have special behaviour when they are looking for host nests. Wood-ants on the other hand seem to be more casual parasites of *Formica fusca* and no behaviour of that kind has been described for them. The small *Teleutomyrmex schneideri* queens fasten themselves to the bodies of alate *Tetramorium caespitum* alate queens in the mother nest, and accompany them on the mating flight (Kutter 1950).

Naturally the parasite queen can only be watched after she has entered the host nest in a laboratory nest. Occasionally a dead parasite queen is found in a wild nest of the host to show that adoption is by no means automatic. When *Lasius umbratus* queens are placed in a laboratory nest of *L. niger* they are closely investigated by the *niger* workers. Although *L. umbratus* queens in the wild, before they have caught and eaten a *niger* worker, repel the attacks of other *niger* workers, inside the nest they behave quite differently. They wash themselves all the time (this may be a substitute activity for fighting) and do not fight back but frequently touch their attackers with their antennae. (Hölldobler 1955.) Unmated *L. umbratus* do not behave so submissively and are usually killed by the *L. niger* workers (Gösswald 1938b). The queens of *Formica difficilis* behave in the same quiet way and usually haunt the brood of their host *F. nitidiventris*. If queens of *F. nitidiventris* itself are placed in strange colonies of *nitidiventris* they show great alarm and rush about: they are soon attacked and killed. So are *F. difficilis* queens in a colony of *F. difficilis*. (Unmated queens with their wings cut off were used in these experiments and their behaviour may not have been adequate to avoid attack, as is the case in *Lasius umbratus* (Wheeler 1904, 1906a).

The part which 'submissive' behaviour seems to play in protecting intruding parasite queens from attack is interesting because it recalls the behaviour of worker honeybees which enter the wrong hive. Successful laden foragers enter the hive without hesitation or challenge from the hive's guard bees. Unladen bees are usually stopped by the guards if they have a 'foreign' odour, especially if the hive has already been alerted by robber bees. An intruder which is stopped in this way adopts a 'submissive' attitude and allows its wings and legs to be mauled by the guards. These submissive intruders are rarely stung. It is only when one tries to escape or is moved rapidly by another guard (or by an experimenter) that a stinging battle starts. The battles are usually fatal to the intruder or to the guard. Intruders that are being mauled often try to feed the guard bees from their crops (Butler and Free 1952).

Submissive behaviour and offering food are ways of averting attack by ants that are also used by, for instance predators of aphids, and by beetle guests of ants (section 5·4, 6·5). Just as many of the latter have repellant glands so many temporary parasites have strong odours. *Lasius umbratus* and *fuliginosus* have powerful odours in all castes which may be repellant and a *Bothriomyrmex decapitans* queen (but not the workers) is said to possess the strong odour of her host *Tapinoma*. Some like *Formica ciliata* have long hairs, which can prevent ants from taking a secure grip: the equation of these with the trichomes of *Lomechusa* (Wheeler 1910) seems unlikely.

Ants which live as permanent parasites in the nests of other ants use much the same ways of avoiding attack as the temporary parasites. This, rather than an imitation of the behaviour of a *Formica fusca* queen (Viehmeyer 1908), seems to be what protects *Polyergus rufescens* queens when they first invade a host colony. *Anergates atratulus* queens often simply walk into colonies of *Tetramorium caespitum* without challenge. Workers that they meet may seize them but soon release them (Wheeler 1910).

The queen of *Formica sanguinea* is exceptional in behaving aggressively towards her potential hosts. Newly mated *F. sanguinea* queens will not lay eggs in isolation (Donisthorpe 1910). If they are placed with *Formica fusca* workers far from being submissive they resist attacks from the *F. fusca* workers and constantly raid the brood of the host until they

have collected their own little pile of pupae (Wasmann 1908, Viehmeyer 1908). If she can the *F. sanguinea* queen seals herself off from the
fusca workers in a corner of their nest. Here she stays with her stolen
pupae until they emerge a few days later. In another week she lays her
first eggs. The first *sanguinea* workers emerge in about 50 days (Eidmann
1926). The theft of pupae has been described as atavistic because it
represents the slave-raiding behaviour which is typical of workers, not
of fertile females (Wasmann 1908). It seems just as reasonable to suppose that the attraction which ant pupae have for the workers reflects
the collection of pupae by a queen, which is an essential part of colony
foundation. This is in line with the facultative, almost casual, nature of
F. sanguinea's slaving raids. Slaves are not essential, slaveless colonies
are found, and *F. sanguinea* can hunt, raise her own brood and build her
own nest. The only time when 'slaves' are essential is in the foundation
of a new colony by a young queen.

7·5·2 *Establishment in the host colony*

In most cases the parasite queen secures the full food resources of the
host colony for herself and her growing brood. The *Formica sanguinea*
queen gets 'her own' little group of workers by kidnapping pupae.
Their feeding relations with their unenslaved sisters do not seem to have
been worked out, but they presumably act as intermediaries between
the foragers of the *F. fusca* colony and the parasite queen. Other parasitic queens operate by replacing the original queen of the host species.
The simplest way in which this can be done is by invading a colony
which is already queenless. *Formica difficilis* may in fact only be successful when her host colony has no queen of its own (Wheeler 1904).
Presumably the attractant substances which ants can lick from their
queens are sufficiently powerful to override a tendency to attack
foreigners. *Lasius umbratus* (Gösswald 1938b) and *Epimyrma gösswaldi*
(Gösswald 1933) are able to compete with the host queen for the attentions of workers, *E. gösswaldi* gradually 'wins workers for herself' by
frequently stroking them and begging for food. Eventually the host
queen is deserted or actually killed by her own workers. The parasite
queen rarely attacks her. In the parasitism of *Tetramorium caespitum* by
Strongylognathus testaceus this competition is so finely balanced however
that both queens survive and both lay eggs. The *T. caespitum* eggs never
produce sexuals, only workers.

Bothriomyrmex decapitans is unusual because its queen, unlike most
other parasites, consistently attacks the larger queen of its host *Tapinoma
nigerrimum*. The *B. decapitans* queen is said to climb onto the back of the
host queen, where she is more or less immune from attack by the host
workers. If the *T. nigerrimum* queen throws her off she climbs on again.
Gradually, after several days of attacks, she gnaws right through the
unfortunate hostess' neck. Decapitation is not directly fatal to an ant,
and the queen starves gradually over several days, attended by her

workers as usual. After this the *Bothriomyrmex* queen is tended and fed by the workers. She also eats *Tapinoma* eggs (Santschi 1919).

However the take-over is achieved the result is the same. The queen is fed by workers of a different species, and they also feed and care for her brood. She for her part, takes over the functions of the host queen as a provider of eggs for the workers to nurse and no doubt of queen pheromones (sections 2·5·1, 6·3·6).

8 — The organisation of an ant colony

So far this book has described how ants set about some of their tasks in the colony. The most important of the tasks were concerned with food collection, care of the young and nest building, and also for alate ants, reproduction and colony foundation. Simply calling them 'tasks' implies that they play some vital part in the existence of the colony. If this is so it is only reasonable to ask what ensures that each task is in fact done. It will have been clear that in most cases we know a little about what starts a certain worker ant digging or hunting, that is to say about the releasing stimuli for ant behaviour. We have spoken to some extent as if these stimuli were the controllers of what an ant does from minute to minute. This is only partly true. If a group of ants are placed in a tube of moist sand most of them will dig in it, and if they are offered pupae they usually carry them about. It would be disastrous for the ant colony if this was the whole of the story. If the brood is attractive to ants why should any ants leave the nest to get food? If hungry ants leave the nest and forage why should not all the colony do so at once? How in fact is the worker force distributed to all the tasks which need to be done?

As well as this problem, which is one of co-ordination of ants doing different tasks, there is another of co-ordination of ants in groups which are doing the same job in the nest. Quite a different problem arises here, for it is not a matter of preventing more than a certain number of ants doing the same thing, but of ensuring that those that are doing a particular job act together in a coherent way.

8·1 Polyethism - the various tasks of ants

As we have said it would be against the interest of the colony if every ant behaved in the same way at the same time. Even if the nest is attacked it would be best for only some of the ants to defend the nest and cover the retreat of others with the brood. It is not unknown for animals which are not social to have individuals which respond in different ways in the same situation. The sexual differences in behaviour are perhaps a rather special case, but other differences may be important in the survival of a species too. Among caterpillars some may be more inclined to move about and disperse than others; in some circumstances one type is valuable, at other times the other (Wellington 1957).

Animals which show these variations in behaviour from one to another can be said to show polyethism—a word formed by analogy with polymorphism, the occurrence of different forms within the single species. Like differences in form, differences in behaviour may be traced back to a variety of origins—different ages or sexes, different genetic endowments and different developmental histories. It is however an easier thing to change behaviour than to change form and we might expect that polyethism would be less fixed than polymorphism. Indeed it would be possible to have a completely unorganised polyethism, in which any ant might respond in a number of ways to the same situation. Then except in very small colonies, mere chance would ensure that some ants would always be doing any particular task. At first sight this idea of variable polyethism is attractive, for it is often found that small colonies are very hard to set up in the laboratory (Peacock, Sudd & Baxter 1955). The idea is probably wrong, for it leads us to expect that in small colonies sometimes one task, sometimes another would be neglected. In fact small colonies neglect care of larvae and show increased food collection (Francfort 1945).

In any case there is plenty of evidence to show that the same ants often keep to the same sort of task for long periods. Marked workers have been seen at the same tasks outside the nest for months in *Formica sanguinea* (Dobrzanska 1959), wood-ants, *Camponotus herculeanus* and *ligniperda* (Kiil 1934), *Myrmica rubra* and *Manica rubida* (Ehrhardt 1931). In reality the tasks a particular worker does are related to two or three sorts of polyethism. Some of the differences in behaviour are associated with differences in size and shape, between for instance large and small workers of the same colony. We can call this *caste polyethism* and it is a fixed polyethism, just as the polymorphism that goes with it is fixed. Even more important differences in behaviour depend on the age of the ant: young ants as a rule specialise in brood care and older ones in hunting. This is *age polyethism*, and of course it is not fixed but changes as the ant's age changes. Lastly, for reasons which we do not understand, some ants concentrate on certain tasks whilst their sisters of the same age and size group do others or else change their tasks very frequently (Otto 1958). We do not know whether these ants are slightly different from their sisters at the start, or whether they become different by learning to specialise.

8·1·1 *Caste polyethism*

In ants like *Pheidole* and *Messor* the workers of a mature nest are of two distinct sorts. There are large workers, sometimes called major workers or soldiers, and smaller or minor workers. In other genera like *Atta* or *Anomma* there is a wide but continuous range of size (Wilson 1953a, Hollingsworth 1960). With the differences in size go differences in form so well described by Darwin: 'The difference was the same as if we were to see a set of workmen building a house, of whom many were five feet four inches high and many sixteen feet high; but we must in addition suppose that the larger workmen had heads four instead of three times as big as those of the smaller men, and jaws nearly five times as big.' So in some ants not only are the females of two castes, queen and worker, but the workers are divided into subcastes. While queens and workers differ most in the relative development of the thorax and of course wings, the differences between workers are most marked in the head and jaws (Wilson 1953a).

The differences in behaviour between large and small workers are easily observed without the need for marking individual ants. The idea that large workers are 'soldiers' and defend the colony is not true for most ants. The soldiers of *Colobopsis truncata* (Goetsch 1953), *Cataglyphis bombycina* (Bernard 1951b) and many species of *Pheidole* are less aggressive than their small sisters, and more likely to run and hide if the colony is attacked. The largest workers of *Anomma nigricans* do however line the edges of migration routes with their forelegs linked. Thieves like *Bengalia* and predators like *Oecophylla longinoda* attack stragglers among the smaller ants in the column and the soldiers' main contribution to safety is probably in preventing other workers from escaping from the route. Large workers of *Camponotus americanus* are said to fight, while building and brood care are the concern of medium and small workers. Isolated medium-sized workers of *Camponotus americanus* are more likely than larger or smaller workers to attack a piece of clean filter paper. Both large and medium workers attack filter paper soaked in formic acid. The smallest workers flee from all interference (Vowles 1953). Many large-headed soldiers defend their nests by stuffing their heads into the entrance holes rather than by fighting (*Colobopsis*, *Cryptocerus* Creighton and Gregg 1954, *Camponotus ulcerosus* Creighton 1953b, *Pheidole m liticida* Creighton and Gregg 1959).

The differences in the behaviour of workers of different sizes are often only of degree and not at all clear cut. Some ants which have very large workers do not send them out foraging. All the searching for food is done by the smaller workers in *Pheidole megacephala*, *P. crassinoda* (Sudd 1960b) and *P. militicida* (Creighton and Gregg 1959). Major workers are eventually recruited to food if the experiment is prolonged, as indeed the queen herself may be in *Pheidole megacephala*, *Monomorium pharaonis* and *Myrmica rubra*. The number of majors attracted in this way depends on how many there are in the colony. Small young colonies often have none or only a few. As the majors develop later in the history of the colony they are often younger than many of the minor workers. Age polyethism ensures that younger ants stay with the brood and this may reduce the number of majors which can be recruited in *Pheidole*. In *Acromyrmex* the large workers are short-lived and may never reach the age at which they turn to duties outside the nest (Goetsch, 1939). Sometimes the large workers appear to specialise in cutting up insect prey or in cracking seeds; both these tasks may be difficult for smaller ants. The story, unfortunately fossilised in its specific name, that *Pheidole militicida* slaughters its major workers after the seed harvest (Wheeler 1910) is untrue (Creighton and Gregg 1959).

The major workers of *Oecophylla longinoda*, unlike the species we have just been discussing, are foragers more often than the minor workers (Weber 1949). The same is true of *Messor* species. In captivity groups of only major workers of *Messor* forage but neglect the brood, whilst groups of minors eat the brood rather than forage (Goetsch 1953). Most experiments with these small colonies are to be suspected how- ever unless some attention has been given to the age of the ants.

Two differences between large and small workers of most ants are pretty certain. Large workers are less active, show less faithfulness than minors to particular tasks. Two major *Messor* workers made 19 changes of task in 10 days while two minors only changed twice (Goetsch 1953). Even in *Formica polyctena*, where the polymorphism is not strong, large workers are twice as likely to change tasks and nearly twice as likely to be inactive (Otto 1958). As a result majors here, as in *Pheidole*, often serve as a reserve to be called on when needed.

8·1·2 *Age polyethism*

All these differences between workers of different types (and no doubt differences between workers which have no visible distinctions too) are overlain by a change of tasks with age which probably occurs in all species of ant. Young workers which have fairly recently emerged from the pupa remain in the nest. Their first work in the nest is tending brood or the queen and they do not forage. Older workers forage out- side the nest and do not tend brood. In addition they are usually more likely to approach, investigate or attack strange objects; young ants usually flee. Since the cuticle of worker ants gets darker during their adult lives, young and old ants can be told apart. By this means the general drift with age has been shown to occur in *Manica rubida*, *Myrmica rubra* (Ehrhardt 1931), *Myrmica scabrinodis* (Weir 1958), *Messor* species (Goetsch 1930), *Acromyrmex* species (Goetsch 1939), *Formica sanguinea* (Dobrzanska 1959) and wood-ants (Otto 1958).

The details of these changes in behaviour have been worked out in detail for *Form ca polyctena* (Otto 1958) and are summarised in figure 8·1. This was done by recording the work done by each of a large number of individually marked worker ants in artificial nests. In *Formica polyctena*, provided that the colony has a reasonably normal balance between old and young workers, the workers do not begin to forage until at least 40 days after they come out of the pupal stage. For the first few days of their adult life they move very little and are treated more or less like pupae by their older nestmates. They have certain parts of the adult behaviour pattern even at this time however, for they can clean themselves and they put themselves in the correct curled posture when their nestmates carry them. They begin to take regurgitated food as early as their third day, and other social activities like cleaning their neighbours, begin on the fourth or fifth day. They begin

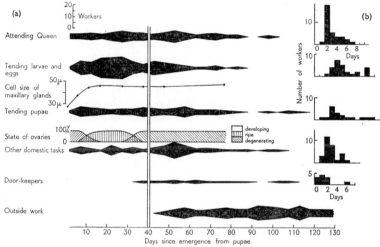

FIG. 8·1 Age polyethism in *Formica polyctena*. (a) The depth of the black bands indicates the number of workers that performed each task on any day of their adult life. These numbers have been corrected slightly to allow for mortality. The condition of the maxillary glands and the ovaries is also shown. (b) The number of days workers persisted in certain tasks. A high column on the left of the diagram implies that the task was done by many ants, each of which soon left it. Columns on the right show the existence of specialists in that task that persisted with it for many days. (Based on Otto, 1958)

to lick the brood around the sixth day. During their service inside the nest the marked workers undertook various tasks of brood care—delivering the queen of eggs, licking young larvae and regurgitating to them and feeding older ones with pieces of insects. The change from inside work to outside work was followed in twelve marked ants and took place from the 45th to the 80th day after their emergence from the pupa. Since workers are not produced early in the year by woodants, this means that few workers leave the nest to forage in their first summer. When an ant reached the age of 40 days or more it began to spend a lot of its time in the nest entrance, where it may be described as a watchman, though its behaviour is not very much like that of the guards in a honeybee colony. An ant's first excursion usually started when a forager returned to the nest and disturbed it as it sat in the nest entrance. During their early adult life *Formica polyctena* workers also become more aggressive, and around the 27th day of their adult life they begin to attack such things as needles when these are thrust at them. They begin to spray formic acid and to attack prey at about this time too. A small proportion of ants however remains timid for as long as 75 days. In general these changes resemble those which occur in the honeybee whose workers do not leave the nest for their first two or three weeks as adults.

At the same time that the ants' behaviour is changing in this way, important changes are going on in their internal organs too. The maxillary glands are increased in size in nursing ants but degenerate in foragers. (No changes seem to occur in the labial glands which are thought to yield a secretion fed to queen larvae.) The most striking changes are in the ovaries of worker ants. Each of the paired ovaries of a *F. polyctena* worker has 2-5 ovariole tubes, whilst a queen's ovary has 63-83. Almost all *Formica* workers caught outside the nest have degenerate ovaries but a large proportion of those inside the nest have well developed ones. Also when the ant is moving to a branch nest, the ants which are being carried have well developed or ripe ovaries and the ants doing the carrying degenerate ones. In a nest in which there is a normal balance of old and young workers the ovaries of the workers increase in size and maturity in the first two weeks after an ant has emerged, so that they can be classed as mature (with two large oöcytes) after about 27 days. During the fifth and sixth weeks of adult life workers' ovaries retrogress and become degenerate. The corpora allata (glands attached to the brain that control the ripening of oöcytes) similarly increase in size in the first three weeks. This normal course of development of the ovaries is altered if the conditions in which the workers live are abnormal. In particular the ovarian development depends on diet and on the company of older workers. Two hundred newly emerged workers were divided into two groups one of which was given a flesh diet the other merely sugar. Each of these groups in turn was divided into a group of fifty workers which were placed with fifty older workers, and a second group which was kept without older workers. Only the fifty workers which both received meat and had older workers with them developed ripe ovaries. (Otto 1958).

This result seems to explain some observations made many years before. In a number of species of ant the full pattern of worker behaviour was not shown by newly emerged workers. Some pieces of behaviour appeared earlier in ants which were reared with older workers. At the time it was thought that the young ants learnt from older ones (Heyde 1924). This seems to have been wrong, or at least not proved, for the company of older workers accelerates ovary development and this in turn is associated with changes in behaviour. Keeping young *Formica* workers with older *Camponotus* did not have this effect of maturing their behaviour (Heyde 1924).

8·1·3 *Specialisation*

The division of the labour force of the colony into two groups—domestic and outside workers—on grounds of age very likely exists in many ant species, at least in the higher subfamilies. It is only these broad categories that appear serially however, even in wood-ants where the appearance of the more slowly maturing pieces of behaviour is later than in other ants (Heyde 1924). Young ants do not distribute themselves among the various tasks inside the nest on grounds of age. Instead some ants specialise in certain tasks and spend most of their time on them. This is shown on the right hand side of figure 8·1. The ants which care for larvae and eggs can be seen at the same task for days on end. Attendance on the queen however is by ants which are sometimes not seen at the same task later; they are fickle and often change. This means that there is no court of permanent attendants, only a shifting set of ants round the queen. Half of the attendants waited on the queen in only three of the twenty periods of observation. Tending pupae is also done by specialists, and so is door-keeping and butchers' work, in the short period for which ants perform these tasks.

We do not know how ants become specialists. It may be that some ants are more likely to become specialists than others and that they are inclined to wait on eggs and larvae. Certainly small workers are more inclined to become specialists than large ones. Specialists in tending eggs and larvae made up 27% of all small workers and a further 5% of them specialised in other tasks. Among large workers only 16% were specialists. This suggests that size influences whether an ant will specialise or not and other fixed factors might be equally important. On the other hand specialists may be made not born. Perhaps ants which happen to tend larvae at an early stage of their adult life become attached to this task more permanently, at least for as long as they work inside the nest.

Workers outside the nest show some specialisation too. Some foragers are attached to honeydew collection others to hunting (Kiil 1934). Again size is important for honeydew collectors are on average smaller than hunters (Otto 1958).

8·1·4 *Polyethism and the needs of the colony*

In a colony which is expanding in a normal way caste and age polyethism should keep a reasonable number of ants on each of the tasks that the colony requires. If the colony should be abnormal in any way can the development of behaviour be accelerated or turned aside to draft in a larger number of builders or hunters after some sort of catastrophe?

Not all the workers in a colony are hard at work. Many of them are in fact doing nothing for a lot of the time. These 'resting' ants stand in a characteristic way, legs close to body and antennae folded on their heads (Wallis 1962b). Where the workers are of various sizes large workers are more often to be seen resting than small ones (Goetsch 1934, 1953). Even in *Formica polyctena* nearly a quarter of the large workers have been recorded as 'specialists in doing nothing' against one in ten of small workers (Otto 1958), and in *Formica sanguinea* 30% of large against 15% of small workers were immobile (Dobrzanska 1959). In both these species medium sized workers are intermediate in activity.

The activity of ants, in the sense of whether they are moving about or 'resting' is very much affected by their social life. Differences in the activity of large and small ants are probably not just differences in the likelihood that an ant will begin to move. How easily it can be disturbed by other ants is at least as important. Many experiments have shown that the smaller a group of worker ants in an artificial nest is the more of the ants in it will be immobile (Barnes 1941, Sturdza 1942, Chauvin 1944, Sudd 1957). A simple explanation of this is suggested by the behaviour of a few ants imprisoned in a small space. If all the ants are quite still, when any one of them does move it will disturb its neighbours, and probably most of the ants in the group will begin to move again. The more ants there are in the group the more likely it is that some of them will begin to move (Sudd 1957). Responsiveness is an important factor in keeping ants active.

There are differences in responsiveness between ants of different ages, and these sometimes show themselves as differences in aggressiveness as we have seen. When an artificial nest of *Myrmica scabrinodis* is disturbed the first workers to run out are all dark coloured and belong to older age groups. The last to leave are pale and therefore young (Weir 1958a). *Formica fusca* is a very dark brown ant, and cannot be sorted into age groups by colour. There are differences in the responsiveness of workers however which are very probably related to age. When groups of 40-50 workers are kept without any brood only a small number of them will leave the nest after a slight disturbance. These ants may be the main searchers for food which leave the nest spontaneously and look for it. Some other workers are slow to leave the nest unless they are disturbed more strongly. They will not forage unless food has already been found by the searchers, but they are ready to accept regurgitated food when it is brought into the nest. The least responsive ants never forage and are slow even to accept food from their more active sisters (Wallis 1962c).

The activity of these different groups of workers (which cannot be told apart by colour or size) is strongly affected by the 'hunger' of the colony. In a nest which has been fed in the last five days the searchers are 'resting' for 30% of the time, but if the nest has not been fed for 5-9 days they are still for only 7% and if no food has been given for 10 days only 2% of the time. Giving food reduces activity almost at once (Wallis 1962b). Hunger has the same effect on *Formica polyctena* and increases the number of ants near the nest exit (Otto 1958).

The traffic in food in the colony tends to spread hunger equally through all the worker force, for the better fed workers feed the hungrier ones. Because of this hunger is not really an individual thing but a property so to speak of the colony. When ants are feeding at food they have found, ants from hungry colonies feed for longer on their first trip than ants from well-fed colonies. On subsequent trips to the food workers from hungry colonies do not necessarily feed for longer. The amount of food which has been taken from them in the nest does affect later trips: the more food it has given to its nestmates the sooner an ant makes another trip to the food and the longer it feeds when it gets there. This has been shown by splitting a laboratory colony in two, one well fed the other not. An ant from the hungry half was diverted into the well-fed half when it came back from feeding. It gave less food, sallied out again later and collected less food next time than sisters which returned to the hungry half of the colony (Wallis 1964). The ants had no brood in these experiments but probably the demands of larvae can also alter the rate at which foragers work (Schneirla 1957a, Vowles 1955a).

In this way the hunger of the colony controls the number of ants that forage by drawing on a pool of unemployed ants. No-one is quite sure whether this pool exists in wild nests as well as in the laboratory or whether these ants perform other tasks in the wild for which artificial nests offer no opportunity. Idle workers are common enough in observation hives of honeybees whose behaviour seems to be fairly normal, so no doubt idle ants are also to be found in wild nests.

Is it possible for ants to change from one major task to another if the colony needs more workers on that task? In *Messor* caste polyethism is rather rigid and majors will not nurse, nor minors forage even in nests made up of only majors or only minors (Goetsch 1953). Is age polyethism any less rigid? In *Messor* apparently it is for young workers which normally spent a month in the nest as domestics began to clean the nest earlier, after only 6 days, when there were no older workers in the nest (Goetsch 1953) and *Manica rubida* workers left off nursing abnormally early when there were no older workers to forage (Ehrhardt 1931). *Formica polyctena* workers too can change from nursing to foraging or the reverse if they are placed in groups all of the same age. The presence of older workers, it will be remembered, is one of the essentials for normal ovary development in workers (Otto 1958). In *Myrmica scabrinodis* small groups of light coloured (that is young) workers paid more attention to the brood when older workers were placed with them. When six workers of the least dark sort were given ten larvae, on average four out of the six were sitting on the pile of larvae at any time. When four pale and two dark workers were used more than three out of the four pale workers were on the brood. These figures, which were more different than chance could explain, can be interpreted in two ways. It may be that young workers prefer to be near the brood but can be forced to

do other tasks if there are no older workers. It may equally likely be
that the young workers will perform several tasks but can be forced onto
the brood by competition from older workers for other tasks (Weir
1958a). So though there are a good many leads into the question of
need altering polyethism no-one yet has carried out a comprehensive
study of it.

8·2 The integration of work in single tasks

We now move from the strategy of ant labour to its tactics. A small
group of worker ants from a single colony put in a small dish of moist
sand usually digs a single hole, not one for each ant, and will place all
the brood it is given in a single pile in the hole. How does this come
about? This experiment can be used to illustrate some of the explana-
tions which have been given. We might perhaps expect that if the sand
was uniform in moistness and texture the ants and their brood would be
distributed at random all over the dish. In practice however there
would always be small differences in temperature and light intensity to
which all the ants would respond in the same way. As a result of
orientations to these differences ants would come to rest, quite independently of one another, in the same places in the dish. Differences
in the number of ants in the various equally attractive parts of the dish
would be due to chance.

The actual behaviour of ants in a dish of sand is more complicated
still for ants do not really behave independently of one another. In the
first place they tend to cluster together, as a result of responses to carbon dioxide and perhaps to other substances too (section 2·5·1). Once
the ants have collected together as a result of this 'interattraction'
(Rabaud 1937) they affect each other in ways like some of those which
were described in the section 8·1·4 of this chapter. These alter the
activity of an ant in amount but do not seem to affect what sort of
things it does. A puzzling feature of the sort of experiment we are discussing is that ants in a dish of sand take longer to form a single group
than they would in an empty dish.

More specific effects of one ant on another do occur however, when
one ant in digging seems to promote the same activity in other ants.
This apparent 'imitation' has often been remarked but hardly ever investigated. A particular activity like digging or moving pupae is started
'by one or a few workers which have more initiative or respond more
quickly to a change of conditions than the bulk of the colony. The
movements of such individuals attract the attention of others in their
immediate neighbourhood and these proceed to "imitate" their more
alert companions' (Wheeler 1910). Clearly a good deal of comment of
this sort is speculation. If the imitators are merely slower to respond to
changes of conditions they may join in the activity later whether they
are affected by more alert ants or not.

Almost the only detailed study of this sort of behaviour was made on workers of *Camponotus japonicus* (Chen 1937a). When these ants were placed in pairs in bottles of moist earth they began to dig sooner, and removed more earth than when they were placed one in a bottle. Not only the number of ants but their individual characteristics were important. Some ants rapidly found patches of moist soil and began to dig, others were much slower. The fast working ants were retested on five successive days and found to be consistently faster than their fellows (Chen 1937a). Unfortunately the ants were not marked but were told apart by their size, for *C. japonicus* has considerable polymorphism. As a result there were no tests of pairs of ants of the same size. Also the ants were collected freshly from an earth nest and so their age, which would affect digging behaviour, was not known. Large workers were more often fast workers than small ants were, but as the history of their colony is not known the significance of this is not clear. Whatever the basis of the differences between ants was, the same ant began digging sooner and dug more earth when it was paired with a fast worker than when it was paired with a slow one (Chen 1937b). It would be extremely interesting if someone repeated these experiments with more control of caste and age polymorphism. As it is we are left with a solitary instance where a companion causes an increase in a specific activity and not just a general increase in movement. In groups of *Formica fusca* and in mixed groups of *F. fusca* and *F. sanguinea* the amount of soil each ant digs is less in larger groups than in small ones (Sakagami and Hayashida 1962).

8·2·1 *The efficiency of group work*

'Imitation' in any case cannot take us very far towards explaining how the work of several ants in a group can be integrated. When groups of ants are working together it often looks as if their work is quite unorientated although they may all be doing the same job. One ant digs a hole which another soon after fills in: one ant carries larvae into the nest another carries them out again. If there is any 'imitation' it is rather inexact, to say the least. This apparent undoing of each others work does not mean that the work is not integrated, as two examples may show. *Myrmica ruginodis* workers, like most ants, collect their brood into a pile. Clearly this concentration of the brood reduces the time nurse workers spend in moving from larva to larva. At the same time piling must not be taken too far or a lot of the larvae will be buried and inaccessible to their nurses. The tendency to move larvae to the pile is balanced by a tendency to spread them (section 6·2, Brian 1953). Although a worker may remove from the pile a larva which another ant has only just put there, there is an integration of their work which results in a compromise between concentration and dispersion of the larvae.

The shape of the nest-mound of *Formica polyctena* is maintained by rather similarly balanced processes. Mostly ants move nest material up the mound but there are also more or less random movements which produce a frequent turn-over of surface material. In addition ants move material downwards to fill in hollows and ledges. The shape of the mound is the result of these opposed tendencies, much as the shape of a fountain arises from upward and downward movements of water. (Section 4·1·2, Chauvin 1958, 1960).

These examples show that one has to be careful in measuring integration by the mere quantity of work the group of ants can do. Integration of behaviour in the arrangement of brood does not and in the colony's interest should not, result in as concentrated as possible a brood pile. Nor is it in the colony's interest to have the steepest and highest dome possible. In other cases it does seem more reasonable to compare the work a single ant does when it works alone with what it achieves as a member of a group. Although casual observation, without measurement, sometimes suggests the reverse, the work output of a group is always higher than that of a single ant. The number of larvae a group of *Myrmica ruginodis* workers can rear from 50 eggs increases more or less in proportion to the number of workers in the group, up to a group size of 15 workers. Increasing the number of workers to 40 does not increase the yield above the level of 11-12 achieved by 15 workers. Larger groups of workers do succeed in raising heavier larvae, and the weight of larvae goes on increasing until there are 80 workers attending them. The contribution each worker in the group makes to rearing larvae gets less as the groups of worker are larger. A solitary worker however is unable to produce much gain in weight in the larvae it tends (Brian 1953).

Pairs of *Formica polyctena* workers can drag prey of a standard size faster than a single worker can (Chauvin 1950). Groups of *Pheidole crassinoda* workers (Sudd 1960b) and pairs of *Formica lugubris* workers (Sudd 1965) exert larger forces than single ants can and work at about twice the rate. The power of a pair of *Formica lugubris* workers is about $8·0 \times 10^{-6}$ H.P. as compared with $3·2 \times 10^{-6}$ H.P. for single ants. However on average only about 75% of the force each ant produces is used to move prey, the rest is wasted in opposing the efforts of the other ant in the pair. As a result the force produced by two ants is less than twice that produced by a single ant. The same is true of *Pheidole crassinoda*.

8·2·2 Co-operation in group work

If two workers can do more work than one there is a clear advantage in group work, for it means that two ants can carry heavier prey, build larger nests or rear more brood than one ant can. This advantage in terms of amount achieved or the time taken to achieve it has been put forward as the sole criterion that the work is co-operative (Chauvin 1950). Although this is reasonable if by co-operation we only mean that the ants work together, and that their efforts do not cancel one another out, it is not what we usually mean by co-operation. If we say that a person is co-operative we imply that he is willing to suit his behaviour to ours. Applied to ants this requirement that one ant should alter its behaviour to suit another's is probably satisfied in many cases.

We can take a first example from nest excavation again. Although, as has been said, a group of ants in a dish of soil dig a common hole, they do not do so from the very start. At first they dig separately, and it is only later that the holes join up to form a common system. Even at this stage there may be several openings and earth may be thrown out of one hole only to fill up another. In the end, after say 48 hours, there is a single nest which looks as if it had been planned from the start (Goetsch 1953). There was however no plan from the start in fact, and the co-ordination of the work of the different ants must have grown up as the work progressed, for until work started there were no marks to guide the ants. If ants are to respond to the work other ants are doing it is not surprising that there is no co-ordination for the first 24 hours in nest excavation.

We need not look far to see where ants might have got a response to each other's work. A single ant working quite solo needs to respond to its own work if it is to achieve any particular goal. Perhaps the question 'Why do ants eventually concentrate on a single excavation?' has the same answer as 'Why does a single ant concentrate on one hole?' The sensory messages that co-ordinate the digging of a single ant can co-ordinate the digging of several. When one ant is digging a hole its behaviour must bring it back to dig over and over again, load of soil after load, in the same place. The same response to a place where there is a hole can bring one ant to a hole dug by another too. This arrangement, where the results of the work give the stimuli to guide further work has been called *Stigmergy* (*stigma*—a prick or stimulus, *ergon*—work) (Grassé 1960).

Similar co-ordinations appear as *Oecophylla longinoda* builds its leaf-nests. Ants collect on certain leaves perhaps as a result of interattraction. They pull the leaf they are standing on and also some of them reach across and pull neighbouring leaves. While some of these ants are very persistent many others move about to other parts of the leaf. They are more likely to settle and begin pulling again at places where the leaf edge is already bent. As a result they concentrate in teams at places where the leaf can be bent. Here again there is no plan, and no 'knowledge' of where a leaf will bend. Instead there is a response to the work of nestmates where this has been successful. As a result nests can be built from a wide variety of shapes of leaf. (In other respects however the building of nests is more firmly determined: in the way that one ant holds another or holds a spinning larva for instance; see section 4·5.)

The transport of prey by groups of ants can be studied in more detail because single ants can move prey successfully. A group of ants which is moving prey often seems to be behaving in a very disorganised way, yet there is no doubt that groups can move prey which a single ant could not move. Each ant in the group would if it was working alone, orientate in the direction of its nest. As all of them come from the same nest agreement about the direction in which they pull might be expected. At least there should be a resultant force in the direction of the nest, rather than away from it (Chauvin 1950). In *Formica lugubris* this is not often what happens. Although two ants may agree about the direction in which prey is to be pulled they still pull against one another. This happens because an ant begins to pull prey by seizing it at any convenient place and then turning with its prey, until its body is orientated for a homeward journey. When two ants take hold of prey at opposite ends they usually make these turns in opposite directions. As a result they pull against one another (Sudd 1965).

In spite of this initial inefficiency the ants later begin to pull their prey home, because their behaviour changes. The transport of prey by *Formica lugubris* has three phases. In the first there is slight transport of the prey at a mean speed of 3·6 cm. a minute; this lasts 2–3 minutes. During the succeeding 5 minutes or so movement almost ceases (mean speed 0·3 cm./min.) but starts again in the last phase even faster than before (mean speed 9·6 cm./min.). Movement stops in the second phase because of a more or less exact balance of forces as the number of ants increases, rather than because the ants are not pulling, and removing some ants usually restarts movement of the prey. The rapid movement in the third phase is due to the better organisation of the work so that the prey is pulled in a straighter line. A progressive improvement in efficiency can also be seen when pairs of ants are pulling prey which is fastened to a spring. In general large forces, up to twice what a single ant can do, are only produced when the ants have been working for ten minutes or more (Sudd 1960b, 1965). These changes depend on the way that the ants apply their efforts to their prey. It is not a simple matter of the arrangement of ants, for an ant is able to exert its maximum force at an angle of 50° to its body. Ants have a repertoire of changes of effort which free the prey of ants pulling singly from various snags and obstacles (section 5·3·1): the same movements probably serve to free them from deadlocks due to the antagonistic work of several ants.

8·2·3 *Co-operation in men and ants*

When men work in groups they often follow a plan thought out before hand, which may be imposed on the group by leadership and command. The plan can be altered in details according to its progress as work proceeds. Also during the work the men in the group may learn more efficient ways of working, within the framework of the plan. The plan, the leadership and some of the learning bulk rather large in our human view because we are conscious of them. Equally important adjustments of posture and muscular co-ordination which we are not conscious of, seem less important to us. Ants do not work to an overall plan, at least not in the sense that the group works to a set pattern. Each ant in the group does however have a pattern of responses to the work as the work is going on. These responses govern the details of how the individual works and not its broad outlines. The work pattern of the group is made up of the interactions of these individual patterns. This means that the group patterns of behaviour are not of any standard type but vary from instance to instance.

There is no real sense in which ants have leaders. Since each ant responds to the work done by the other ants in the group any one ant may, for a time, determine how others work, but their work will in turn effect its ways. In some cases an ant which works faster or which happens to be in a critical position may determine the way the whole group works. An *Oecophylla* worker which succeeds in bending the edge of a leaf or a wood-ant which is well placed to pull prey certainly can dominate the rest of the group. It does not of course issue commands on how the work is to be done.

It is also clear that ants do not 'think out' problems in prey transport or in building. 'Thinking out' involves using some sort of mental model to simulate the results of different courses of action. This is precisely what ants do not do. Instead they 'work out' the problem by trying various expedients until one solves the problem. Unfortunately we have no idea what 'trying' means as far as ant behaviour is concerned. An ant which is pulling prey has a set of 'trial-and-error' responses to difficulty, we do not know how it acquires them. The change from carrying to dragging as the weight of the prey increases is probably inborn but it is possible that the 'swings', by which an ant dragging prey rounds an obstacle, are partly learnt. During its early life as an adult inside the nest the worker may move pupae and gain experience in the general properties of loads. It is not likely that ants learn how to co-operate with other ants, for each problem in group transport is different from previous ones. It would not be any use for ants to adopt by preference solutions which have been successful in previous, totally different, difficulties.

8·3 The learning powers of ants

In other cases however it has very clearly been shown that ants can learn, but how they use this power in their natural lives is not so clear.

Ants can be trained so as not to show their usual inborn responses to certain stimuli. The failure to respond after the stimulus has been experienced many times is called habituation. Ants in laboratory nests can be habituated to handling and to the company of other species of ants in mixed nests (Fielde 1904) and to illumination of the nest

(Wilson 1962a). They can also be trained to respond to a stimulus which at first had no effect on them. This is called associative learning (Thorpe 1956). Ants can for instance be trained to come for food at particular times of day (section 2·4). The learning of routes and directions by wood-ants and other ants also seems to involve associative learning.

The behaviour of ants in mazes has been studied and has the advantage over more natural observations that the ability of an ant to learn its way through a maze can be compared with that of a rat or for that matter a man. Both habituation and associative learning play a part when an ant learns a maze. During the first eight attempts or so a *Formica pallide-fulva* worker becomes habituated to the new conditions in the maze, and starts to explore it without making sudden trips back to the start (Schneirla 1941). A maze can be made in which the ant can run through one part from nest to feeding-place, and then return through a reversed section, to which the solution in terms of right or left turns is the same. It can also be made to pass either way along direct passages through small plastic gates. Its learning of the route is measured by the number of 'wrong' turns it makes. In a maze which has six points where the ant might go wrong, a *Formica pallide-fulva* worker will at first make about 70 errors on its way through the maze. By its tenth trip it may make less than ten errors. The reduction of errors is usually faster on trips from food to nest than on the outward journey (Schneirla 1933b). No ant ever succeeded in learning the combination of the same maze on both outward and return journeys (Schneirla 1934).

The learning process really begins when the ant is habituated to the maze. At first ants favour certain directions of turning in the maze. If the maze passage bends to the left before a side-alley the ant is more likely to take a right turn than a left, because it will already be following the right-hand wall round the bend. Where the solution to the maze asks the ant to turn to the inner wall the ant will learn more slowly. A maze of only four 'inward turns' may only be learnt after 150 trips, but a six-point maze where all the turns are outwards can be learnt in 40. Also at first the ant follows blind alleys to their very end after a false turn. Its correction of the error goes through several stages: first it stops at the first bend in the wrong alley, then it runs only a short way down the first arm. In the final stages it occasionally does not turn at all until, after say 20 trips, it consistently makes the correct turn (Schneirla 1943).

Although *Formica pallide-fulva* has considerable powers of learning a maze it is a much slower learner than a rat. Faced with similar mazes (built however to different scales) rats reduce the number of wrong turns they make much more quickly. Rats can learn in 14 trips a six-point maze for which ants need over 30 runs. Rats, like ants, find inward turns difficult but rats can be trained to make them in about 60 runs where ants need 100. The way that ants learn seems to differ from

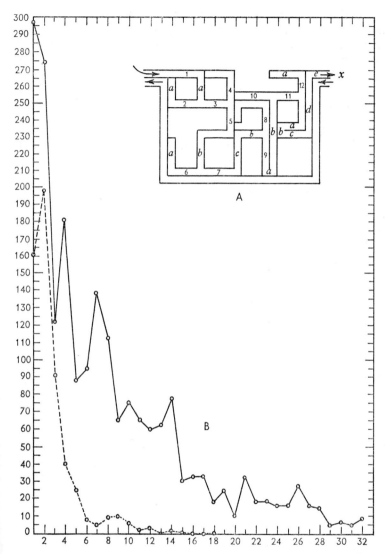

FIG. 8·2 (A) A six-point maze used in testing the learning powers of *Formica pallide-fulva*. (B) Learning curves for *Formica pallide-fulva* (solid line) and for hooded-rats (broken line). Ordinate number of errors per trial, abscissa—number of trial. (Roeder 1953)

that of rats more fundamentally too. Ants learn mazes in smaller bits than rats do; as a result the ants' learning curve is smooth, showing many small improvements. The learning curves of rats improve by sudden jumps, and rats are more likely to avoid a blind alley altogether

IBA M

than to show the stages of learning that an ant has. Ants are apparently unable to transfer their learning to other circumstances. Once they have learnt a maze on a trip from food to the nest, they can neither run the mirror maze from nest to food nor the original maze backwards from point 6 to point 1. Their learning is entirely bound to the one-way trip. However the way ants learn in small units seems to protect them from 'neurotic' effects. If one choice in a maze is continually reversed, so that first left, then right, then left again is the correct choice a rat's performance in other parts of the maze also deteriorates. This does not happen with *Formica pallide-fulva*, although it may feed for a shorter time at the feeding place (Schneirla 1962).

It is extremely difficult to find how much ants use their learning powers in nature. For example a wood-ant might be expected to learn a twisted searching route to food, just as a *Formica pallide-fulva* does in a maze. Although it does learn it transforms the experience of turns and distances into a straight-line course to or from the nest (section 3·1·1). Watching an ant in the field might suggest that it could not learn a maze simply because it does not learn it in some way we have, wrongly, anticipated.

9 — The evolution of social behaviour in ants

Now that the details of ant behaviour have been described it is time to take a more panoramic view of the varieties of ant behaviour. Everyone is agreed that ants evolved from some sort of solitary wasp which hunted insect prey to feed to its young in a burrow. From the point of view of a student of behaviour it is not very important which particular group of solitary wasps are favoured as ancestors. In the first place there are no wasps sufficiently close to the ants to be thought of as solitary ants in the way that we have solitary bees (Wheeler 1928). In the second place all the possible candidates among living Hymenoptera for the honour of standing close to the ants have obviously specialised behaviour. For example the family Tiphiidae (Brown 1954), which are the favourites on anatomical grounds, are found living parasitically in the nests of solitary bees and wasps. It is unlikely that their behaviour will illuminate the early evolution of ant behaviour. However it is clear that the ancestors of ants must have been well-equipped with sense organs. Other features of ants: loss of wings, the heavily sculptured cuticle of Myrmeciinae and Ponerinae, the elongated shape and dark colour, are characteristic of soil-dwelling insects. The most obvious way of life which combines subterranean life with the need for good eyesight is that of a burrowing wasp which hunts above ground.

It is not easy to see how the earliest ants evolved from this state, for many of the ways we should expect an ancestral ant to behave would not suit a solitary life at all. This is particularly true of colony foundation. We may take the characteristics of the earliest ant, as far as we can guess them, in the order in which they have appeared in earlier chapters of this book.

1. Early ants nested in the soil or in moist rotting wood or humus. Nests in dry crevices and all the sorts of arboreal nests were later developments.

2. Early ants hunted insect prey or collected dead insects. At the same time they took nectar and possibly honeydew (as the Tiphiid

Myrmosia still does—Krombein 1939). Feeding on seeds or fungi, and greater dependence on honeydew, were later developments. Early ants hunted singly and all sorts of group-hunting and group collection of food were later developments. Early ants hunted on the ground; hunting below the soil and in trees were later developments.

3. Early ants mated in the air, the flight is still a behavioural necessity even in many ants which make no use of the flight for dispersal. Mating on the ground or in the nest developed later.

4. The colonies of early ants were founded by solitary queens. There is only weak evidence that early ant queens, like some *Myrmecias*,

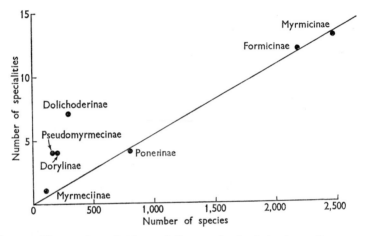

FIG. 9·1 The number of advanced features in the behaviour of seven sub-families of ant in relation to the number of species in each. (Original)

hunted prey for themselves. Foundation by large solitary queens which do not feed seems more likely to have evolved after ants became social, because a solitary species might be hard put to produce large enough queens. The large numbers of queens which most ants produce is also hard to fit into the picture of a solitary insect practising parental care of its young. All forms of adoption and social parasitism must of course have appeared later.

5. Ants occur in greatest numbers in the tropics. There are forty times more species in Trinidad than in Alaska and the numbers of species fall off with altitude too (Kusnezov 1957). Probably therefore they first evolved in the tropics. The evidence that they evolved in a dry rather than a humid region is not convincing (Wheeler 1928). From the tropics they later moved to other regions, developing habits which allowed them to live in cool climates. These include mound nests and perhaps parasitic methods of founding colonies.

9·1 The systematics of ant behaviour

The different subfamilies of ants depart to different extents and in different directions from the characteristics of early ants which have just been listed. Figure 9·1 was drawn by counting for seven of the subfamilies the number of 'later developments' and plotting this against the number of species in the subfamily. The 'late development' was scored one or two according to its frequency in the subfamily. It is clear that the number of ways the ants in each subfamily depart from 'early ant ways' and the number of species in the subfamily are related to one another. It is impossible to say whether a large number of species makes more sorts of advance possible, or whether the relationship is the other way round and groups which have many advanced ways of life develop more species. Probably both these ideas are correct: a large group has more lines of advance and this in turn allows it to become even larger. This might explain why the two large subfamilies are so much larger, and why there are no subfamilies of one to two thousand species.

The Myrmeciinae, Ponerinae, Myrmicinae and Formicinae all lie very nearly on the same line in figure 9·1. The two primitive subfamilies Myrmeciinae and Ponerinae have few species and few departures from the ways of early ants. The two higher subfamilies Myrmicinae and Formicinae have far more specialised members, but not more than we might expect from their large number of species. The Pseudomyrmicinae, Dorylinae and Dolichoderinae all lie above the line with more 'later developments' than their number of species justifies. Dorylinae and Pseudomyrmicinae are small subfamilies with a high degree of specialisation in nesting habits and in feeding habits. Each has however only one main line of specialisation not several. The Dolichoderinae are a small subfamily which still presents about half as many 'later developments' as the much larger Myrmicinae.

The cavalier treatment of behavioural patterns and taxonomy on which figure 9·1 is based conceals at least one important point. In the Formicinae and the Myrmicinae the same 'later development' has been attained independently by several unrelated groups in each subfamily. It can also be attained in several different ways, that is by different patterns of behaviour. Crevice-nesting Myrmicines may be as different as *Leptothorax* and *Cataulacus* for example. The variety of ant life in large families is underemphasised in figure 9·1.

At the same time the same piece of behaviour can serve different functions in different ants (or even in the same ant). The turning movements of a feeding ant may tear out pieces of flesh from the prey in *Anomma* or *Monomorium pharaonis* or free the prey from obstacles in *Formica lugubris* or cut out a piece of leaf in *Atta cephalotes*. Nest construction is promoted by rain in soil-building *Messor*, in mound-building *Formica* and in carton nesting *Crematogaster*. The existence of this groundwork of similar behavioural units, which can be combined in various ways, has been mentioned before.

9·2 The geography of ant behaviour

Comparisons of the behaviour of ants from different regions are also interesting. Often the same habits are found in ants from different regions. Sometimes, when we compare the ants of North America and Eurasia for instance, the ants are closely related. The members of the *Formica rufa* and *F. exsecta* group have very similar habits on both sides of the Atlantic. These similarities only reflect the recent connection of the two parts of the Holarctic zoogeographical region. Large Ponerine ants and the driver- and army-ants in the Dorylinae similarly have close similarities in behaviour throughout the tropics. The harvesting ants of the Mediterranean and Africa on one hand and North America on the other are related at about the same level as the Dorylines. *Pheidole* species are common to both regions but the Old World *Messor* is replaced by *Veromessor* and *Pogonomyrmex*. All the harvesting ants however belong to the same section of the subfamily Myrmicinae. Among ants which always live in hollow twigs and thorns both Africa and America have Pseudomyrmicine ants (like *Pseudomyrma*, *Pachysima* and *Viticola*) but *Azteca* is peculiar to America and *Crematogaster* much more common in Africa.

In other cases there is a less close relationship between ants of similar behaviour in different regions. *Azteca* and *Crematogaster* are a case in point. Not only do they both, in different regions, inhabit the thorns of *Acacia* bushes, but both build very populous nests in hollow trees and carton nests on tree branches too. Trap-jawed species of *Odontomachus* and Dacetini are found throughout the tropics but the superficially similar, though unrelated, *Myrmoteras* is confined to Asia.

Lastly a few types of behaviour seem to have only evolved on one occasion, in one group of ants in a particular region. Fungus culture is practised by no ants except the Attini and they are found only in the New World tropics. No ant practises fungus culture in Africa or Asia. Yet termites can build nests and grow fungus in them there so that there is no reason to think that it is impossible for ants to do so. Fungus cultivation of the Attine type has simply never arisen in the Old World. To redress the balance the Old World *Oecophylla* and its leaf-nests occur in all the tropics from Queensland to West Africa but are absent from America.

These facts suggest that some of the habits of ants are of more ancient origin than others. The general way of life of Dorylines must have been acquired before the separation of the Old and New World portions of the subfamily (Wheeler 1910). Broadly speaking the Doryline ants have kept these habits, for no ant of conceivably Doryline descent has any other way of life. The greater tendency to move underground in

African *Anomma* compared with American *Eciton* may have arisen because of the more broken forest conditions in Africa (Schneirla 1957a). The extreme specialisation of Pseudomyrmicines for crevice nesting may also be very ancient but many other ants have taken it up so that it must have evolved several times. In the same way a large number of only moderately closely related Myrmicines collect seeds in desert and savannah regions. Fungus cultivation and building leaf-nests are evidently very difficult habits for ants to evolve. Accordingly their evolution is exceedingly improbable and has only occurred once.

9·3 The social history of ants

The evolution of ants has seen at least five sorts of departure from the habits that the group had at the start of its existence. In many ways this has taken the ants away from habits which might be found in other animals to more extraordinary ones, from hunting to fungus cultivation, from earth nests to leaf nests. A good many older workers saw the history of ants as one of increasing intelligence from Ponerinae to Formicinae. Chapter 8 showed how far this is from the truth. All sorts of analogies with human society and lessons for man have been drawn from the supposed evolution of ants too, from the importance of providing for winter to the inevitability of totalitarianism. The most famous parallel with human history was drawn by Lubbock (Lubbock 1882). He suggested that the history of men and ants went through three phases, based on hunting, pastoral life and agriculture. As far as ants were concerned his idea of agriculture was the false one that American harvesting ants planted some of the seeds they collected round their nest to provide a field crop in place of a wild one. However we could substitute fungus-growers for harvesting ants without doing any violence to this notion.

This view of the history of ants as an escape from hunting, in which the amount of food available, and the difficulty of catching it, limit the size of the society, is very probably correct. Certainly many hunting ants have only small colonies, or depend for their food on large colonies of plant-eating termites, or are nomadic. The further idea, that the horticulture of Attini is in some way more advanced than the collection of honeydew is not so certain. Everyone has his prejudices and no entomologist who is aquainted with wood-ants and with *Oecophylla* will be happy to see them placed so low in the second class. Perhaps those who are better acquainted with *Atta* feel differently. Modern knowledge of aphids shows them to be a very efficient way of collecting food from plants from the ants' point of view. Unlike the fungi of Attines, aphids do not convert plant material and pass it on to ants, they merely pass it on without change. Once this is admitted it seems pointless to grade ants that feed from root aphids as more 'agricultural' than those that milk aphids on trees.

In any case food collection is only one of five ways in which ants have advanced from the state of early ants. We might just as easily argue that control of the temperature in the nest was the best criterion for marking advancedness. As far as our knowledge goes wood-ants or *Camponotus ligniperdus*, which nest so far north would compete for the prize.

This perhaps is the lesson figure 9·1 teaches. Some subfamilies of ants are conservative in habits, others advanced. There are several ways of being advanced and it is difficult to grade one as more advanced than others. If ants could write their own history each species would no doubt see itself as the inevitable climax of a long historical process. The picture never looks quite so simple to an outsider.

9·4 The 'superorganism'

Yet another way of looking at an ant colony is to see it as like the body of a single living organism (Emerson 1939, Schneirla 1946). The individual ants are then compared with one or other of the functional units of the body, cells, tissues or organs, at the writer's convenience. The virtues of this point of view are the three important analogies between an organism and an ant society, or for that matter any other society, for bodies have been called states and states bodies for many centuries. Individual ants, like individual cells, have different functions in the running of the whole to which they belong. The most striking of these of course is the specialisation of the alate sexual forms. This can be compared with the specialisation of the germ cells of an organism. The sorts of polyethism among worker ants however are not on the whole analogous with the specialisations of tissue cells.

Both organisms and societies show integrated activity. When the activities of the colony are controlled by chemical signals the analogy with the hormonal control of an organism is clear. Pheromones, like hormones, can be divided into those which have general effects (primer pheromones and metabolic hormones) and those which produce immediate changes in behaviour (releaser pheromones and hormones such as those that control alarm and colour change) (Wilson and Bossert 1963). There are however other sorts of integration in organisms as well as in societies, and it is hard to draw analogies between them. Some sorts of integrated behaviour especially control of nest temperature and colony migration in *Eciton* do have rather close counterparts in organisms.

Last of all each society has a characteristic form, in terms of the sort of individuals which make it up, and a characteristic life-history. In many species early colony development draws on the food stores acquired by the queen in her maternal colony, and the active search for food only begins when workers are developed. The colony then grows vegetatively in size, later becomes reproductive, and may finally grow old and die out. There is a good resemblance here to the development of an organism from a yolky egg. Other sorts of ant live parasitically, either temporarily or permanently.

For many zoologists the analogy will be spoilt by the question 'What *sort* of organism does an ant colony resemble?' Clearly it would be a very curious sort of animal with no central nervous system and no sense organs. It would grow in a curious way too, for all the workers are produced by specialised queens and there are no cell lineages to study. (There are no hereditary social classes either.) Naturally as our knowledge of organisms and of societies becomes more detailed we can expect more flaws in the analogy to turn up. Possibly the time for analogies has gone by. The main efforts of students of ant behaviour now are in describing in detail how ants actually behave, and how the behaviour of one ant reacts on another ant. As this sort of research multiplies a truer picture of the workings of ant society will appear.

References

NOTE. The titles of books are given, but for papers in journals only a brief indication of subject.

ANDRASFALVY, A. (1961). Time of marriage flights. *Ins. Soc.*, **8**, 299-310.

ANDREWS, E. A. (1929). Aphis shelters. *Ann. ent. Soc. Amer.*, **22**, 369-91.

ARNOLD, G. (1915). African ants (part I) *Ann. S. Afr. Mus.*, **14**, 1-578.

—— (1916). African ants (part II) *Ann. S. Afr. Mus.*, **14**, 159-220.

ARNOLDI, K. V. (1932). *Rossomyrmex*—slave raids. *Zeits. Morph. Ökol. Tiere*, **24**, 319-28.

ASSMUTH, J. (1907). *Prenolepis longicornis* habits. *Zeits. wiss. Insektenbiol.*, **3**, 301-9, 328-34, 357-68.

AUCLAIR, J. L. (1963). Composition of honeydew. *Ann. Rev. Entomol.*, **8**, 439-90.

AUTRUM, H. (1936). Hearing. *Zeits. vergl. Physiol.*, **23**, 332-73.

AUTRUM, H. and SCHNEIDER, K. (1948). Subgenual organ. *Zeits. vergl. Physiol.*, **31**, 77-88.

AUTRUM, H. and STUMPF, H. (1950). Polarised light perception. *Naturforsch.*, **5b**, 116-22.

AYRE, G. L. (1958a). Daily rhythms. *Ins. Soc.*, **5**, 147-57.

—— (1958b). Guests of *Formica subnitens*. *Ins. Soc.*, **5**, 1-7.

—— (1959). Diet of *F. subnitens*. *Ins. Soc.*, **6**, 105-14.

BAILEY, I. W. (1924). Ant-plants. *Bull. Amer. Mus. nat. Hist.*, **45**, 585-620.

BANKS, C. J. (1958). Effect of ants on aphids. *Bull. ent. Res.*, **49**, 701-14.

BANKS, C. J. and NIXON G. E. J. (1950). Honeydew production. *J. exper. Biol.*, **35**, 703-11.

BARLOW, H. B. (1952). Capabilities of compound eyes. *J. exper. Biol.*, **29**, 667-74.

BARNES, T. C. (1941). Activity of ants. *J. gen. Psychol.*, **25**, 249-58

BARTH, R. (1953). Biology of *Monomorium floricola*. *Naturwiss.*, **40**, 40.

BARTLETT, B. R. (1961). Effect of ants on aphids. *Ann. ent. Soc. Amer.*, **54**, 543-51.

BEARD, R. L. (1963). Insect venoms. *Ann. Rev. Entomol.*, **8**, 1-18.

BECK, H. (1961). *Polyergus* and *Formica sanguinea*, slavery. *Ins. Soc.*, **8**, 1-11.

BEQUAERT, J. (1912). Stridulation, seed-collection. *Rev. Zool. Afric.*, **2**, 396-431.

—— (1922). Predators of ants. *Bull. Amer. Mus. nat. Hist.*, **45**, 271-331; Ant-plants. Ibid., 332-584.

—— (1930). Defence from enemies. *Zool. Anz.*, **88**, 163-76.

BERNARD, F. (1951a) Formicoidea. *Traité de Zoologie*, **10** (2), 997-1104. Masson, Paris.

—— (1951b). Ants of the Sahara. *Bull. Soc. Hist. nat. Toulouse*, **86**, 88-96.

—— (1955). *Epixenus*. *Ins. Soc.*, **2**, 273-83.

BETHE, A. (1898). Recognition of nestmates, trails. *Arch. gesamt. Physiol.*, **70**, 15-100.

BIER, K. (1954). Oviposition by workers. *Ins. Soc.*, **1**, 7-21.

BINGHAM, C. T. (1903). Glands of *Crematogaster inflata*. *Fauna of British India; Hymenoptera*, **2**.

BIRUKOW, G. (1958). Functions of antennae. *Z. Tierpsychol.*, **15**, 265-76.

BLUM, M. S. and CALLAHAN, P. S. (1963). Venom. *Psyche*, **70**, 69-74.

BLUM, M. S. and PONTECARRERO, C. A. (1964). Scent trail of *Eciton hamatum*. *Ann. ent. Soc. Amer.*, **57**, 793-4.

BLUM, M. S. and ROSS, G. N. (1965). *J. ins. Physiol.*, **11**, 857-68.

BLUM, M. S., WALKER, J. R., CALLAHAN, P. S. and NOVAK, A. F. (1958). Venom. *Science*, **128**, 306-7.

BLUM, M. S. and WILSON, E. O. (1964). Sources of trail-chemicals. *Psyche*, **71**, 28-31.

BODENHEIMER, F. S. and KLEIN, H. Z. (1930). Activity and temperature. *Z. vergl. Physiol.*, **11**, 345-85.

BOMBOSCH, S. (1962). Predators of aphids. *Z. angew. Entomol.*, **50**, 81-88.

BORGMEIER, T. (1953). Ant guests. *Naturwiss.*, **40**, 36.

BOSSERT, W. H. and WILSON, E. O. (1963). Scent-trails. *J. theoret. Biol.*, **5**, 443-69.

BRAUNS, J. (1901). *Aenictus* habits. *Z. Syst. Hymen. Dipt.*, **1**, 14-17.

BRIAN, M. V. (1953). Care of larvae. *Physiol. Zool.*, **26**, 355-68.

—— (1955). Hunting. *J. anim. Ecol.*, **24**, 336-51.

—— (1956). Care of larvae. *Physiol. Zool.*, **29**, 173-94.

—— (1957a). Care of larvae. *Physiol. comp. et ecol.*, **4**, 329-45.

—— (1957b). Colony foundation. *Ins. Soc.*, **4**, 178-90.

—— (1957c). Caste determination. *Ann. Rev. Entomol.*, **2**, 107-20.

—— (1964). Nesting preferences. *J. anim. Ecol.*, **33**, 451-61.

BRIAN, M. V. and BRIAN, A. D. (1949). Colony foundation. *Trans. Roy. ent. Soc. London*, **100**, 393-409.

—— (1951). Nesting preferences. *Trans. Roy. ent. Soc. London*, **102**, 303-30.

—— (1952). Larval secretions in wasps. *Trans. Roy. ent. Soc. London*, **103**, 1-26.

—— (1955) Mating swarms, foundation. *Evolution*, **9**, 280-90.

BRIAN, M. V. and DOWNING, B. M. (1958). Nest structure. *Proc. Xth Int. Congr. Entomol. Montreal*, **2**, 539-40.

BRIAN, M. V. and HIBBLE, J. (1963). Larval care. *Ins. Soc.*, **10**, 71-82.

BROOKS, J. L. (1942). *Platyarthrus hofmanseggi*. *Ecology*, **23**, 427-37.

BROWN, W. L. (1954). Subfamilies of ants. *Ins. Soc.*, **1**, 21-31.

—— (1955). Parasitic ants. *Ins. Soc.*, **2**, 181-6.

—— (1958). Slave raids. *Psyche*, **65**, 39-40.

—— (1959). Alarm scents. *Psyche*, **66**, 25-27.

—— (1960). Ants in *Acacia*. *Ecology*, **41**, 587-92.

BROWN, W. L. and WILSON, E. O. (1959). Dacetini. *Quart. Rev. Biol.*, **34**, 278-94.

BRUN, R. (1914). *Die Raumorientierung der Ameisen*. Jena.

BRUNS, H. (1954). Daily rhythms. *Z. Tierpsychol.*, **11**, 151-4.

BUGNION, E. (1929). Infrabuccal pouch. *Zool. Anz.*, **82**, 58-78.

BÜNZLI, G. H. (1935). Scale-insects, nest construction. *Mitt. schweiz. entom. Ges.*, **16**, 453-593.

BURKHARDT, D. (1960). Antennal function. *J. insect Physiol.*, **4**, 138-45.

BUTLER, C. G. and FREE, J. B. (1952). Robber bees. *Behaviour*, **4**, 262-92.

BUXTON, P. A. (1924). Activity and temperature. *Trans. ent. Soc. London*, 538.

CARTHY, J. D. (1951a). Visual navigation. *Behaviour*, **3**, 275-303.

—— (1951b). Scent trails. *Behaviour*, **3**, 304-18.

CHAPMAN, J. A. (1957). Mating swarms. *Canad. Ent.*, **89**, 389-95.

CHAUVIN, R. (1944). Activity. *Bull. Biol.*, **78**, 197-205.

—— (1948). Scent trails. *Année Psychol.*, **45**, 148-55.

—— (1950). Prey transport. *Behaviour*, **2**, 249-56.

—— (1952). *Oecophylla*, nest repair. *Behaviour*, **4**, 190-202.

—— (1958). Nest construction, wood-ants. *Ins. Soc.*, **5**, 273-86.

—— (1959a and b). Nest construction, wood-ants. *Ins. Soc.*, **6**, 1-11 and 308-11.

—— (1960). Nest construction, wood-ants. *Ins. Soc.*, **7**, 201-5.

—— (1962). Wood-ant routes. *Ins. Soc.*, **9**, 311-21.

CHAUVIN, R., COURTOIS, G. and LECOMTE, J. (1961). Food-traffic between nests. *Ins. Soc.* **8**, 99-107.

CHEN, S. C. (1937a). Nest excavation, co-operation. *Physiol. Zool.*, **10**, 420-36.

—— (1937b). Nest excavation, leaders. *Physiol. Zool.*, **10**, 437-55.

CLARK, J. (1951). *The Formicidae of Australia*. C.S.I.R.O., Melbourne.

CLAUSEN, R. (1938). Mating. *Mitt. schweiz. ent. Ges.*, **17**, 233-46.

CLOUDESLEY-THOMPSON, J. L. (1958). Nest temperature. *Ent. mon. Mag.*, **94**, 43-47.

—— (1961). *Rhythmic activity in animal physiology and behaviour*. Academic Press, London.

COLE, A. C. (1957). Daily rhythms. *J. New York ent. Soc.*, **65**, 129-31.

COLLART, A. (1925). *Megaponera foetans*, raids. *Rev. Zool. Afric.* supplement B.C.Z.C. (26)-(27).

—— (1927). *Megaponera foetans* raids. *Rev. Zool. Afric.*, **14**, 249-53.

COLLINGWOOD, C. A. (1958). Mating swarms. *Ent. Rec.*, **70**, 65-67.

CORNETZ, V. (1911). Visual orientation. *Rev. suisse de Zool.*, **19**, 153-73.

—— (1914). *Les explorations et les voyages des fourmis*. Flammarion, Paris.

CORNWELL, P. B. (1956). Plant-lice. *Bull. ent. Res.*, **47**, 137-66.

CORY, E. N. and HAVILAND, E. E. (1938). Hunting. *Ann. ent. Soc. Amer.*, **31**, 50-56.

CREIGHTON, W. S. (1950). Ants of North America. *Bull. Mus. comp. Zool. Harvard*, **104**.

—— (1953a). *Leptothorax silvestri*, nests. *Amer. Mus. Novitates*, **1635**, 1-7.

—— (1953b). Phragmotic soldiers. *Psyche*, **60**, 82-84.

—— (1954). *Pseudomyrma apache*, nest. *Psyche*, **61**, 9-15.

CREIGHTON, W. S. and CRANDALL, R. H. (1954). Repletes. Biol. rev. City College New York, **16**, 12-16.

CREIGHTON, W. S. and GREGG, R. E. (1954). Phragmotic soldiers. *Psyche*, **61**, 41-57.

—— (1959). *Pheidole militicida*, soldiers. *Psyche*, **66**, 1-12.

DARCHEN, R. (1952). Exploratory behaviour. *Z. Tierpsychol.*, **9**, 362-72.

—— (1955). Exploratory behaviour. *Z. Tierpsychol.*, **12**, 1-11.

DAS, G. M. (1959). Effects of ants on plant-lice. *Bull. ent. Res.*, **50**, 437-8.

DELAGE, B. (1962). Digestion of starch, *Messor*. *Ins. Soc.*, **9**, 137-43.

DENNIS, C. A. (1938). Mound nests. *Ann. ent. Soc. Amer.*, **31**, 267-72.

DETHIER, V. G. (1963). *The physiology of insect senses*. Methuen, London.

DIVER, C. (1935). Wood-ants, routes. *J. anim. Ecol.*, **4**, 32-34.

DIXON, A. F. G. (1958). Responses of plant-lice. *Trans. Roy. ent. Soc. London*, **110**, 319-34.

DOBRZAŃSKA, J. (1958). Wood-ants, hunting *Acta Biol. exper.* (*Lodz*), **18**, 55-67.
—— (1959). Polyethism. *Acta Biol. exper.* (*todz*), **19**, 57-71.
DOBRZAŃSKA, J. and DOBRZAŃSKI, J. (1960). *Polyergus rufescens. Ins. Soc.*, **7**, 1-8.
DOBRZAŃSKI, J. (1961). *Formica sanguinea*, raids. *Acta Biol. exper.* (*Lodz*), **21**, 56-73.
DONISTHORPE, H. (1910). Colony foundation. *Trans. ent. Soc. London*, 142-50.
—— (1911). Colony foundation. *Trans. ent. Soc. London*, 175-83.
—— (1927). *British Ants*. Routledge, London.
DONISTHORPE, H. and CRAWLEY, W. C. (1911). Colony foundation, *Lasius fuliginosus. Trans. ent. Soc. London*, 664.
DUNCAN-WEATHERLEY, A. H. (1953). Daily rhythms. *Austral. J. Zool.*, **1**, 178-92.
EHRHARDT, S. (1931). Polyethism. *Z. Morph. Ökol. Tiere*, **20**, 755-812.
EIDMANN, H. (1926). Colony foundation. *Z. vergl. Physiol.*, **3**, 776-826.
—— (1927a). Scent-trails, hunting. *Rev. Zool. russe*, **7**, 39-47.
—— (1927b). Plant-lice. *Biol. Zentr.*, **47**, 537-56.
—— (1928a). Colony foundation. *Z. vergl. Physiol.*, **7**, 39-55.
—— (1928b) *Camponotus herculeanus*, food and nest. *Z. angew. Entomol.*, **14**, 229-53.
—— (1931). Colony foundation. *Biol. Zentr.*, **51**, 657-77.
—— (1932). Nest construction, *Atta sexdens. Z. Morph. Ökol. Tiere*, **25**, 154-83.
—— (1938). Fungus cultivation. *Rev. de Entomol.*, **8**, 291-314.
EISNER, T. (1957). Proventriculus of ants. *Bull. Mus. comp. Zool. Harvard*, **116**, 439-90.
EISNER, T. and BROWN, W. L. (1958). Proventriculus of ants. *Proc. Xth Int. Congr. Entomol.*, **2**, 503-8.
ELLIOT, J. S. B. (1915). Fungus in nest of *Lasius fuliginosus. Trans. Brit. mycol. Soc.*, **5**, 138-42.
EL-ZIADY, S. (1960). Effects of ants on aphids. *Proc. Roy. ent. Soc. London*, A **35**, 30-38.
EL-ZIADY, S. and KENNEDY, J. S. (1956). Effects of ants on aphids. *Proc. Roy. ent. Soc. London*, A **31**, 61-65.
EMERSON, A. E. (1939). 'The Superorganism'. *Amer. Midl. Nat.*, **21**, 182-209.
EMERY, C. (1892). Ants and acacia. *Zool. Anz.*, **15**, 237.
—— (1915). *Polyergus rufescens* raids. *Rev. suisse Zool.*, **23**, 384-400.
ESCHERISCH, K. (1907). Daily activity, Paussid beetles. *Z. wiss. Insektenbiol.*, **3**, 1-8.
—— (1911). Daily rhythms, nest construction. *Biol. Zentr.*, **31**, 44-51.
FELTON, J. C. (1958). Collection of nectar. *Ent. mon. Mag.*, **94**, 279-80.
FIELDE, A. (1904). Temperature sense. *Biol. Bull.*, **7**, 170-4.
—— (1905). Recognition of nestmates. *Biol. Bull.*, **10**, 1-16.
FLANDERS, S. E. (1957). Plant-lice. *Ecology*, **38**, 535.
FORBES, J. (1952). Mating. *J. New York ent. Soc.*, **60**, 157-71.
FOREL, A. (1892). Ants and *Acacia. Zool. Anz.*, **15**, 140-3.
—— (1905). Nests of *Azteca. Biol. Zentr.*, **25**, 170-81.
—— (1908). *The senses of insects*. Methuen, London.
—— (1920). *Fourmis de la Suisse*. 2nd edition, La Chaux au Fonds. (Reprint 1948, Rotapfel Verlag, Zürich.)
—— (1928). *The social world of ants*. Translated by Ogden, C. K. Putman, London and New York.
FRANCFORT, R. (1945). Activity. *L'Année Psychol.*, 280.

FREE, J. B. (1956). Food-sharing in bees. *Brit. J. anim. Behaviour*, **4**, 94-101.

FREELAND, J. (1958). *Myrmecia*, care of larvae. *Austral. J. Zool.*, **6**, 1-18.

GOETSCH, W. (1928). Seed collection. *Z. Morph. Ökol. Tiere*, **10**, 353-419.

—— (1929). Seed collection. *Naturwiss.*, **17**, 221-6.

—— (1930). Seed collection. *Z. Morph. Ökol. Tiere*, **16**, 371-457.

—— (1932). Seeds and nests. *Z. Morph. Ökol. Tiere*, **25**, 1-30.

—— (1934). Scent trails, hunting. *Z. Morph. Ökol. Tiere*, **28**, 319-401.

—— (1939). Leaf-cutting ants. *Zoologica Stuttgart*, **96**, 1-105.

—— (1941). Food-traffic. *Z. angew. Entomol.*, **27**, 271-320.

—— (1953). *Die Staaten der Ameisen.* Springer Verlag. Translated Manheim, A. (1957). *The ants.* Chicago Univ. Press.

GOETSCH W. and KÄTHNER, B. (1937). Colony foundation. *Z. vergl. Physiol.*, **33**, 202-60.

GOIDANICH, A. (1959). Plant-lice. *Boll. ist. entomol. univ. Bologna*, **23**, 93-131.

GÖSSWALD, K. (1930). Parasitic ants, *Epimyrma*. *Z. wiss. Zool.*, **136**, 464-84.

—— (1933). *Epimyrma*. *Z. wiss. Zool.*, **144**, 262-88.

—— (1938a). Temperature and humidity. *Z. wiss. Zool.*, **151**, 337-81.

—— (1938b). Parasitic ants, *Lasius umbratus*. *Z. wiss. Zool.*, **151**, 101-48.

—— (1941a). Wood-ants, hunting. *Forst. wiss. Zbl.*, **63**, 139-43.

—— (1941b). Temperture and humidity. *Z. wiss. Zool.*, **154**, 277-344.

—— (1943). Wood-ants, hunting routes. *Z. Morph. Ökol. Tiere*, **40**, 37-59.

—— (1950). Parasitic ants, colony foundations. *Umschau* (Frankfort-a-M.), **17**, 527-30.

—— (1952). Colony foundation. *Z. angew Entomol.*, **34**, 1-44.

GÖSSWALD, K. and BIER, K. (1954). Caste determination. *Ins. Soc.*, **1**, 229-46.

GÖSSWALD, K. and KLOFT, W. (1956). Food-traffic, radioactive markers. *Waldhygiene*, **1**, 200-2.

—— (1958). Food-traffic, radioactive markers. *Umschau* (Frankfort-a-M.), **24**, 743-45.

—— (1960). Food-traffic, radioactive markers. *Zool. Beitr.*, **5**, 519-56.

GÖSSWALD, K. and SCHMIDT, G. H. (1960). Mating flight. *Ins. Soc.*, **7**, 298-319.

GRABENSBERGER, W. (1933). Rhythms, learning. *Z. vergl. Physiol.*, **20**, 1-54.

—— (1934). Time sense. *Z. vergl. Physiol.*, **20**, 338-42.

GRASSÉ, P.-P. (1959) Co-operation. *Ins. Soc.*, **6**, 41-81.

GRAY, R. A. (1962). Honeydew composition. *Science*, **115**, 129-33.

GREEN, A. A. and KANE, J. (1958). Nest of *Lasius brunneus*. *Ent. mon. Mag.*, **94**, 181.

GREGG, R. E. (1954). *Myrmoteras*. *Psyche*, **61**, 20-30.

GRENSTEAD, L. W. (1956). Nectar collection. *Ent. mon. Mag.*, **92**, 405.

GRESSIT, J. L. (1958). *Oecophylla*, hunting. *Proc. Xth int. Congr. Entomol.*, **2**, 747-53.

HALDANE, J. B. S. and SPURWAY, H. (1954). Information in dances of honeybee. *Ins. Soc.*, **1**, 247-83.

HANNA, A. D., JUDENKO, E. and HEATHERINGTON, W. (1957). Shelters for plant-lice. *Bull. ent. Res.*, **47**, 216-219.

HARKER, J. (1961). Diurnal rhythms. *Ann. Rev. Ent.*, **6**, 131-46.

HASKINS, C. P. and HASKINS, E. F. (1950). Myrmecinæ. *Ann. ent. Soc. Amer.*, **43**, 461-91.

—— (1955). Myrmecinæ, colony foundation. *Ins. Soc.*, **2**, 115-26.

HASKINS, C. P. and WHELDEN, R. M. (1954). Food-traffic, *Myrmecia. Ins. Soc.*, **1**, 33-37.

HAYASHIDA, K. (1960). Nest site selection. *Ins. Soc.*, **7**, 126-62.

HEADLEY, A. E. (1941). Arrangement of brood in nest. *Ann. ent. Soc. Amer.*, **34**, 649-57.

HEIKERTINGER, F. (1927). Guests which mimic ants. *Biol. Zentr.*, **47**, 462-501.

HERAN, H. (1957). Function of antennae. *Naturwiss.*, **44**, 475.

HERTER, K. (1924). Temperature sense. *Z. vergl. Physiol.*, **1**, 221-88.

—— (1925). Temperature sense. *Z. vergl. physiol.*, **2**, 226-32.

HERZIG, J. (1938a). Plant-lice. *Z. angew. Entomol.*, **24**, 367-436.

—— (1938b). Guests milking aphids. *Zool. Anz.*, **121**, 18-20.

HEYDE, K. (1924). Development of worker behaviour. *Biol. Zentr.*, **44**, 623-54.

HINGSTON, R. W. G. (1928). *Problems of instinct and intelligence.* Arnold, London.

HINTON, H. E. (1951). Myrmecophilous Lepidoptera. *Trans. South London entom. nat. Hist. Soc.*, 1949-50, 111-75.

HODGSON, E. S. (1955). Behaviour of *Atta cephalotes. Ecology*, **36**, 293-304.

HÖLLDOBLER, B. (1961). Hibernation etc. of *Camponotus herculeanus* and *ligniperda. Ins. Soc.*, **8**, 13-22.

HÖLLDOBLER, K. (1928). *Solenopsis fugax*, habits. *Biol. Zentr.*, **48**, 129-42.

—— (1936). Colony foundation. *Biol. Zentr.*, **56**, 230-48.

—— (1938a). Colony foundation. *Zool. Anz.*, **121**, 66-72.

—— (1938b). Diet etc. of *Myrmica rubra. Z. angew. Entomol.*, **24**, 268-76.

—— (1941). Relations of *Atemeles* and *Myrmica. Mitt. Münchener entom. Ges.*, **31**, 1054-9.

—— (1948). Behaviour of ants to guests. *Z. Parasitenk.*, **14**, 3-26.

—— (1953). Behaviour of ant guests. *Naturwiss.*, **40**, 34-35.

—— (1955). Colony Foundation. *Z. angew. Entomol.*, **37**, 598-606.

HOLLINGSWORTH, J. (1960). Polymorphism of *Anomma. Ins. Soc.*, **7**, 17-37.

HOLT, S. J. (1955). Hunting, wood-ants. *J. anim. Ecol.*, **24**, 1-34.

HOMANN, H. (1924). Function of ocelli. *Z. vergl. Physiol.*, **1**, 541-78.

HUBER, J. (1905). Colony foundation, *Atta sexdens. Biol. Zentr.*, **25**, 606-19, 628-35.

HUBER, P. (1810). *Vie et moeurs des fourmis indigènes.* Paris and Geneva.

IBBOTSON, J. and KENNEDY, J. S. (1959). Plant-lice. *J. exper. Biol.*, **36**, 377-90.

IHERING, H. VON (1898). Colony foundation *Atta sexdens. Zool. Anz.*, **21**, 238-45.

JACKSON, W. B. (1957). Army-ant bivouacs, climate. *Ecology*, **38**, 276-85.

JACOBY, M. (1953). *Atta sexdens*, nest structure. *Z. angew. Entomol.*, **34**, 145-69.

—— (1955). *A. sexdens*, nest structure. *Z. angew. Entomol.*, **37**, 129-52.

JANDER, R. (1957). Visual orientation, wood-ants. *Z. vergl. Physiol.*, **40**, 162-238.

JANDER, R. (1963). Insect orientation. *Ann. Rev. Ent.*, **8**, 95-114.

JANET, C. (1897a). *Limites morphologiques des anneaux postcephaliques.* Lille.

—— (1897b). *Rapports des animaux myrmecophiles avec les fourmis.* Ducoutieux, Limoges.

—— (1898a). *Aiguillon de la Myrmica rubra.* Carre et Naud, Paris.

—— (1898b). Cuticular glands of ants. *C. R. Acad. Sci. Paris*, **126**, 1168-72.

—— (1904). *Observations sur les fourmis.* Cuticular sense organs. *Ducoutieux*, Limoges.

—— (1906). Resorption of flight muscles by queens. *C.R. Acad. Sci. Paris*, **142**, 1095-7. (1907). *C.R. Acad. Sci. Paris*, **144**, 393-6, 1070-3.

JORDAN, K. H. C. (1913). Glands of *Lomechusa* and *Atemeles. Z. wiss. Zool.*, **107**, 346-86.

JUNG, K. (1937). Cleaning procedure. *Zool. Jahrb.*, **69**, 373-416.

KALMUS, H. and RIBBANDS, C. R. (1952). Recognition of nestmates by bees. *Proc. Roy. Soc. (B)*, **140**, 50-59.

KANNOWSKI, P. B. (1959a). Food-traffic. *Ecology*, **40**, 162-4.

—— (1959b). Mating flights. *Ins. Soc.*, **6**, 115-62.

KARLSON, P. and BUTENANDT, A. (1959). Insect pheromones. *Ann. Rev. Ent.*, **4**, 39-58.

KASCHEF, A. H. and SHEATA, M. N. (1963). Daily rhythm, *Camponotus maculatus*. *Ins. Soc.*, **10**, 83-90.

KATÔ, M. (1939). Nest temperature, wood-ants. *Tôhuko Imperial University, Science Rep.*, **4**, series 14, 53-64.

KELLER, C. (1892). Ants in *Acacia*. *Zool. Anz.*, **15**, 137-43.

KEMP, P. B. (1951). Daily rhythms. *Bull. ent. Res.*, **42**, 201-6.

KIIL, V. (1934). Routes and polyethism wood-ants. *Biol. Zentr.*, **54**, 114-46

KLOFT, W. (1959). Recognition of aphids by ants. *Biol. Zentr.*, **78**, 863-70.

KRAUSSE, A. H. (1910). Stridulation. *Zool. Anz.*, **35**, 523-6.

KROMBEIN, K. V. (1939). Habits of Tiphiidae. *Trans. ent. Soc. Amer.*, **65**, 415-66.

KUSNEZOV, N. (1957). Ant species and latitude. *Evolution*, **11**, 298-9.

KUTTER, H. (1920). *Strongylognathus huberi*, slave raids. *Biol. Zentr.*, **40**, 52-83.

—— (1950). Parasitic ants, *Teleutomyrmex*. *Mitt. schweiz. ent. Ges.*, **23**, 81-94.

KUZNETZOV-UGAMSKY, N.Y. (1927). Mating flights. *Rev. Zool. russe*, **7**, 102-4.

LANGE, R. (1958). Food-traffic. *Naturwiss.*, **9**, 196.

—— (1959). Nest construction, wood-ants. *Entomophaga*, **4**, 47-55.

—— (1960). Food-traffic between nests. *Z. Tierpsychol.*, **17**, 389-401.

—— (1962). Hunting, wood-ants. *Z. angew. Entomol.*, **50**, 56-64.

LEDOUX, A. (1949). *Oecyphylla*, nests, mating flights. *Ann. Sci. nat. Zool.*, **12**, 313-461.

—— (1958). Arboreal nests. *Proc. Xth int. Congr. Entomol. Montreal*, **2**, 521-8.

LE MASNE, G. (1948). Males of *Ponera edouardi*. *C. R. Acad. Sci. Paris*, **226**, 2009-11.

—— (1953). Care of larvae. *Ann. Sci. nat. Zool.*, **15**, 1-56.

LIVINGSTONE, D. (1857). *Missionary journeys. Megaponera foetans* raids. Murray, London.

—— (1880). *The last journals of David Livingstone*. Group raids. Murray, London.

LOWE, G. H. (1948). *Carebara*, colony foundation. *Proc. Roy. ent. Soc. London*, A **23**, 51-53.

LUBBOCK, J. (1882). *Ants. bees and wasps*. Reprint 1929. Kegan Paul, London.

LÜSCHER, M. (1956). Ventilation of termite nests. *Ins. Soc.*, **3**, 273-6.

LUTZ, F. E. (1929). *Atta*, leaf collection. *Amer. Mus. nat. Hist. Novitates*, **388**, 1-21.

MARAK, G. E. and WOLKEN, J. J. (1965). Colour vision. *Nature London*, **205**, 1328-9.

MARIKOVSKY, P. I. (1961). Mating flights. *Ins. Soc.*, **8**, 23-30.

MARKIN, G. P. (1964). Nest structure. *Ann. ent. Soc. Amer.*, **57**, 360.

MARKL, H. (1962). Hair plates and gravity sense. *Z. vergl. Physiol.*, **45**, 475-569.

—— (1963). Hair plates. *Nature London*, **198**, 173-5.

—— (1964). Orientation to gravity. *Z. vergl. Physiol.*, **48**, 552-86.

MASSCHWITZ, U. N. (1964). Alarm scents. *Nature London*, **204**, 324-7.

MEYER, E. (1927). *Messor*, nest and colony foundation. *Biol. Zentr.*, **47**, 264-307.

MIEHE, H. (1911). Ant-plants, *Myrmecodia*. *Biol. Zentr.*, **31**, 733-8.

MITCHELL, S. D. and PIERCE, W. D. (1912). Crevice-nesting, *Monomorium pharaonis*. *Proc. ent. Soc. Washington*, **14**, 67-76.

MITTELSTAEDT, H. (1962). Insect orientation. *Ann. Rev. Ent.*, **7**, 177-98.

MITTLER, T. E. (1958). Honeydew production. *Proc. Roy. ent. Soc. London*, A **33**, 49-55.

MUIR, D. A. (1959). Plant-lice. *J. anim. Ecol.*, **28**, 133-40.

MÜLLER, E. (1931). Functions of ocelli. *Z. vergl. Physiol.*, **14**, 348-84.

MYERS, J. G. and SALT, G. (1926). Spiders imitating ants. *Trans. Roy. ent. Soc. London*, **74**, 427-36.

MCCLUSKEY, E. S. (1958). Daily rhythms. *Science*, **128**, 536.

—— (1963). Daily rhythms. *Physiol. Zool.*, **36**, 273-92.

MCGREGOR, E. G. (1948). Scent trails. *Behaviour*, **1**, 267-96.

NEWELL, W. (1909). Care of larvae. *J. econ. Ent.*, **2**, 174-92.

ÖKLAND, F. (1938). Hunting, wood-ants. *Z. Morph. Ökol. Tiere*, **20**, 63-131.

ORLOB, G. B. (1963). Plant lice. *Ent. exper. et applic.*, **6**, 95-106.

OSMAN, M. F. H. and KLOFT, W. (1961). Venom. *Ins. Soc.*, **8**, 383-95.

OTTO, D. (1958). Polyethism, wood-ants. *Deutsche Akademie der Landwirtschaftswissenschaften zu Berlin, Wissenschaftliche Abhandlung Nr 30*, Akademie Verlag, Berlin.

OTTO, D. (1960). Venom. *Zool. Anz.*, **164**, 42-57.

PAVAN, M. (1961). Nest transplantation, wood-ants. *Collana Verde, Ministr. agric. Forest. Roma*, **7**, 161-9.

PAVAN, M. and RONCHETTI, G. (1955). Glands of ants. *Atti. Soc. ital. Sci. nat. e museo civico storia nat. Milano*, **94**, 379-477.

PEACOCK, A. D., WATERHOUSE, F. L. and BAXTER, A. T. (1955). Nest temperature. *Ent. mon. Mag.*, **91**, 37-42.

PEACOCK, A. D., SUDD, J. H. and BAXTER, A. T. (1955). Colony foundation. *Ent. mon. Mag.*, **91**, 125-9.

PEAKIN, G. J. (1960). Nest temperature and humidity. Ph.D. Thesis, University of London.

—— (1965). Colony foundation. *Proc. XIIth int. Congr. Entomol. London*, 303.

PERTUNEN, V. (1955). Humidity responses. *Ann. entomol. Fenn.*, **21**, 38-45.

PICKLES, W. (1935). Hunting. *J. anim. Ecol.*, **4**, 22-31.

—— (1942). Nest excavation. *Ent. mon. Mag.*, **78**, 38-39.

—— (1944). Desert ants. *Ent. mon. Mag.*, **80**, 61-63.

PLATEAUX, L. (1960). Adoption of larvae of other species. *Ins. Soc.*, **7**, 163-70, 221-6, 345-8.

POLDI, B. (1963). Colony foundation. *Symposia genetica et biologica ital.*, **12**, 132-99.

POLIMANTI, O. (1911). Light responses. *Biol. Zentr.*, **31**, 222-4.

PONTIN, A. J. (1958). Plant-lice. *Ent. mon. Mag.*, **94**, 9-11.

—— (1959). Plant-lice. *Ent. mon. Mag.*, **95**, 154-5.

—— (1960a). Colony foundation. *Ins. Soc.*, **7**, 227-30.

—— (1960b). Plant-lice. *Ent. mon. Mag.*, **96**, 198-9.

—— (1961). Hunting. *Ent. mon. Mag.*, **97**, 135-7.

RABAUD, E. (1937). *Phénomènes sociales et sociétés animales*. Alcan, Paris.

RAIGNIER, A. (1948). Nest temperature. *La Cellule*, **51**, 281-368.

—— (1959). Colony division, *Anomma. Medelingen Kon. Vlaamse Acad.*, **21**, 3-24.

RAIGNIER, A. and BOVEN, J. VAN (1955). *Anomma* biology. *Ann. Mus. Roy. Congo Belge, Teervuren N.S. Sci. Zool.*, **2**. Also 1954 *Verh. Kon. Vlaamse Acad.*, **44**.

RETTENMEYER, C. W. (1963a). Army Ants. *Univ. Kansas. Sci. Bull.*, **44**, 281-465.

—— (1963b). Guests of Army Ants. *Ann. ent. Soc. Amer.*, **56**, 170-4.

REYNE, A. (1954). Plant-lice. *Zool. Mededel.*, **32**, 233-57.

RICHARDS, O. W. (1953). *The social insects.* Macdonald, London.

RIORDAN, D. F. (1960). *Camponotus pennsylvanicus* nest. *Ins. Soc.*, **7**, 353-5.

SAKAGAMI, S. F. and HAYASHIDA, K. (1962). Nest excavation, co-operation. *Anim. Behaviour*, **10**, 96-105.

SANTSCHI, F. (1911). Orientations. *Rev. suisse Zool.* **19** 303-38.

—— (1919). Parasitic ants, *Bothriomyrmex. Rev. Zool. Afr.*, **7**, 201-23.

—— (1923). Orientations. *Rev. Zool. Afr.*, **11**, 111-43.

SCHERBA, G. (1958). Nest construction, *Formica. Ins. Soc.*, **5**, 202-13.

—— (1959). Nest humidity. *Amer. Midl. Nat.*, **61**, 499-508.

—— (1961). Nest construction. *J. New York ent. Soc.*, **69**, 71-87.

—— (1962). Nest temperature. *Amer. Midl. Nat.*, **67**, 373-85.

—— (1964). Inter-colony relations. *Anim. Behaviour*, **12**, 508-12.

SCHIMPER, A. F. W. (1898). Ant-plants. *Pflanzengeographie auf physiologischer Grundlagen.* Jena.

SCHMIDT, A. (1938). Chemical senses. *Z. vergl. Physiol.*, **25**, 351-78.

SCHNEIRLA, T. C. (1933a). *Eciton*, raids. *J. comp. Psychol.*, **15**, 267-301.

—— (1933b). Learning. *J. comp. Psychol.*, **15**, 243-66.

—— (1934). Learning. *J. comp. Psychol.*, **17**, 303-28.

—— (1941). Learning. *J. comp. Psychol.*, **32**, 41-82.

—— (1943). Learning. *J. comp. Psychol.*, **35**, 149-76.

—— (1944). Scent trails. *Amer. Mus. nat. Hist. Novitates*, **1253**, 1-26.

—— (1946). The Superorganism. *J. abnorm. soc. Psychol.*, **41**, 385-402.

—— (1956a). Army-ants, *Eciton. Smithsonian Rep.*, 1955, 379-406

—— (1956b). Colony division, *Eciton. Ins. Soc.*, **3**, 49-69.

—— (1957a). Dorylinae behaviour. *Ins. Soc.*, **4**, 259-98.

—— (1957b). *Eciton*, raids. *Proc. Amer. phil. Soc.*, **101**, 106-33.

—— (1958). *Neivamyrmex*, raids. *Ins. Soc.*, **5**, 215-55.

—— (1962). Learning. *Psychol. Beitr.*, **6**, 509-20.

—— (1965). Dorylinae, behaviour. *Proc. XIIth int. Congr. Entomol. London*, 1964, 336-8, also (1966). *Animal Behaviour*, **14**, 132-148.

SCHNEIRLA, T. C. and BROWN, R. Z. (1952). Mating season. *Zoologica, New York*, **37**, 5-22.

SCHNEIRLA, T. C., BROWN, R. Z. and BROWN, F. (1954). Nests, *Eciton. Ecol. Monogr.*, **24**, 269-96.

SCHWENKE, W. (1957). Hunting. *Beitr. Entomol.*, **7**, 226-46.

SCUDDER, G. G. E. (1961). Sting anatomy. *Trans. Roy. ent. Soc. London*, **13**, 25-40.

SERNANDER, R. (1904). Seeds. *Kungl. s.v. vet. Akademiens Hdl.*, **41**, no. 7, 1-410.

SHARP, D. (1893). Stridulation. *Trans. ent. Soc. London*, 199-213.

SKAIFE, S. F. (1961). *The study of ants. Crematogaster* nests. Longman, London.

SMITH, K. G. V. and HARPER, J. L. (1957). Nectar collection. *J. Ecol.*, **45**, 342.

SMITH, M. R. (1957). *Plagiolepis allaudi*, habits. *J. New York ent. Soc.*, **65**, 195-8.

SMITH, C. C. and BRAGG, A. N. (1949). Predators of ants. *Ecology*, **30**, 333-49.

SOULIÉ, J. (1961). *Crematogaster*, nests. *Ins. Soc.*, **8**, 213-97.

—— (1962). Colony foundation. *Ins. Soc.*, **9**, 181-95.

STÄGER, R. (1924). *Formicoxenus nitidulus*, habits. *Z. Morph. Ökol. Tiere*, **3**, 452-76

—— (1929a). Seeds. *Z. wiss. Insektenbiol.*, **24**, 199-213.

—— (1929b). Hunting. *Z. wiss. Insektenbiol.*, **24**, 227-30.

—— (1930). Hunting. *Z. wiss. Insektenbiol.*, **26**, 125-37.

—— (1935a). Hunting. *Mitt. schweiz. ent. Ges.*, **16**, 344-57.

—— (1935b). Nests in Alps. *Mitt. schweiz. ent. Ges.*, **16**, 732-3.

STAHEL, G. and GEIJSKES, G. C. (1940). Temperature in nests. *Rev. de Entomol.*, **11**, 243-68, 766-75.

STÄRCKE, A. (1941). Blind ants. *Tijdschrift v. Entomol.*, **84**, ii-iv.

STEINER, A. (1924). Nest temperature. *Z. vergl. Physiol.*, **2**, 23-56.

—— (1929). Nest temperature. *Z. vergl. Physiol.*, **9**, 1-66.

STEYN, J. J. (1954). Daily rhythms, mating flight. *Mem. ent. Soc. S. Africa*, no. **3**.

STITZ. H. (1939). Nest of *Monomorium pharaonis. Tierwelt Deutschlands*, **37**.

STRICKLAND, A. H. (1951a). Plant-lice. *Bull. ent. Res.*, **42**, 65-103.

—— (1951b). Plant-lice. *Bull. ent. Res.*, **41**, 725-48.

STRONG, F. (1965). Honeydew composition. *Nature London*, **205**, 1242.

STUMPER, R. (1953). Alarm scents. *Naturwiss.*, **40**, 33-34.

—— (1955). Antennae and eyes. *Bull. Soc. nat. Luxembourgeois*, **60**, 82-86.

—— (1956). Attractive secretions of queens. *Mitt. schweiz. ent. Ges.*, **29**, 373-80.

—— (1961). Repletes, radioactive marking. *Naturwiss.*, **48**, 735-6.

—— (1962). Colony foundation. *Ins. Soc.*, **9**, 329-33.

STURDZA, S. A. (1942). Activity. *Bull. Sect. Sci. Acad. Roum.*, **24**, 543.

SUDD, J. H. (1957). Communication. *Brit. J. anim. Behav.*, **5**, 104-9.

—— (1960a). Hunting. *Anim. Behaviour*, **8**, 67-75.

—— (1960b). Prey transport. *Behaviour*, **16**, 295-308.

—— (1960c). *Aenictus*, habits. *Ent. mon. Mag.*, **95**, 262.

—— (1960d). Scent trails. *Nature London*, **183**, 1588.

—— (1962a). Alarm scents. *Ent. mon. Mag.*, **98**, 62.

—— (1962b). Nesting habits. *Ent. mon. Mag.*, **98**, 164-6.

—— (1965). Prey transport. *Behaviour*, **25**, 234-271.

TALBOT, M. (1943). Nest, *Prenolepis imparis*, repletes. *Ecology*, **24**, 31-44.

TALBOT, M. and KENNEDY C. H. (1940). Slave raids. *Ann. ent. Soc. Amer.*, **33**, 560-77.

TEVIS, L. (1958a). Seeds. *Ecology*, **39**, 688-95.

—— (1958b). Seeds. *Ecology*, **39**, 695-704.

THORPE, W. H. (1956). *Learning and instinct in animals*. Methuen, London.

TOROSSIAN, C. (1959, 1960, 1961). Care of larvae. *Ins. Soc.*, **6**, 369-379; **7**, 171-175; **8**, 189-91.

—— (1960). Colony foundation. *Ins. Soc.*, **7**, 383-93.

VANDERPLANCK, F. L (1960). *Oecophylla*, nests. *J. anim. Ecol.*, **29**, 15-23.

VIEHMEYER, H. (1908). Colony foundation. *Biol. Zentr.*, **28**, 18-32.

—— (1910). Colony foundation. *Zool. Anz.*, **35**, 450-7.

—— (1921). Slave raids. *Biol. Zentr.*, **41**, 269-78.

VOWLES, D. M. (1950). Sensitivity to polarised light. *Nature London*, **165**, 282.

—— (1953). Polyethism. *Advancement of Science*, **10**, 18-21.

—— (1954a). Orientation. *J. exper. Biol.*, **31**, 341-55.

—— (1954b). Orientation. *J. exper. Biol.*, **31**, 356-75.

—— (1955a). Hunting. *Brit. J. Animal Behaviour*, **3**, 1-13.

—— (1955b). Corpora pedunculata. *Quart. J. Micros. Sci.*, **96**, 239-56.

WALKER, T. J. (1957). Hunting. *Ecology*, **38**, 262-76.

WALLIS, D. I. (1960). Cocoon spinning. *Ins. Soc.*, **7**, 187-99.

—— (1961). Food sharing. *Behaviour*, **17**, 17-37.

—— (1962a). Washing, nest excavation etc. *Anim. Behaviour*, **10**, 105-11.

—— (1962b). Aggression. *Anim. Behaviour*, **10**, 267-74.

—— (1962c). Food-traffic. *Proc. Zool. Soc. Lond.*, **139**, 589-605.

WALLIS, D. I. (1963). Aggression. *Anim. Behaviour*, **11**, 164-71.
—— (1964). Foraging. *Behaviour*, **23**, 149-76.
WALOFF, N. (1957). Colony foundation. *Ins. Soc.*, **4**, 391-408.
WASMANN, E. (1897a). Ant guests, Acarina. *Zool. Anz.*, **20**, 170-3.
—— (1897b). *Lomechusa*. *Zool. Anz.*, **20**, 463-71.
—— (1898). *Thorictus*. *Zool. Anz.*, **21**, 536-46.
—— (1899). Antennal language. *Zoologica Stuttgart*, **11**, 1-132.
—— (1902). *Antennophorus*. *Zool. Anz.*, **25**, 66-76.
—— (1903). Ant guests. *Zool. Anz.*, **26**, 581-90.
—— (1908). Parasitic and slave-making ants. *Biol. Zentr.*, **28**, 251-71, 289-306, 321-33, 353-82, 417-41.
—— (1910). Colony foundation. *Zool. Anz.*, **35**, 129-41.
WAY, M. J. (1953). Plant-lice. *Bull. ent. Res.*, **44**, 669-91.
—— (1954a). *Oecophylla*, routes etc. *Bull. ent. Res.*, **45**, 93-112.
—— (1954b). Plant-lice. *Bull. ent. Res.*, **45**, 113-34.
—— (1963). Plant-lice. *Ann. Rev. Entomol.*, **8**, 307-44.
WEBER, N. A. (1937). *Atta cephalotes*. *Tropical Agriculture*, **14** (8), 223-6.
—— (1941). Attini nests. *Rev. de Ent.*, **12**, 93-130.
—— (1943). Ants of Imatong Mts. Sudan. *Bull. Mus. comp. Zool. Harvard*, **93**, 263-389.
—— (1946). Fungus culture. *Rev. de Ent.*, **17**, 114-72.
—— (1949). Polyethism *Oecophylla*. *Ecology*, **30**, 397.
—— (1957). Fungus culture. *Ecology*, **38**, 480-94.
—— (1958). Fungus culture. *Proc. Xth. int. Congr. Entomol. Montreal*, **2**, 459-73.
WEIR, J. S. (1958a). Polyethism. *Ins. Soc.*, **5**, 97-128.
—— (1958b). Polyethism. *Ins. Soc.*, **5**, 315-39.
—— (1959a). Worker oviposition. *Physiol. Zool.*, **32**, 63-77.
—— (1959b). Larval care. *Ins. Soc.*, **6**, 188-201.
WELLENSTEIN, G. (1952). Hunting, plant-lice. *Z. Pflanzenkrankh.*, **59**, 430-51.
—— (1954). Hunting. *Z. angew. Entomol.*, **36**, 118-217.
WELLINGTON, W. G. (1957). Polyethism. *Canad. J. Zool.*, **35**, 293-323.
WERRINGLOER, A. (1932). Eyes of Dorylinae. *Z. wiss. Zool.*, **141**, 432-524.
WESSON, L. (1939). Slave raids. *Trans. Amer. ent. Soc.*, **65**, 97-122.
WHEELER, G. C. and WHEELER, J. (1954). Larval feeding. *Psyche*, **61**, 111-45.
WHEELER, W. M. (1904). Colony foundation. *Bull. Amer. Mus. nat. Hist.*, **20**, 347-75.
—— (1906a). Colony foundation. *Bull. Amer. Mus. nat. Hist.*, **22**, 33-104.
—— (1906b). Nest construction. *Bull. Amer. Mus. nat. Hist.*, **22**, 403-18.
—— (1907). Fungus culture. *Bull. Amer. Mus. nat. Hist.*, **23**, 669-807.
—— (1910). *Ants* (reprinted 1960). *Columbia University Press.*
—— (1915). Cocoons. *Ann. ent. Soc. Amer.*, **8**, 332-42.
—— (1916). Mating flights. *J. anim. Behaviour*, **6**, 70-73.
—— (1917a). *Lasius subumbratus*. *Psyche*, **24**, 167-76.
—— (1917b). Mating flights. *Psyche*, **24**, 177-80.
—— (1922). African ants. *Bull. Amer. Mus. nat. Hist.*, **45**, 1-269.
—— (1928). *The social insects*. Columbia University Press.
—— (1930). *Prenolepis imparis*. *Ann. ent. Soc. Amer.*, **23**, 1-26.
WHEELER, W. M. and BAILEY, I. W. (1925). Ant plants. *Proc. Amer. Phil. Soc. Phila.*, **22**, 235-79.
WICHMANN, H. E. (1955). Hunting. *Z. angew. Entomol.*, **37**, 507-10.

WILSON, E. O. (1953a). Polymorphism. *Quart. Rev. Biol.*, **28**, 136-56.

—— (1953b). Dacetini. *Ann. ent. Soc. Amer.*, **46**, 469-95.

—— (1955). Hunting. *Psyche*, **62**, 82-87.

—— (1957). Mating flight. *Psyche*, **64**, 46-50.

—— (1958a). Alarm scents. *Psyche*, **65**, 41-51.

—— (1958b). Cerapachyini. *Ins. Soc.*, **5**, 129-40.

—— (1958c). Group raids. *Evolution*, **12**, 24-31.

—— (1959a). Trails. *Psyche*, **66**, 29-34.

—— (1959b). Trails. *Science*, **129**, 643-4.

—— (1959c). New Guinea forest ants. *Ecology*, **40**, 437-47.

—— (1962a). Scent trails. *Anim. Behaviour*, **10**, 134-64.

—— (1962b). *Daceton*, hunting. *Bull. Mus. comp. Zool. Harvard*, **127**, 403-21.

—— (1963). Social biology of ants. *Ann. Rev. Entomol.*, **8**, 345-68.

—— (1964). Ants of Florida Keys. *Mus. comp. Zool. Harvard Breviora*, **210**, 1-14.

WILSON, E. O. and BOSSERT, W. H. (1963). Scent trails. *Recent Progr. in Hormone Research*, **19**, 673-716.

WILSON, E. O., DURLACH, N. I. and ROTH, L. M. (1958). Chemical stimuli. *Psyche*, **65**, 108-14.

WILSON, E. O. and EISNER, T. (1957). Food traffic. *Ins. Soc.*, **4**, 159-66.

WILSON, E. O. and PAVAN, M. (1959). Scent trails. *Psyche*, **66**, 70-76.

WILTSHIRE, E. P. (1966). *Agtora and Cecropia*. *Proc. XIIth int. Congr. Entomol. London*, 507-81.

WRAY, D. L. (1938). Nests. *Ann. ent. Soc. Amer.*, **31**, 196-201.

YARROW, R. H. (1955). Wood-ants taxonomy. *Trans. Soc. Brit. Entomol.*, **12**, 1-48.

ZAHN, M. (1958). Nest construction. *Zool. Beitr.*, **3**, 127-94.

Index

Note.

The index shows the subfamily and geographical distribution of each ant genus mentioned in the text by means of the following abbreviations:

Mr = Myrmeciinae; **P** = Ponerinae; **Dr** = Dorylinae; **Ps** = Pseudomyrmecinae; **My** = Myrmicinae; **Dl** = Dolichoderinae; **F** = Formicinae; **C** = Cosmopolitan; **H** = Holarctic; **Pa** = Palaearctic; **N** = Nearctic; **T** = Neotropical; **E** = Ethiopean; **O** = Oriental; **A** = Australasian; **G** = any guest.